AF292199

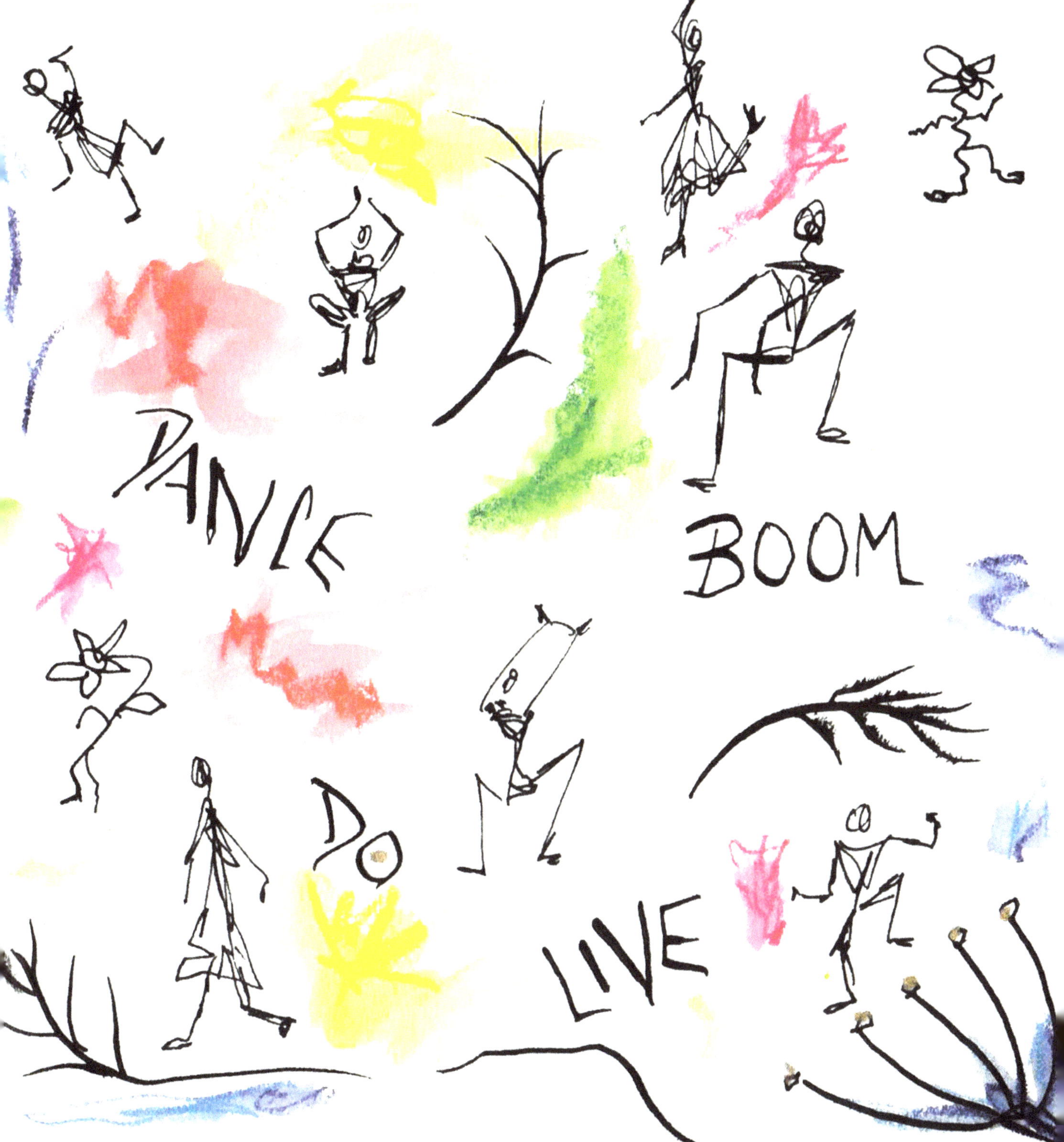
DANCE
BOOM
DO
LIVE

Doodle 2 Intent
Book 2 in the series 'Doodle with Intent'
Published by NoooBooks, 2020
Tweed Heads, NSW, Australia.
Copyright: Dude Ll © NoooBooks©
Illustrations By Dude Ll © 2020 All rights reserved.

Imagery is a blend of traditional pen and ink, and brush and ink illustrations.

The paper this book is printed on is FSC® certified (Forest Stewardship Council®). FSC promotes environmentally responsible, socially beneficial and economically viable management of the world's forests.

A catalogue record for this book is available from the National Library of Australia.
ISBN: 978-1-925991-81-9
ISBN: 978-1-925991-82-6

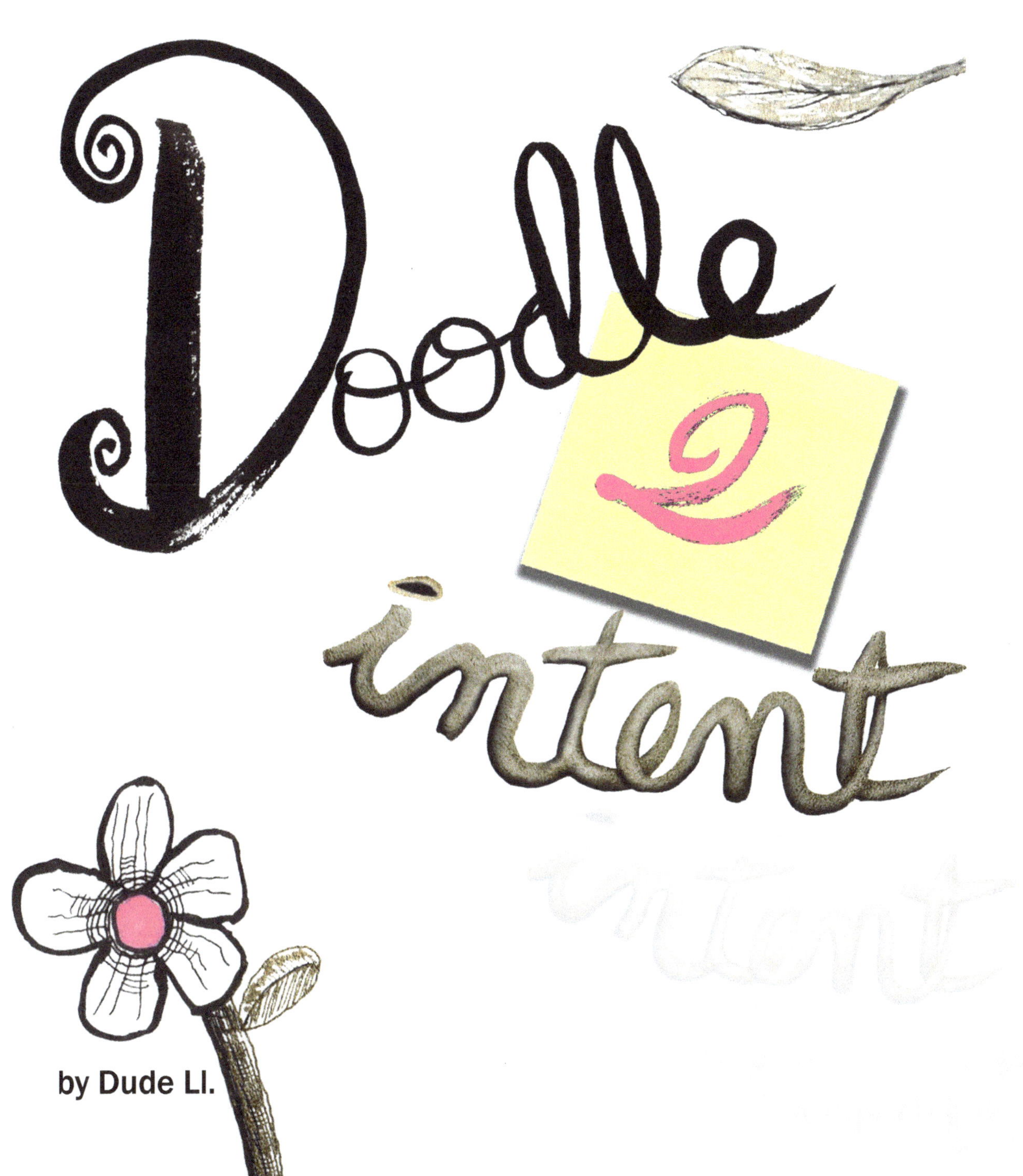

Doodle
2
intent
by Dude Ll.

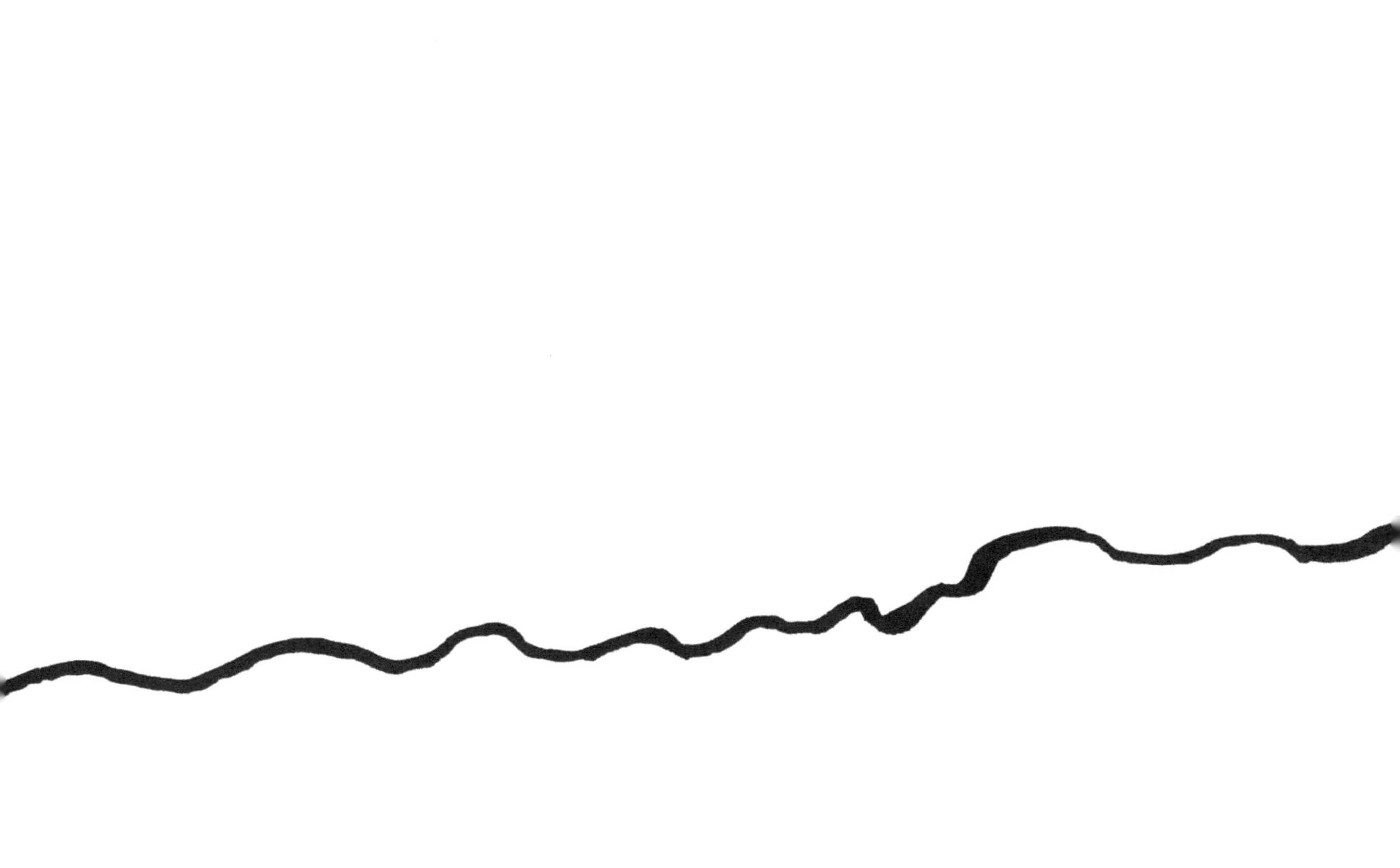

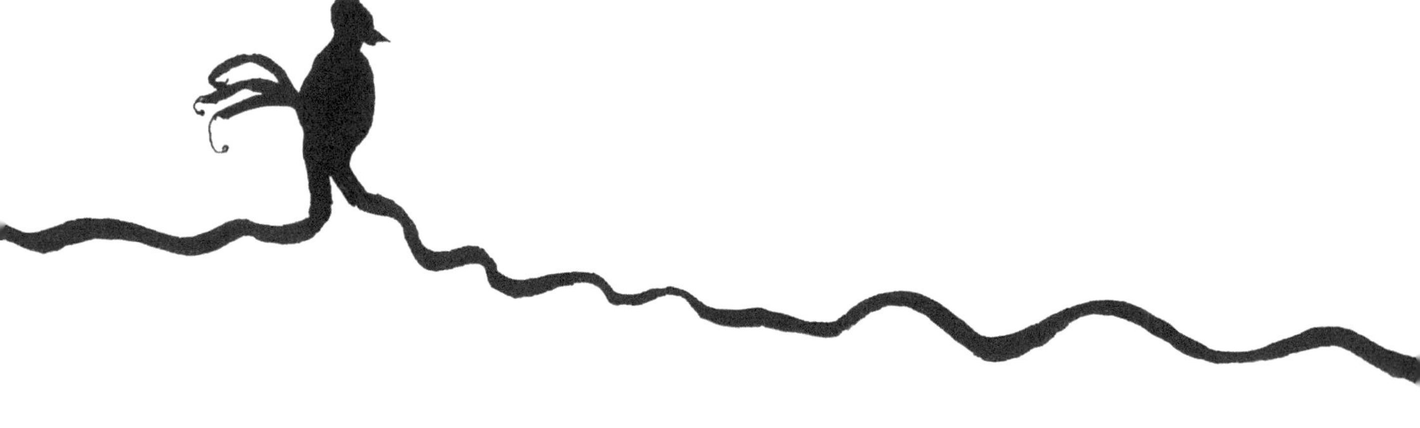

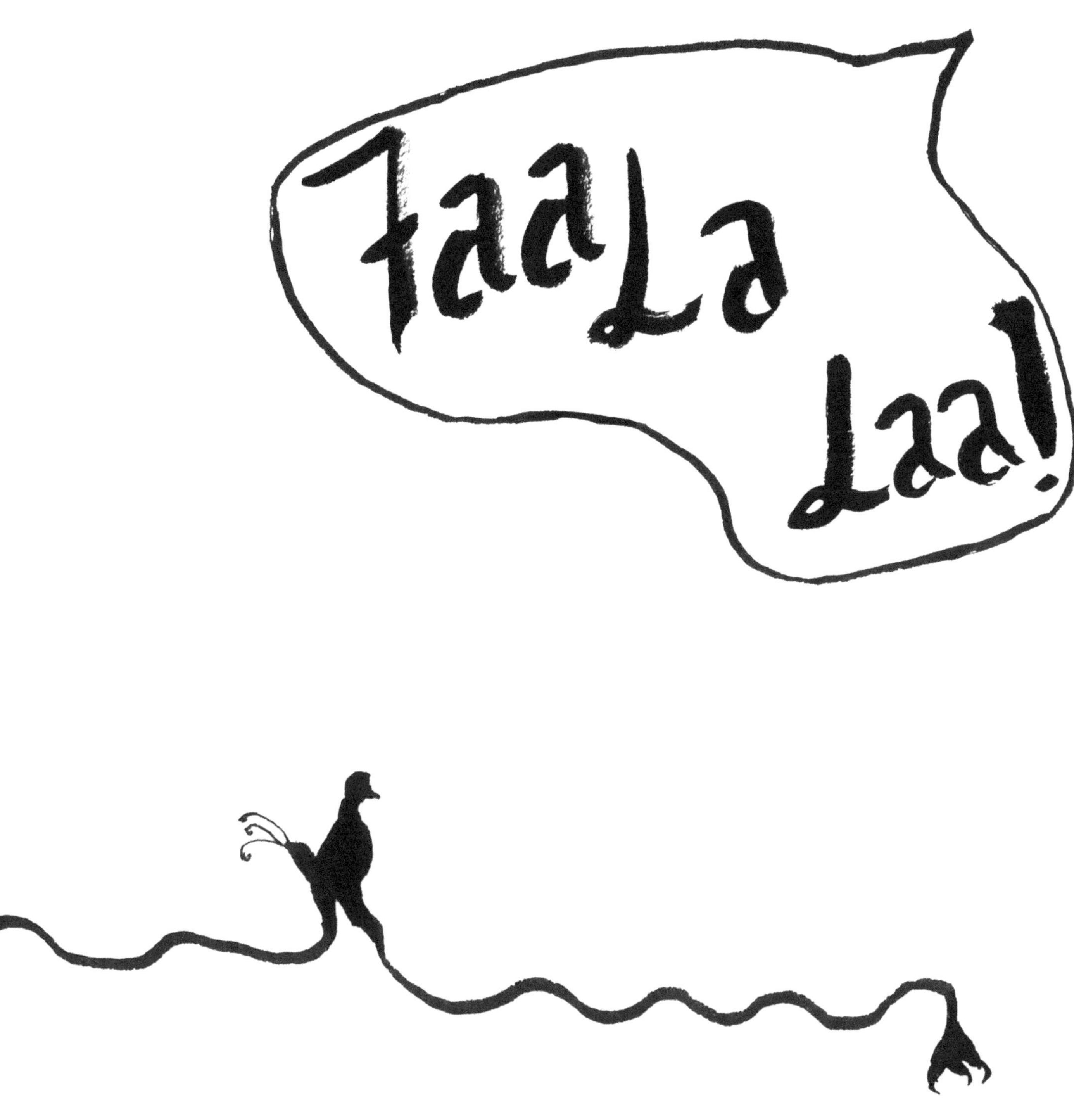

FaaLa
Laa!

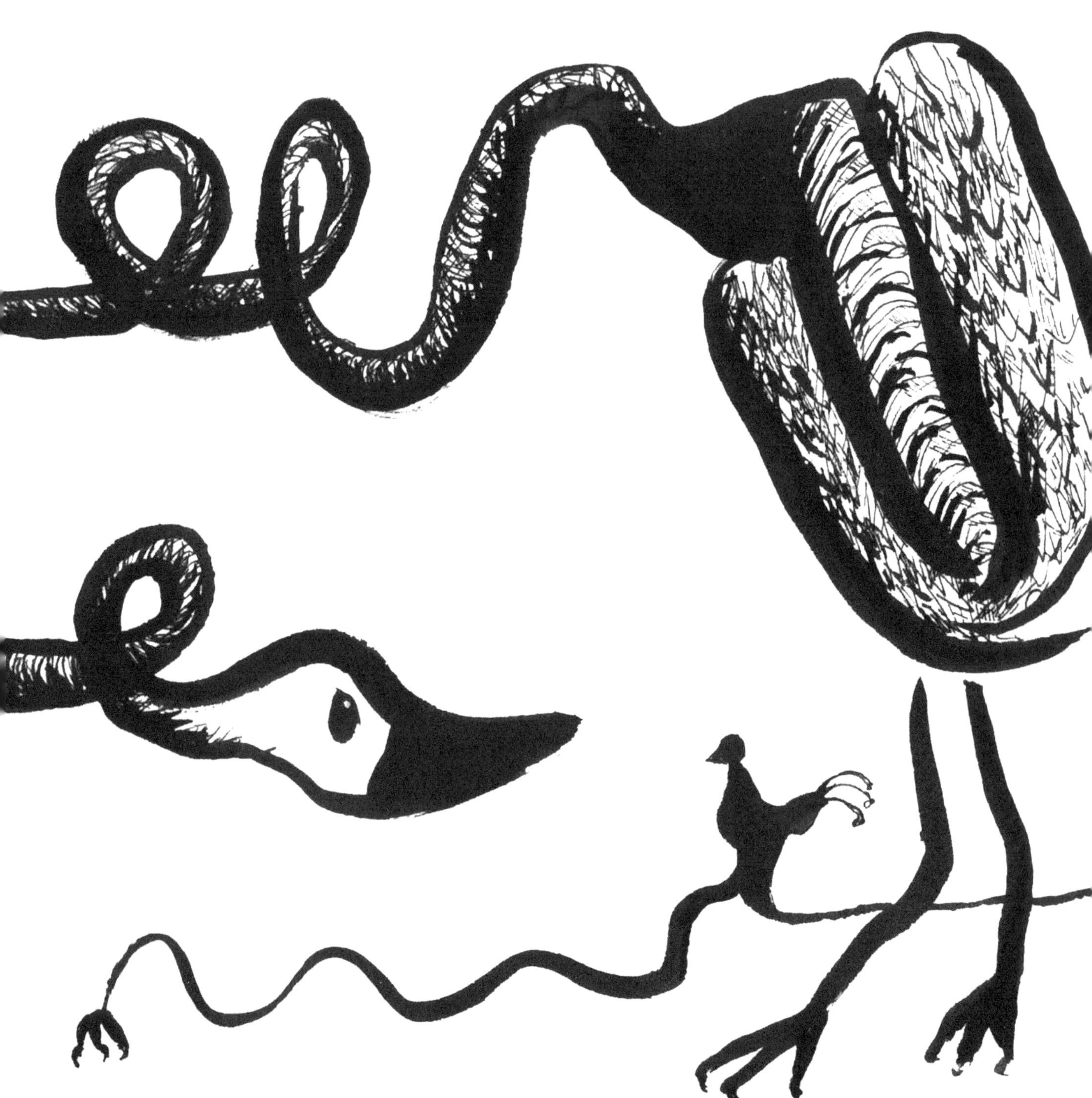

"Where did you get such a nice long neck?"

"Faa la
land"

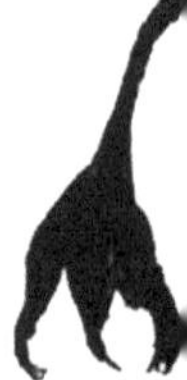

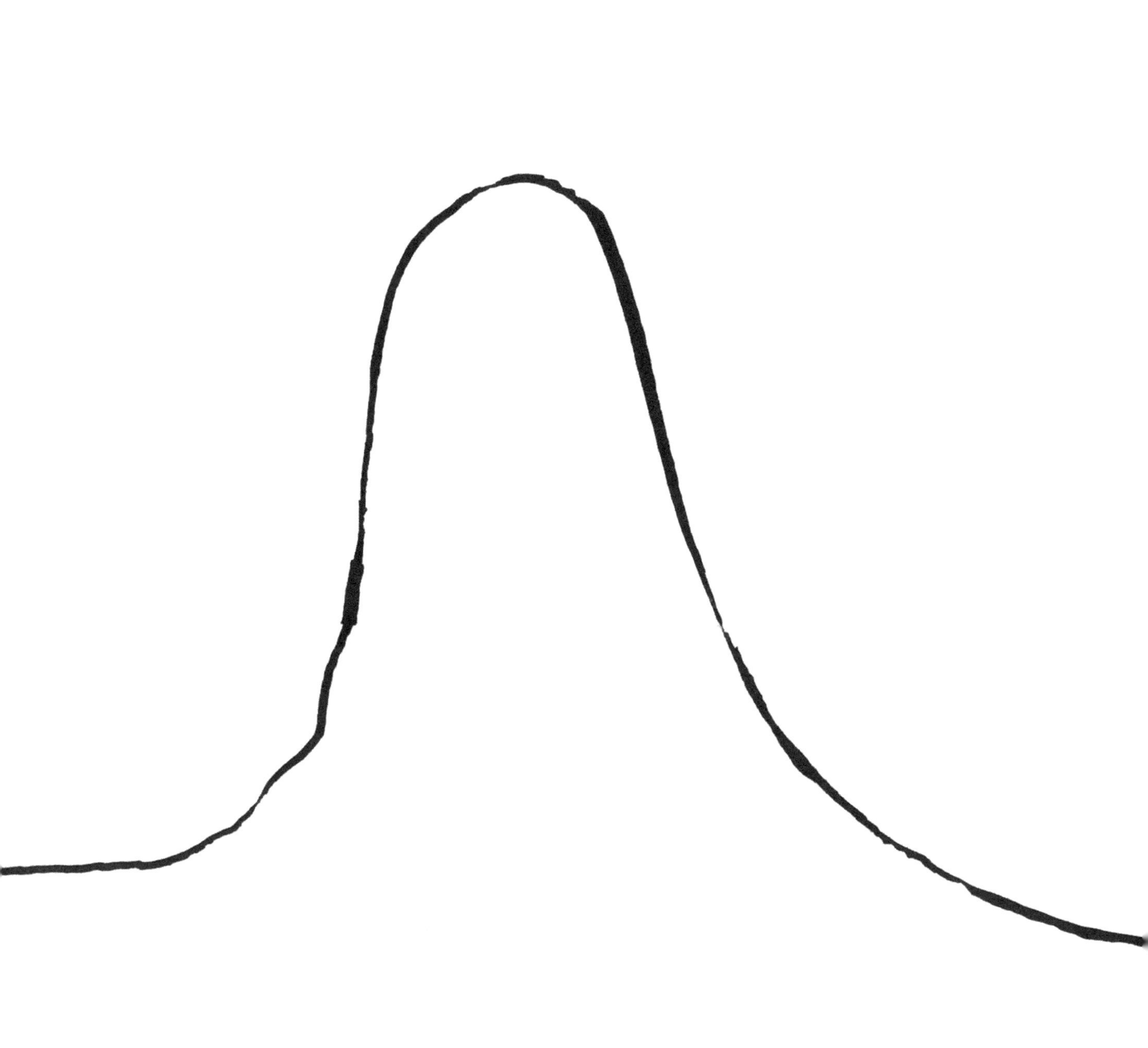

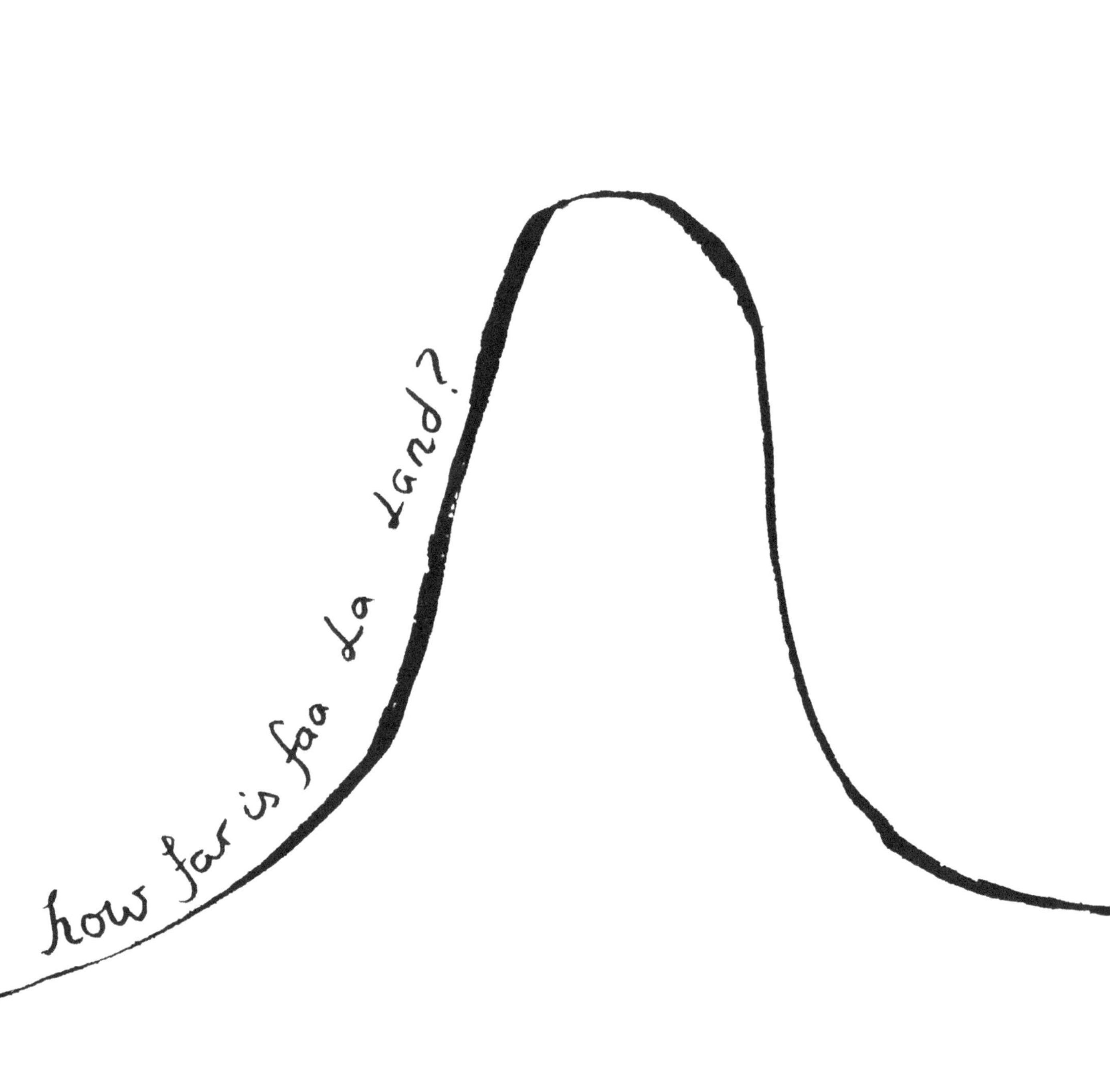
how far is fao la land?

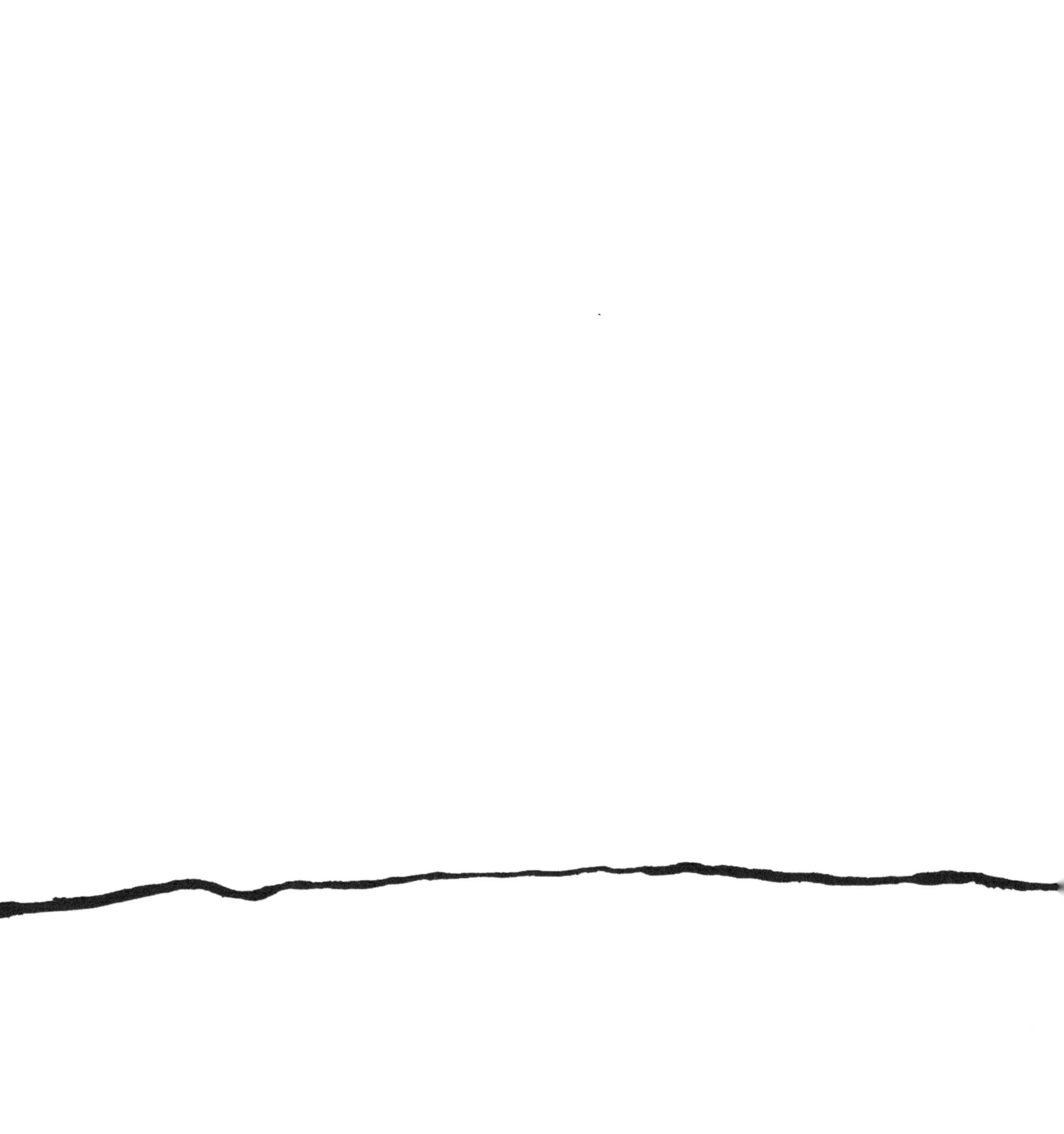

7a

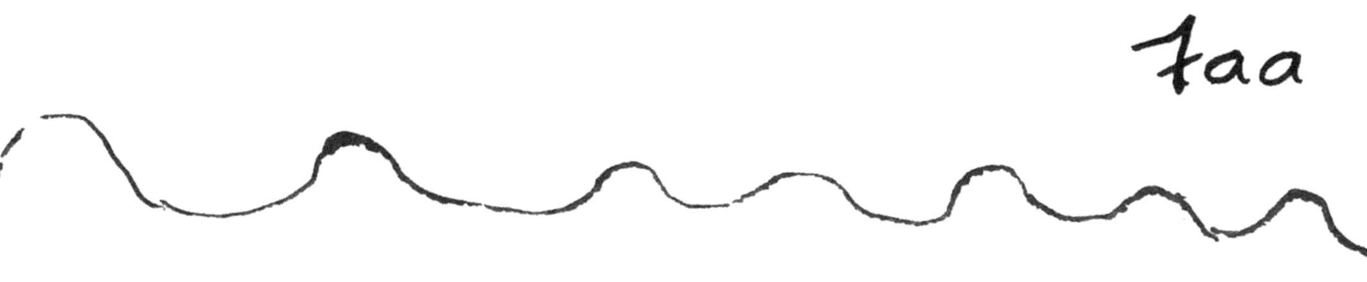

Faa

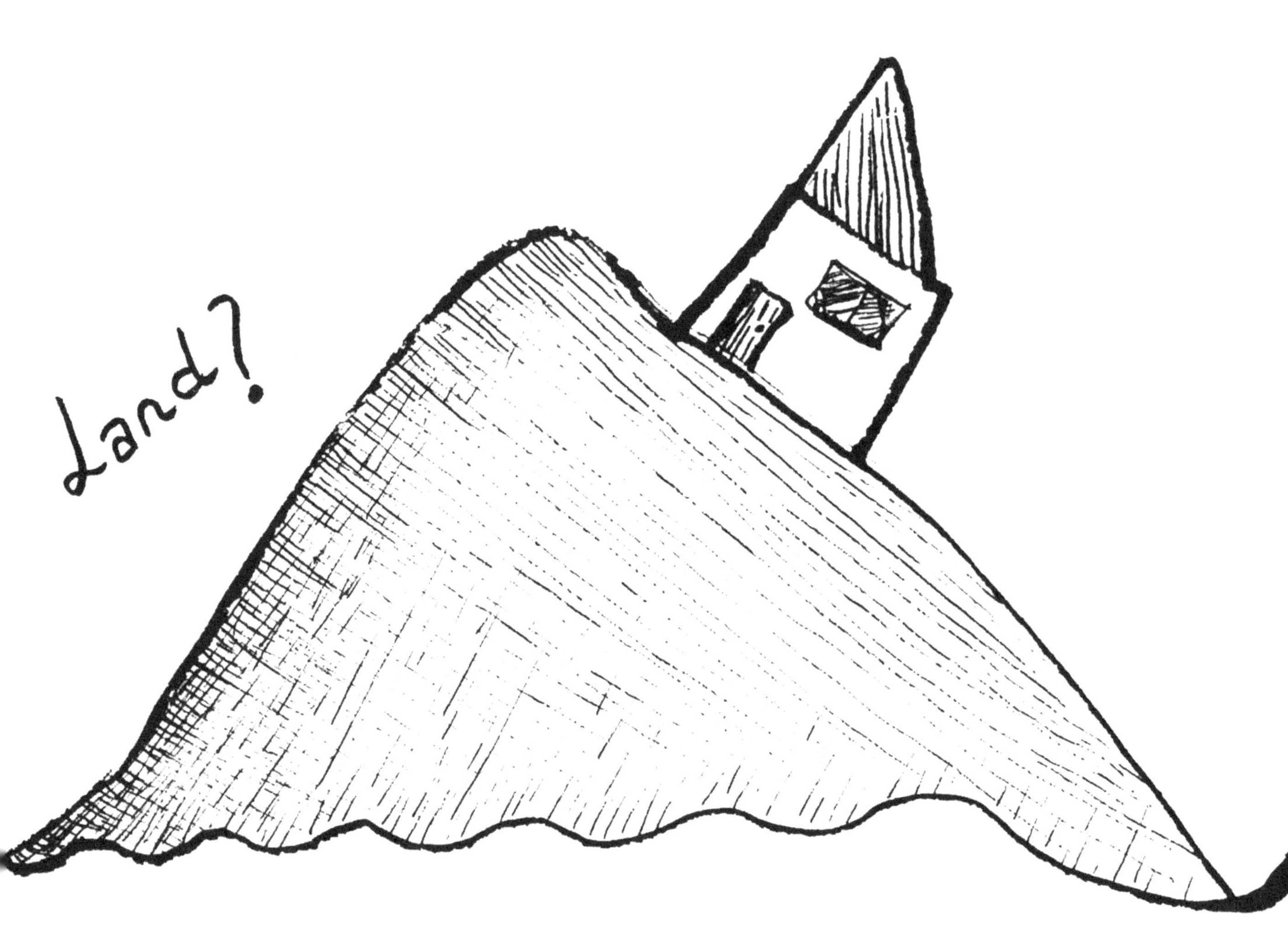
Land?

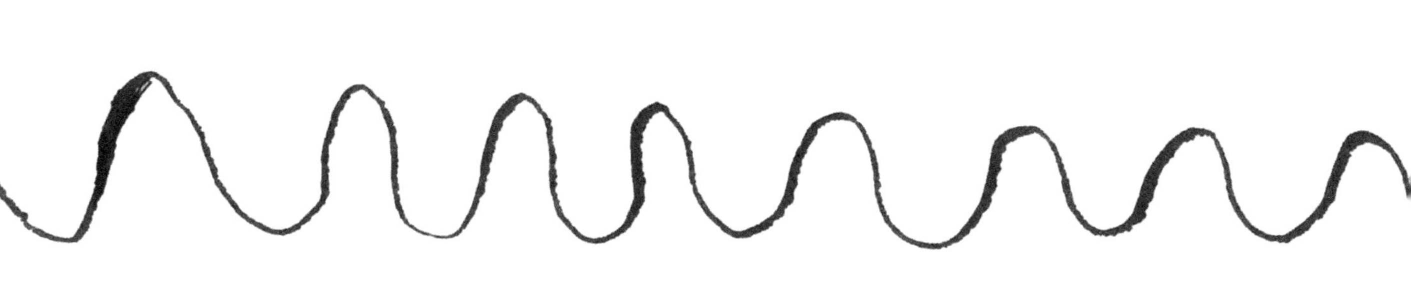

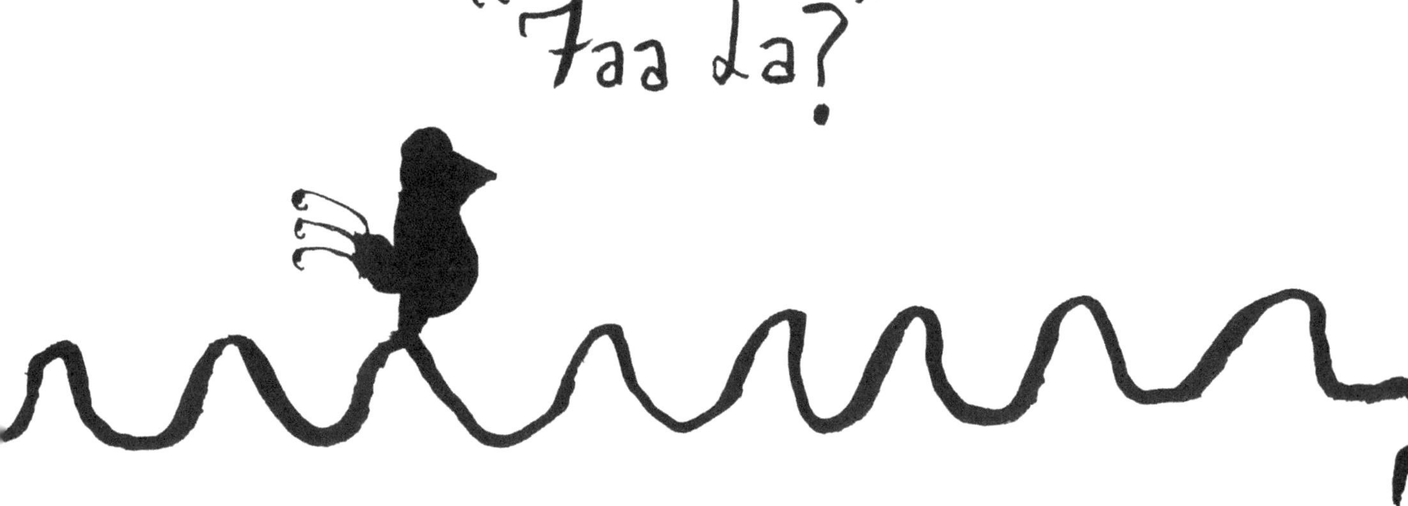

"Faa da?"

"No,
but I'm going there,
hop on,"

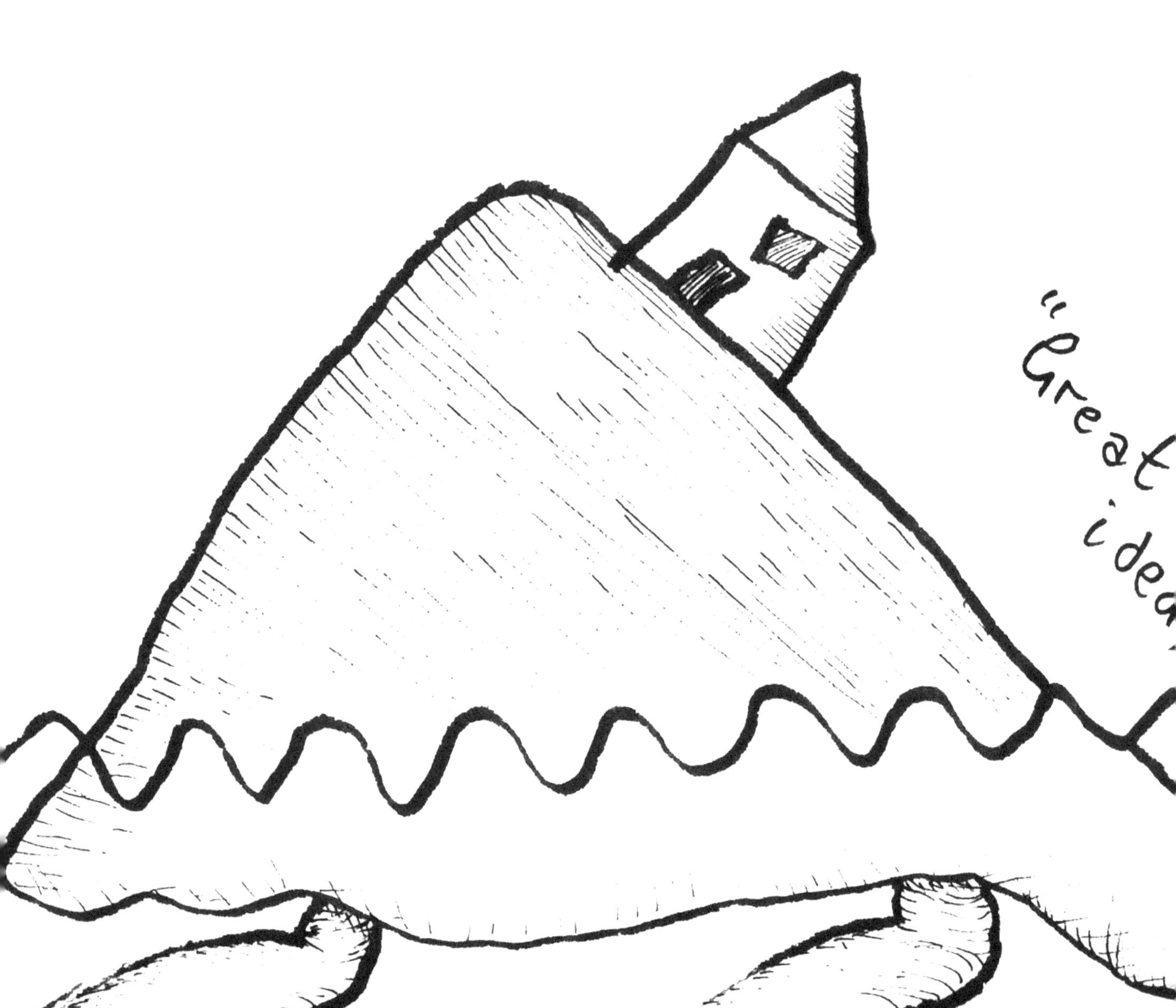
"Great
idea"

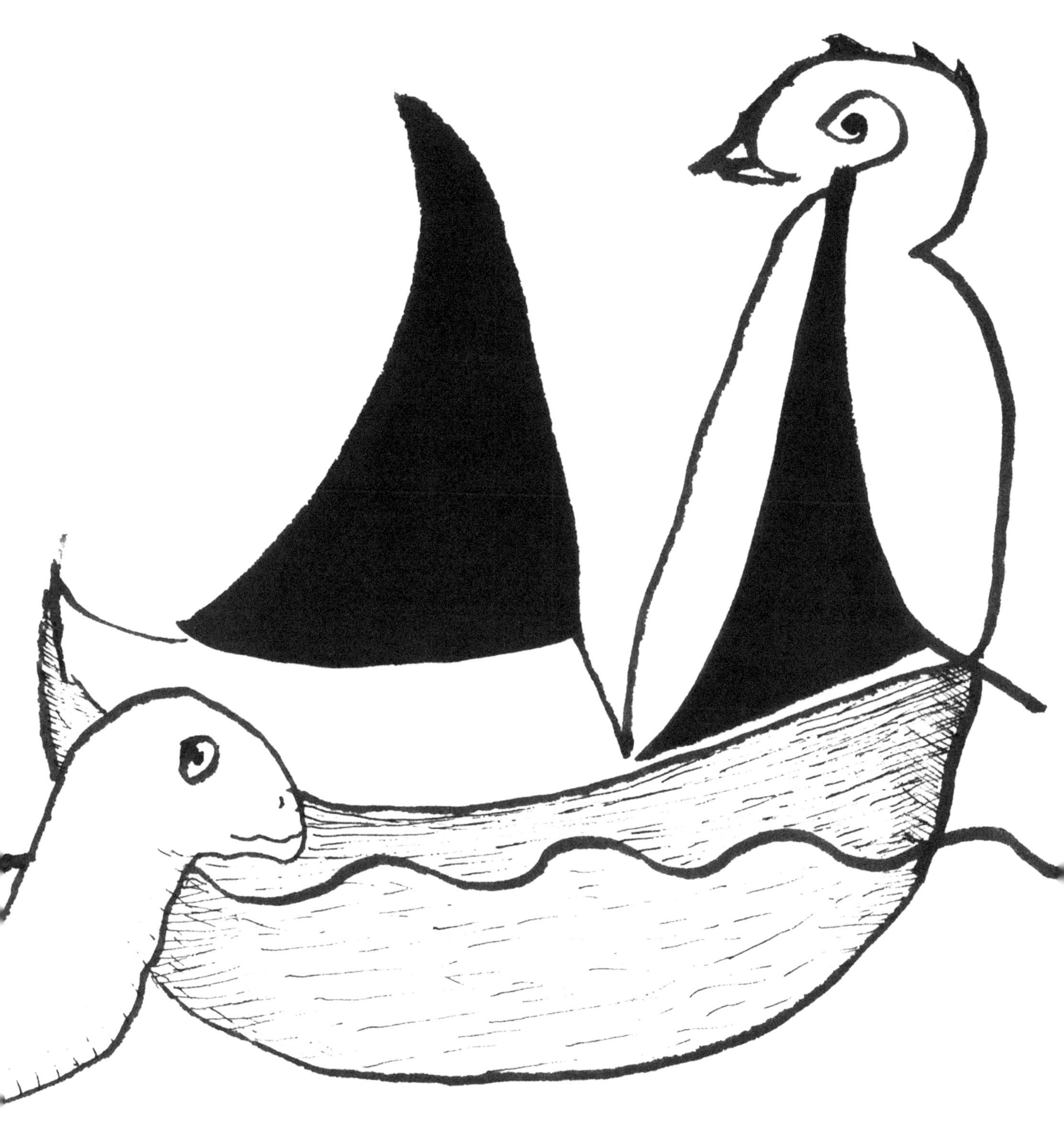

with sails, We'll get 7aa la faster,"

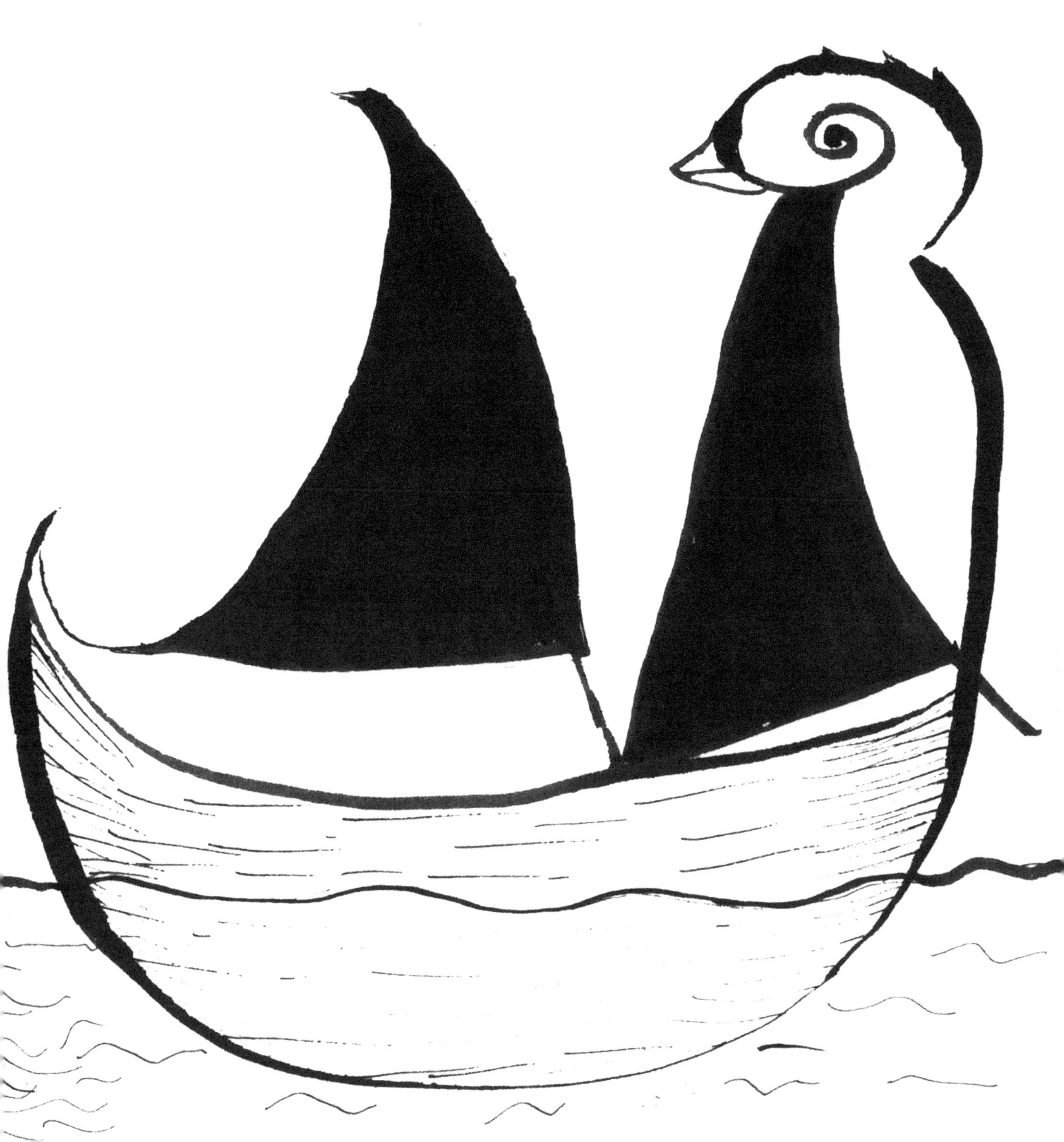

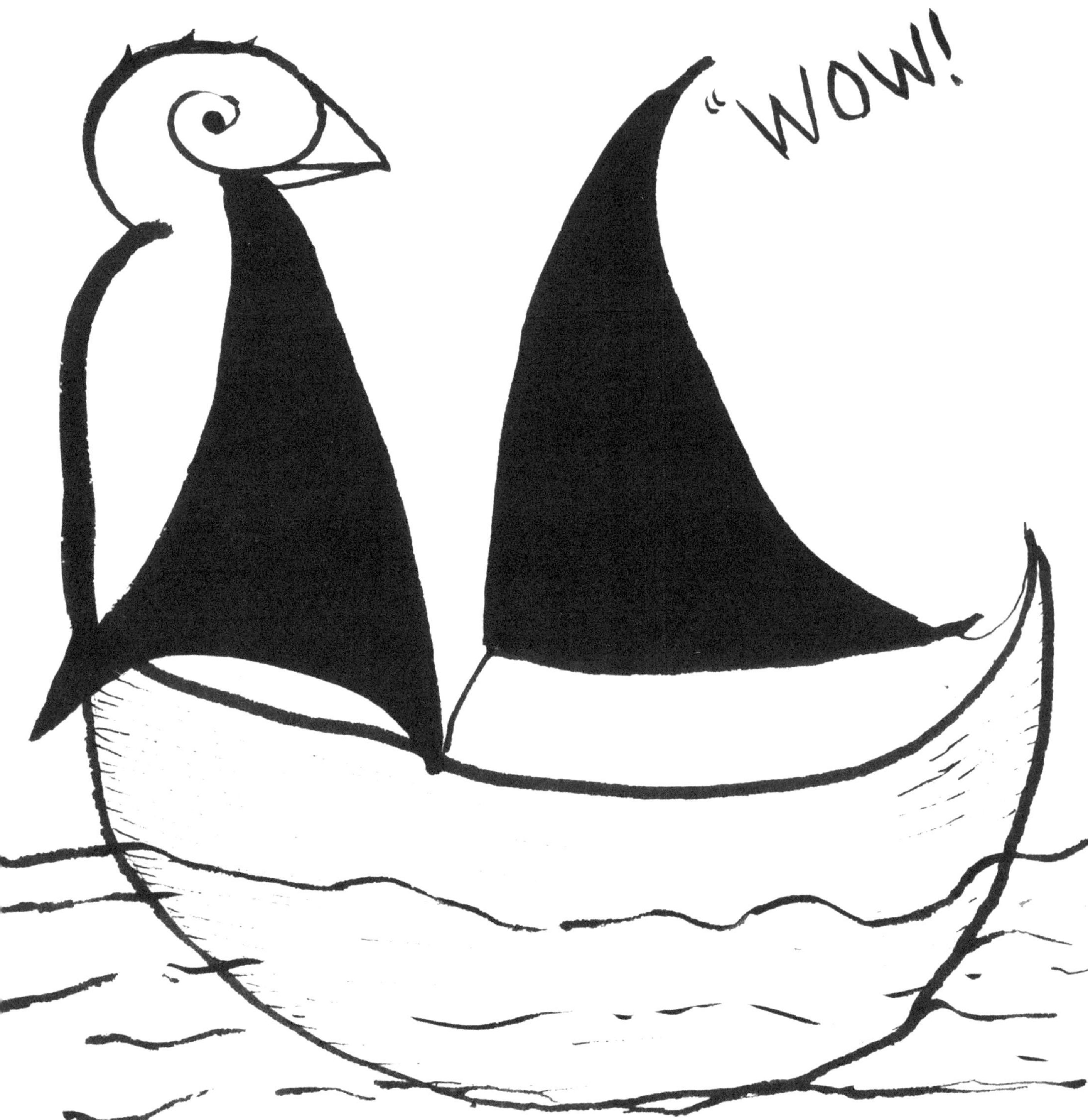

"WOW!

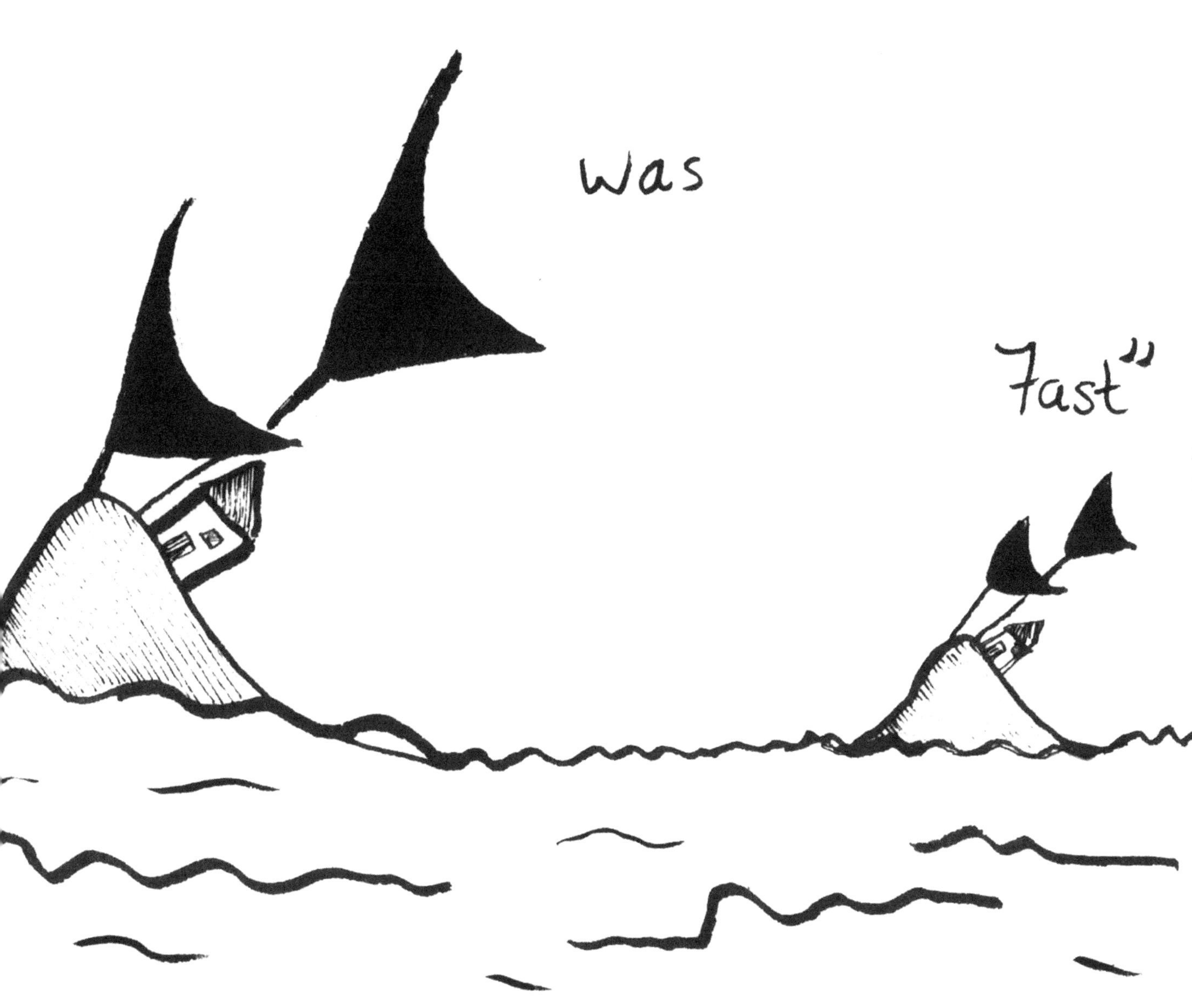
That
was
Fast"

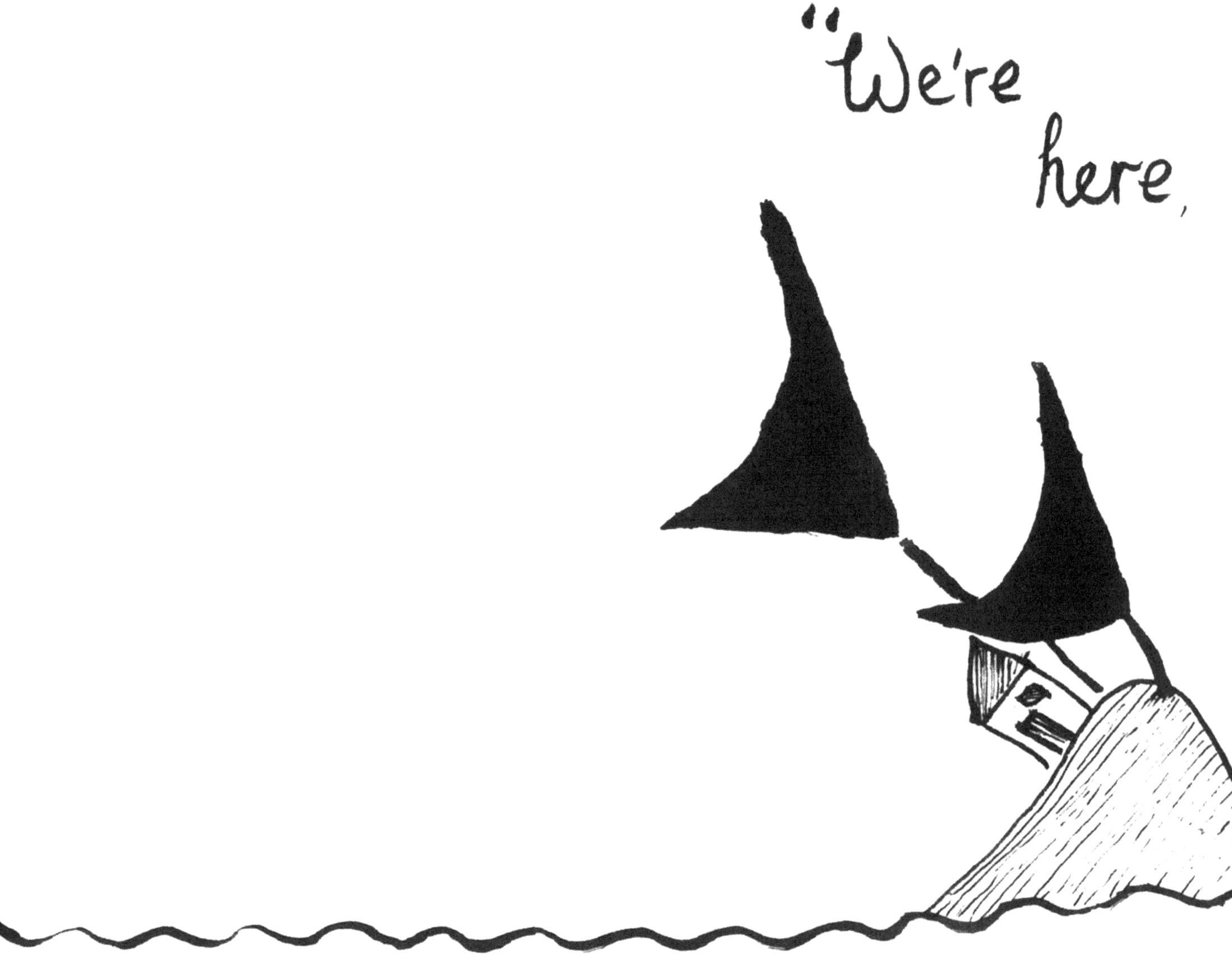
"We're here,

enjoy faa da "
" Thank you "

why is it called

Faa la Land?

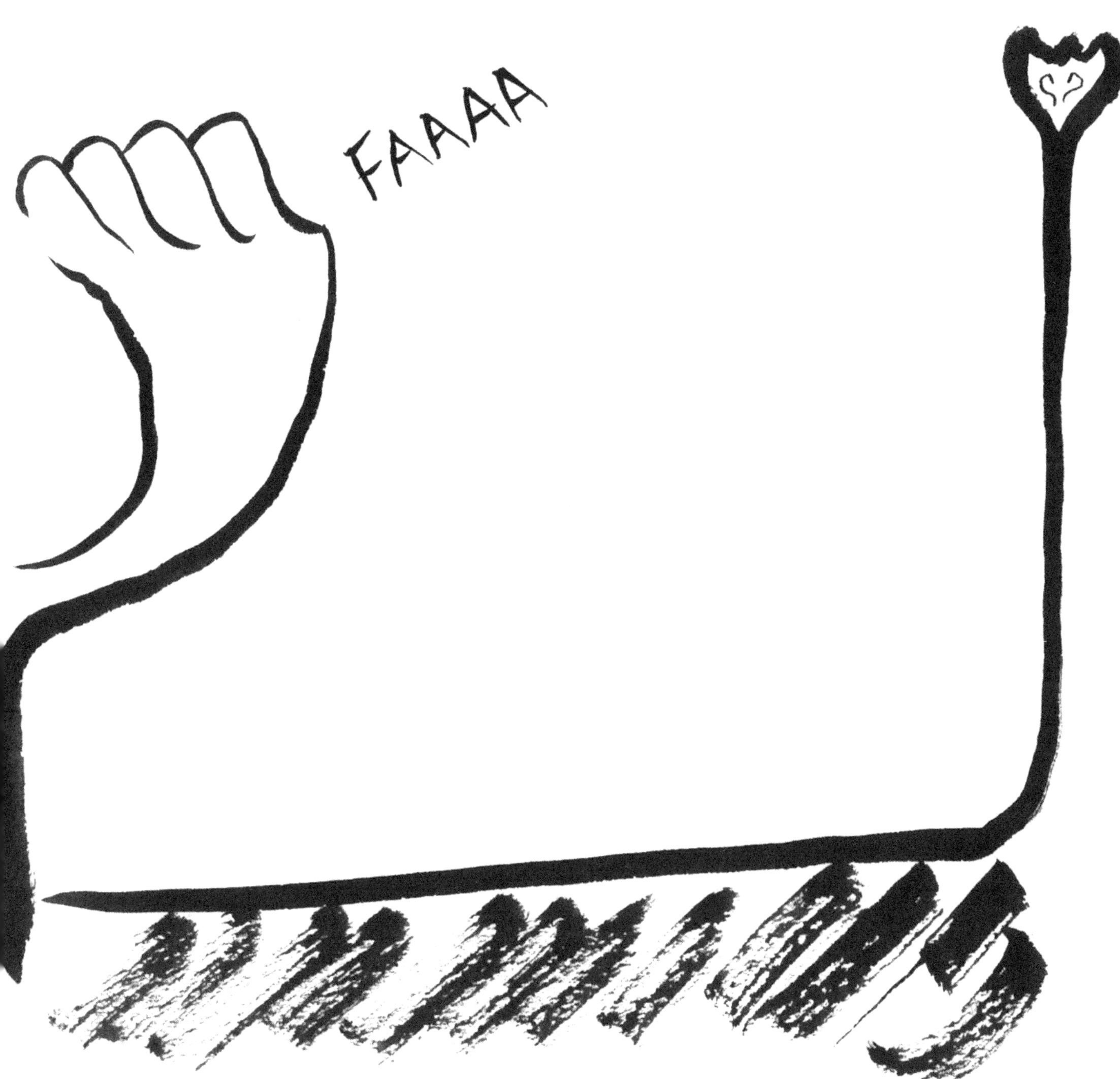
FAAAA

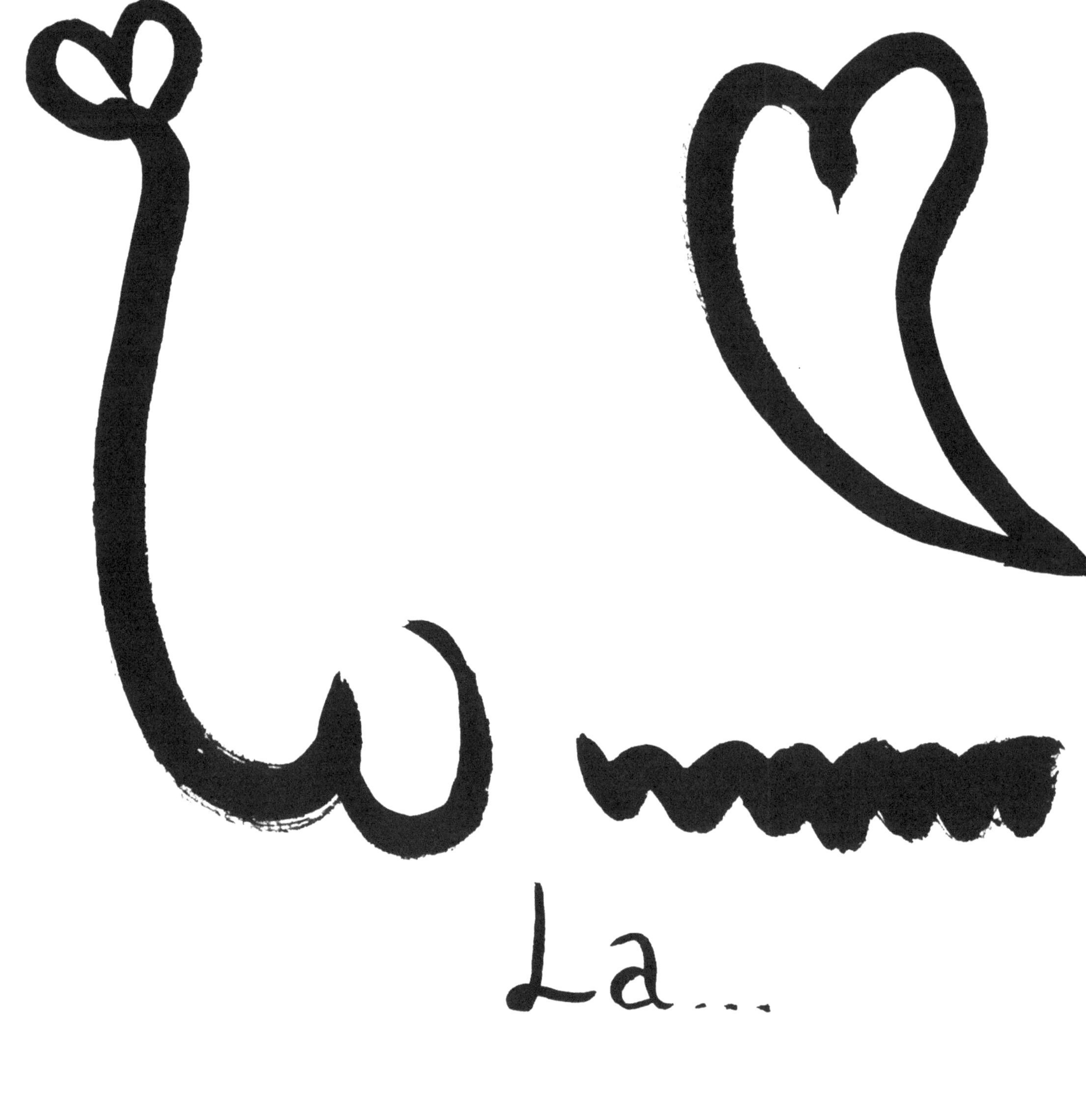
La...

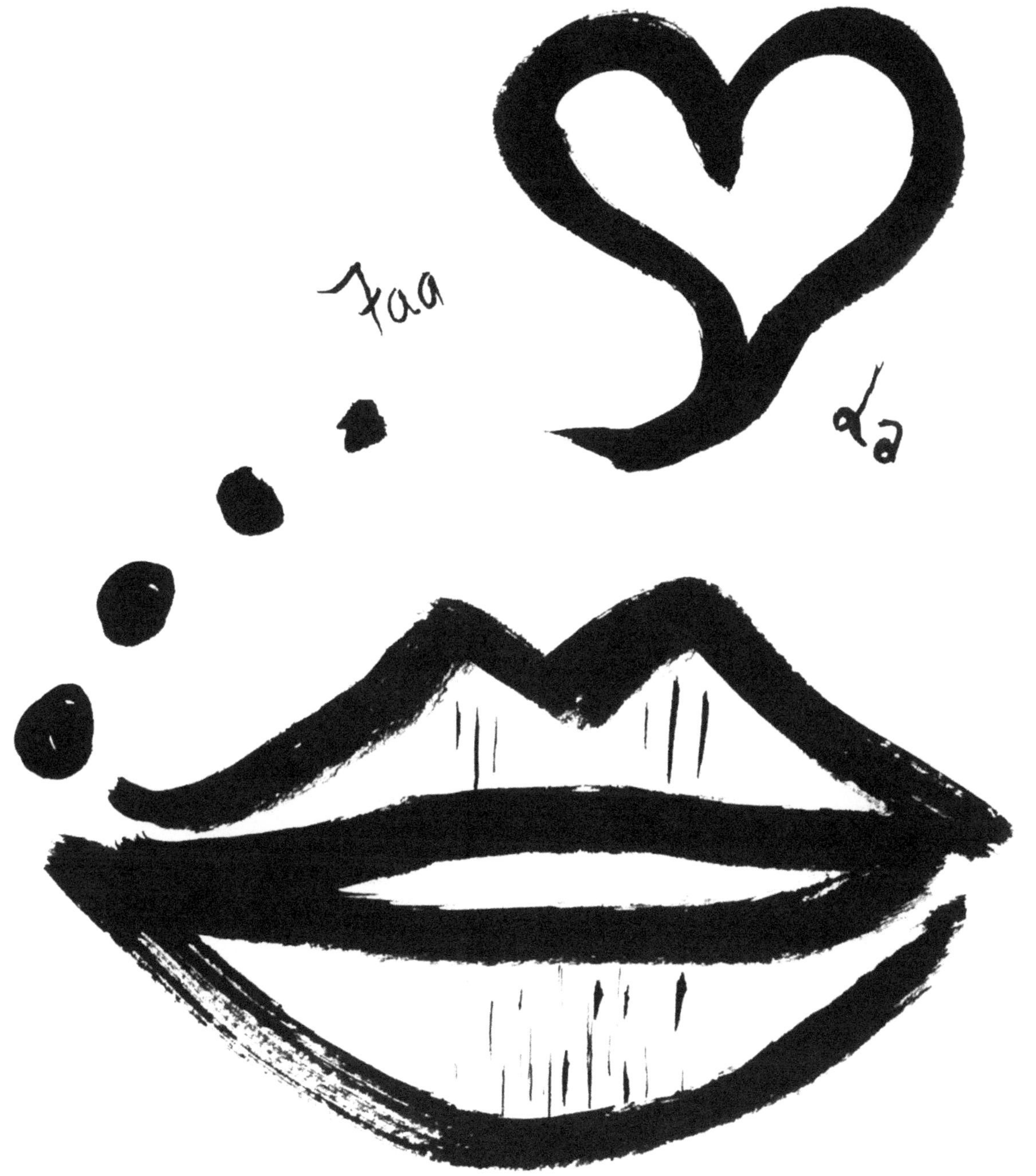

Faa
da

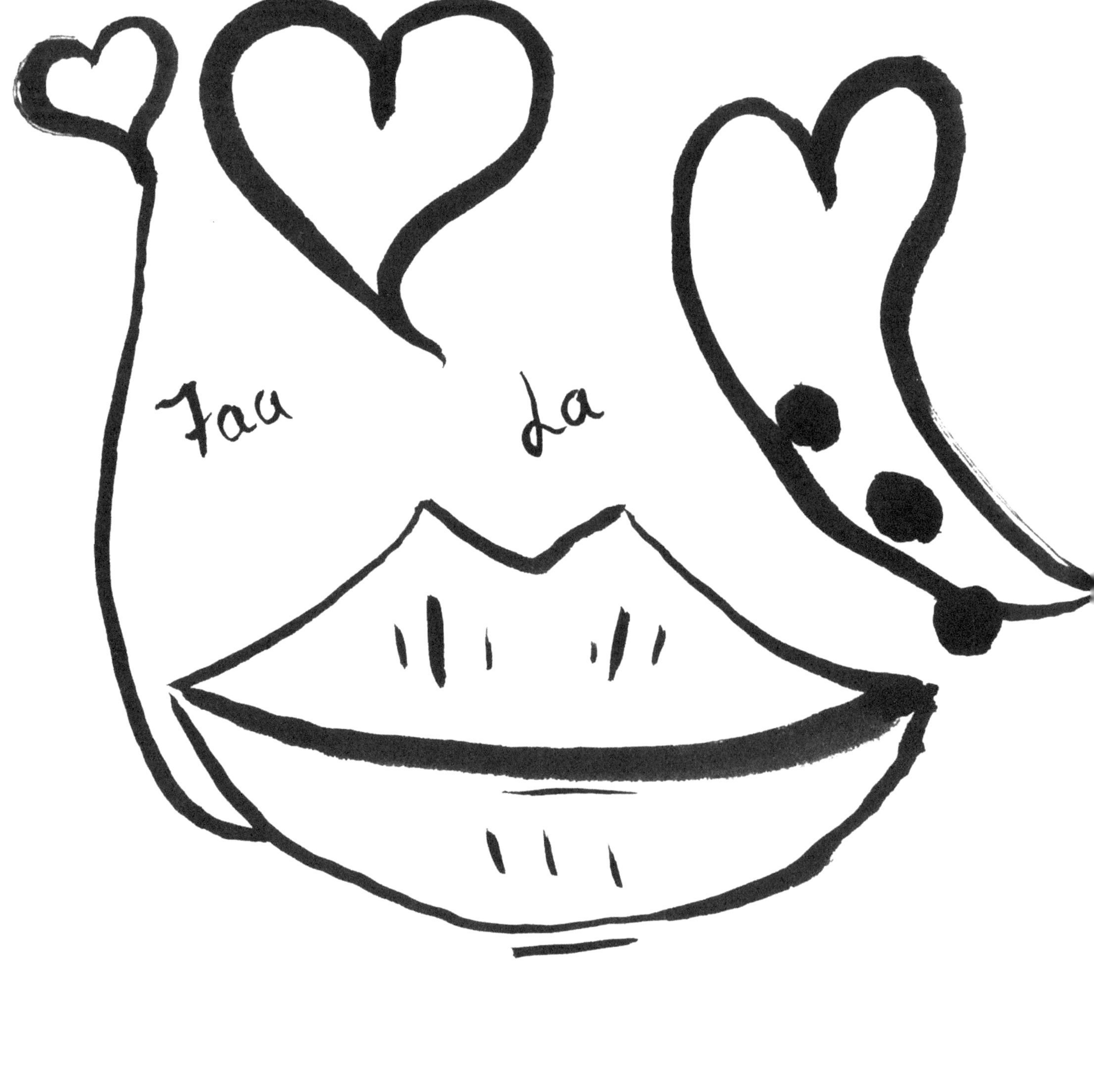

Faa
La

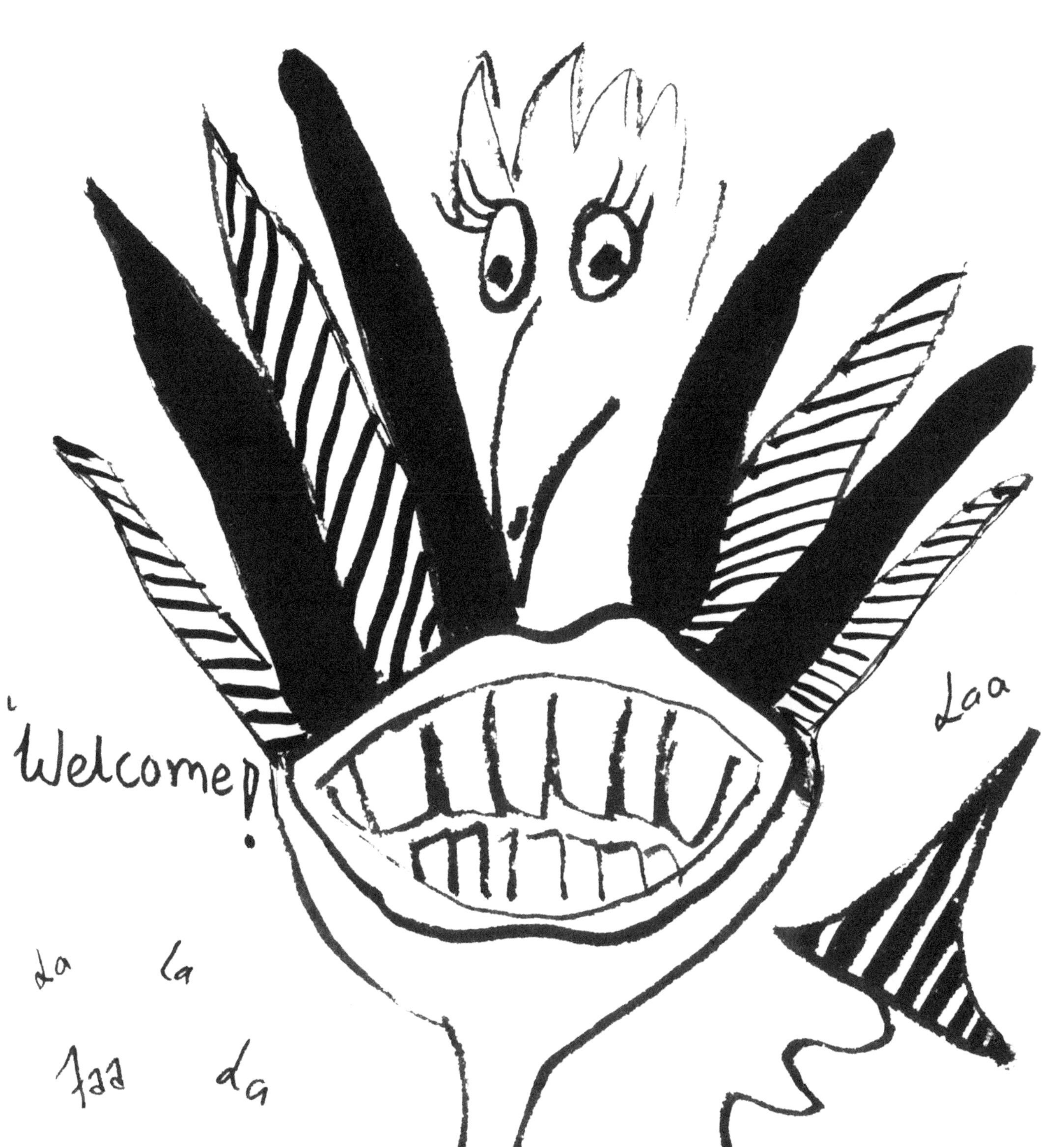
'Welcome!
Laa
da la
Jaa da

this land will take you faa

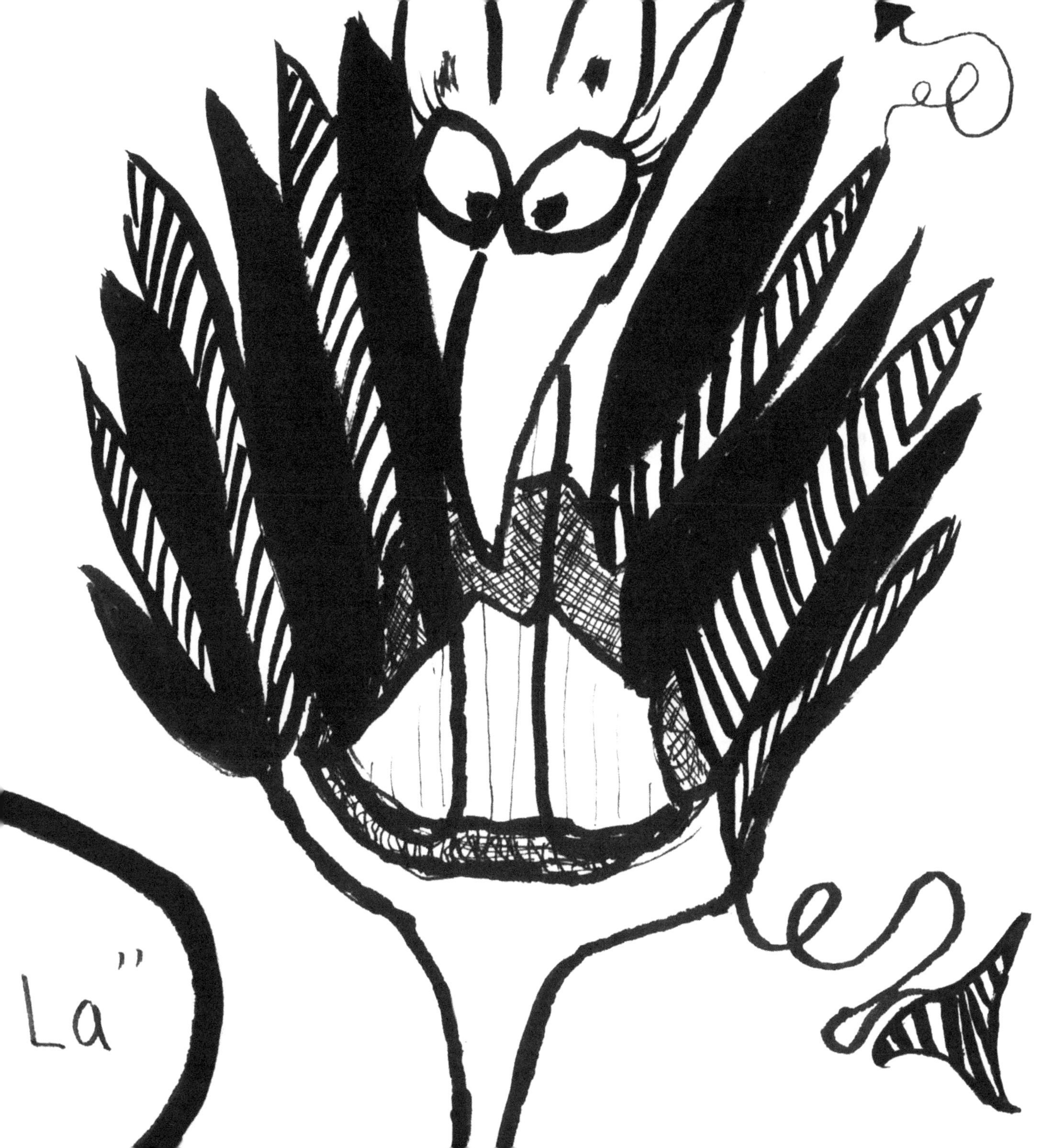
La"

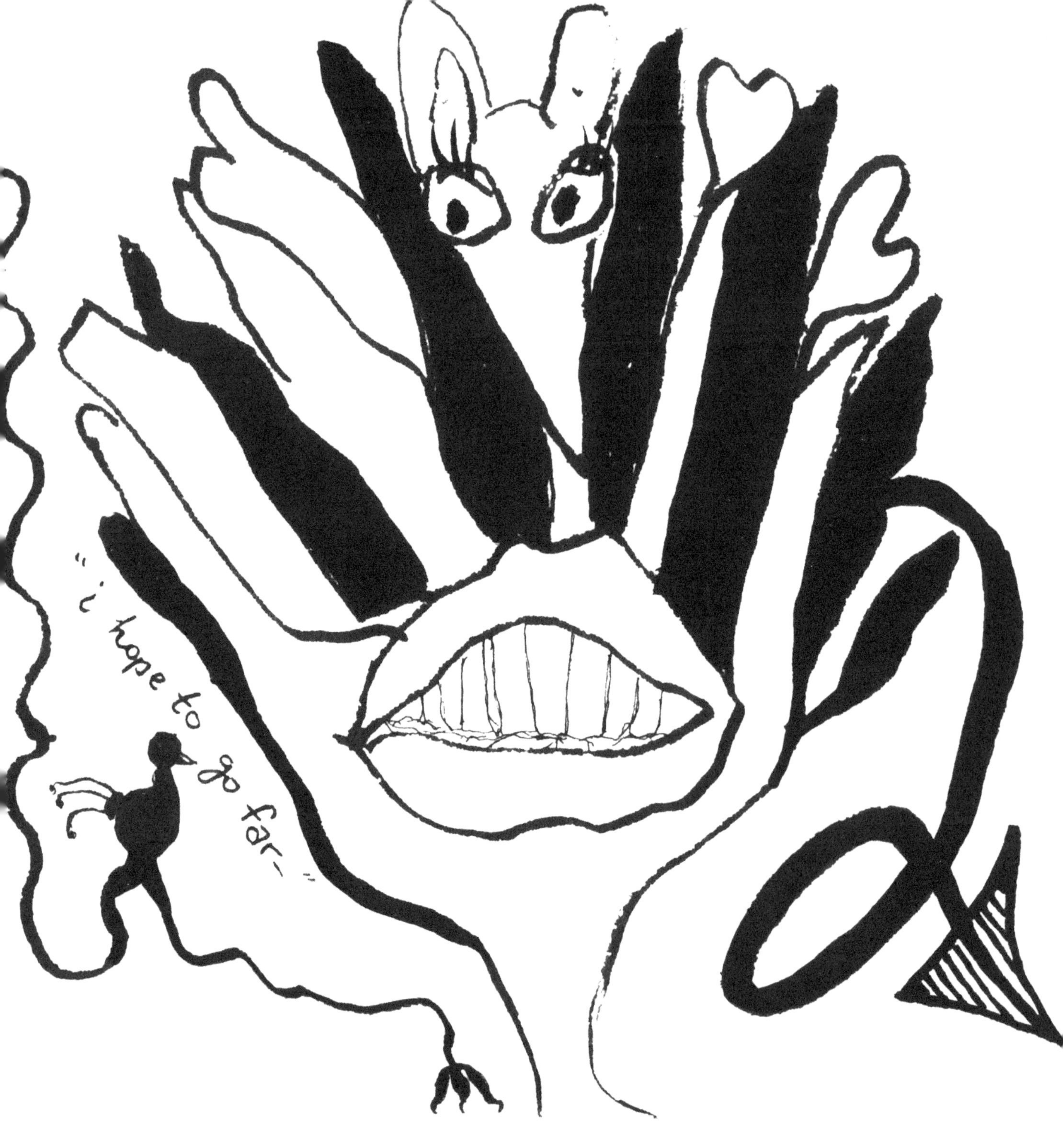
"i hope to go far-"

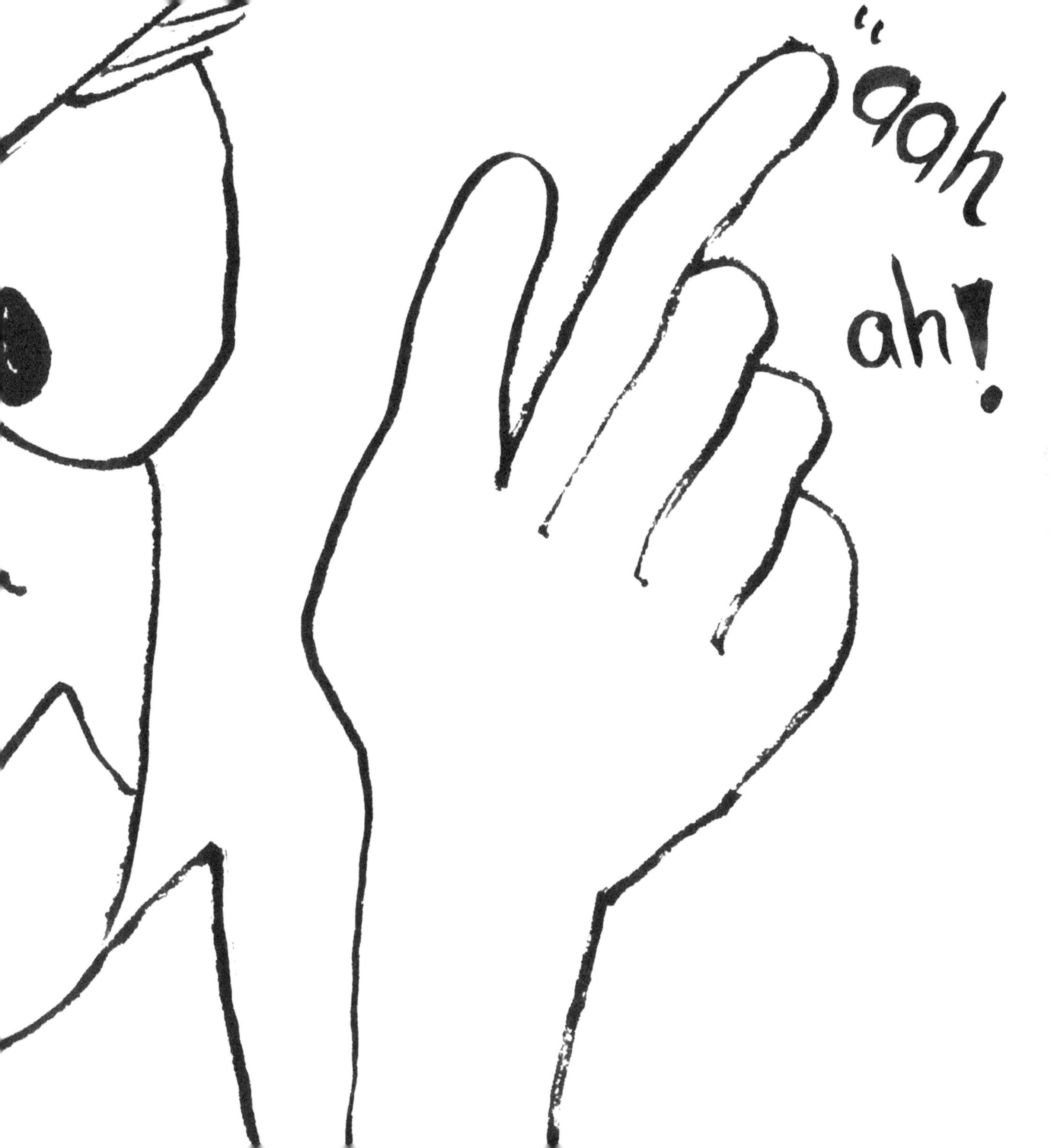
"aah
ah!

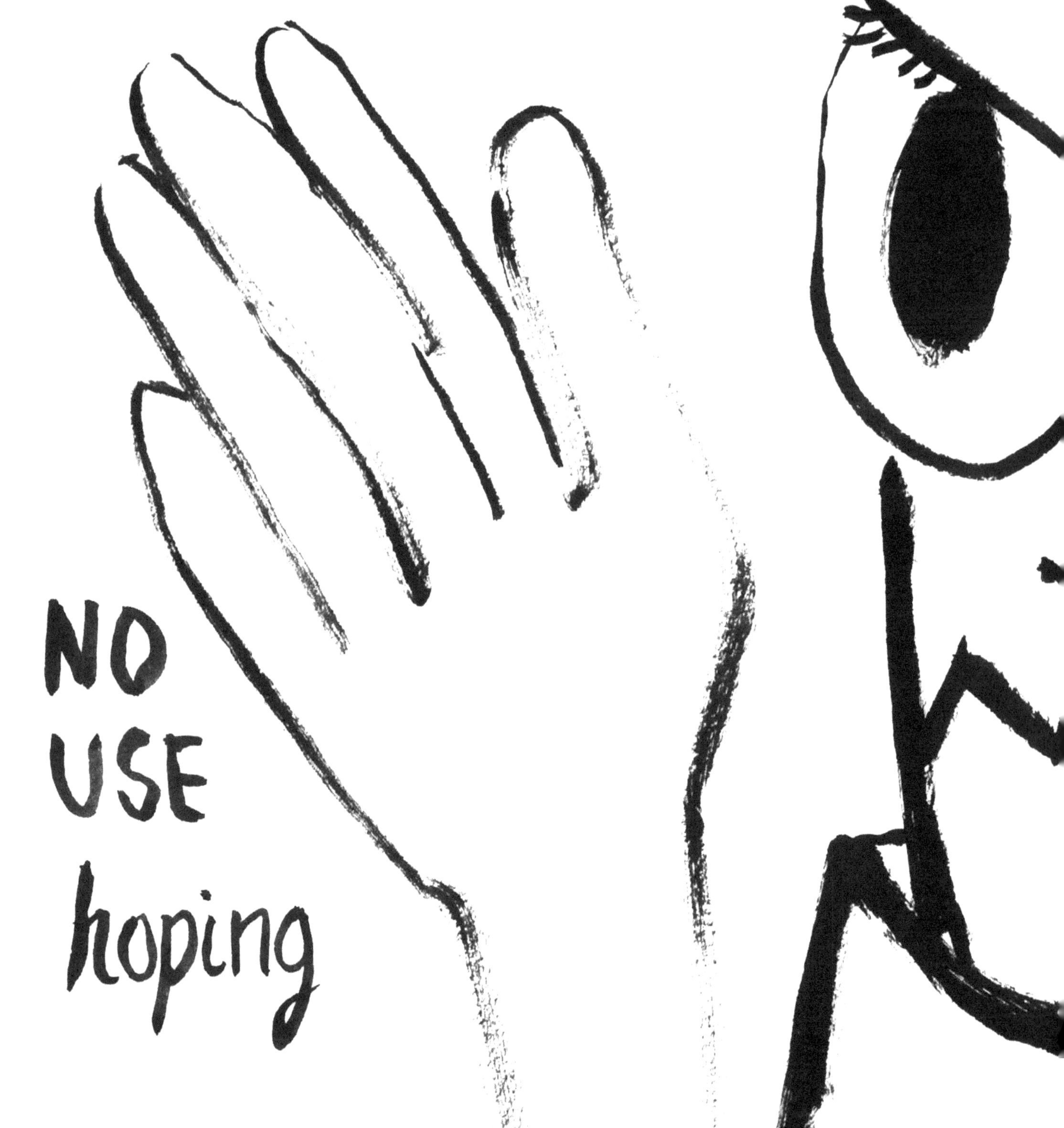

NO
USE
hoping

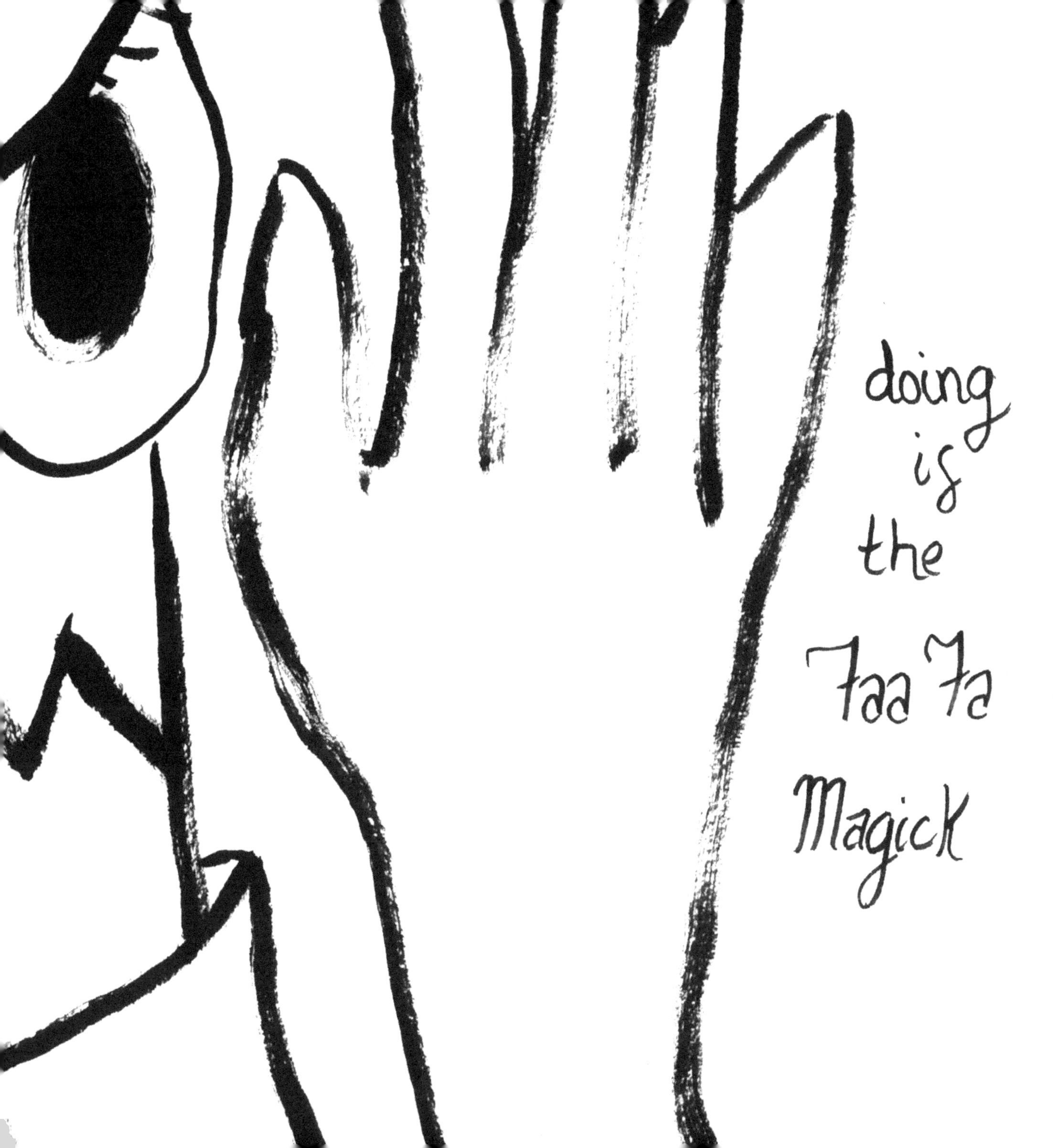
doing
is
the
Faa Fa
Magick

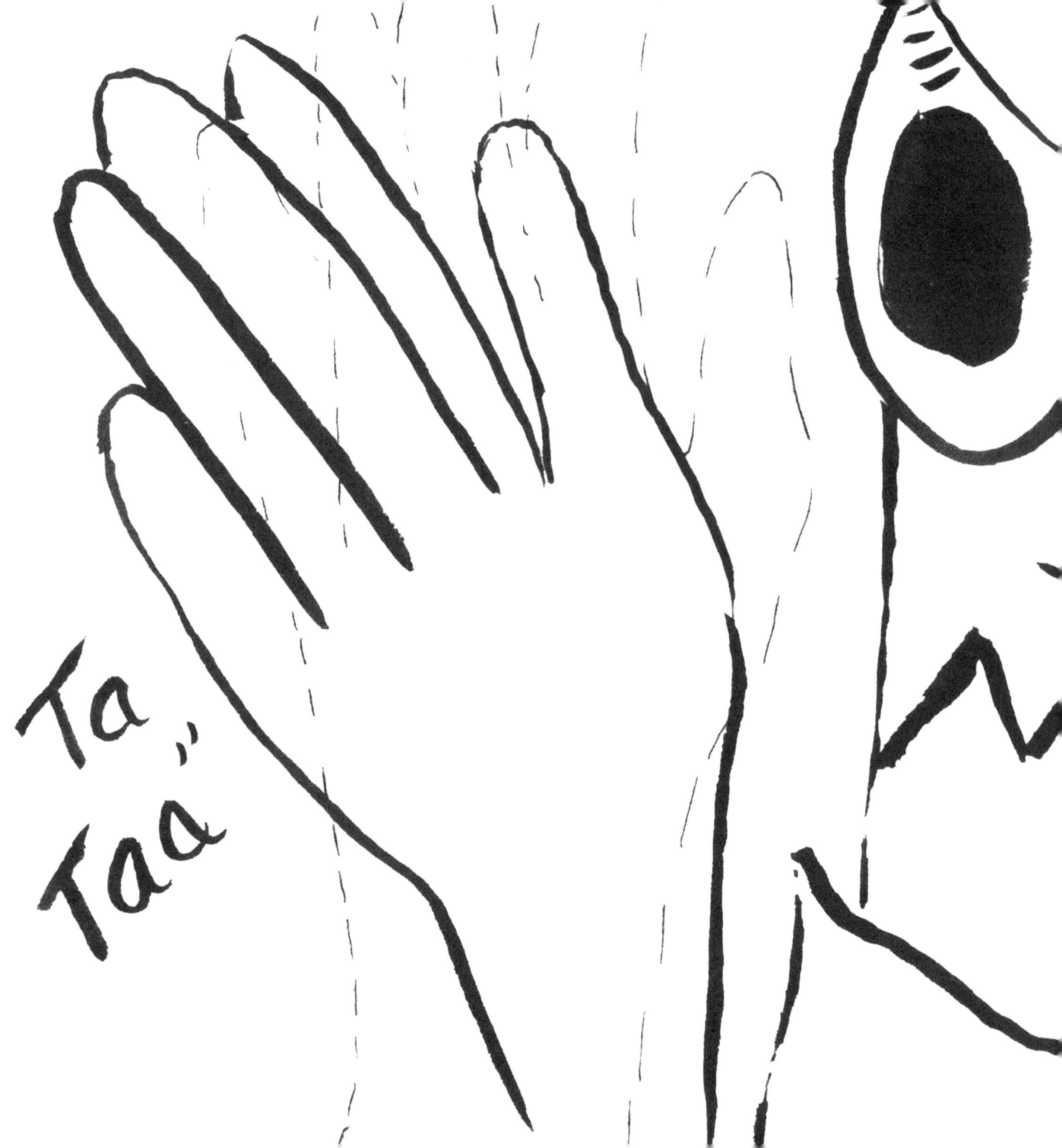

Ta,
Taa

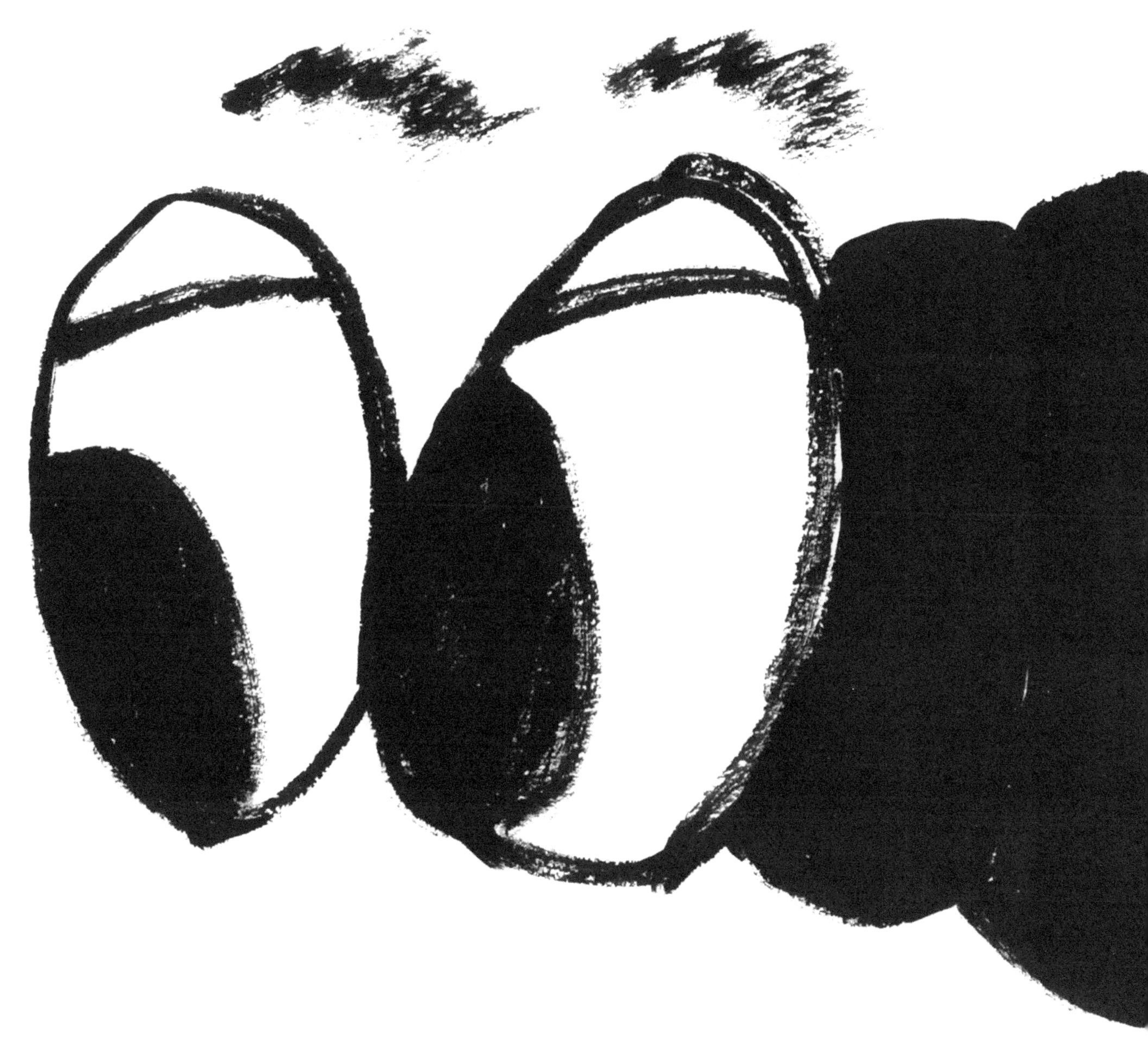

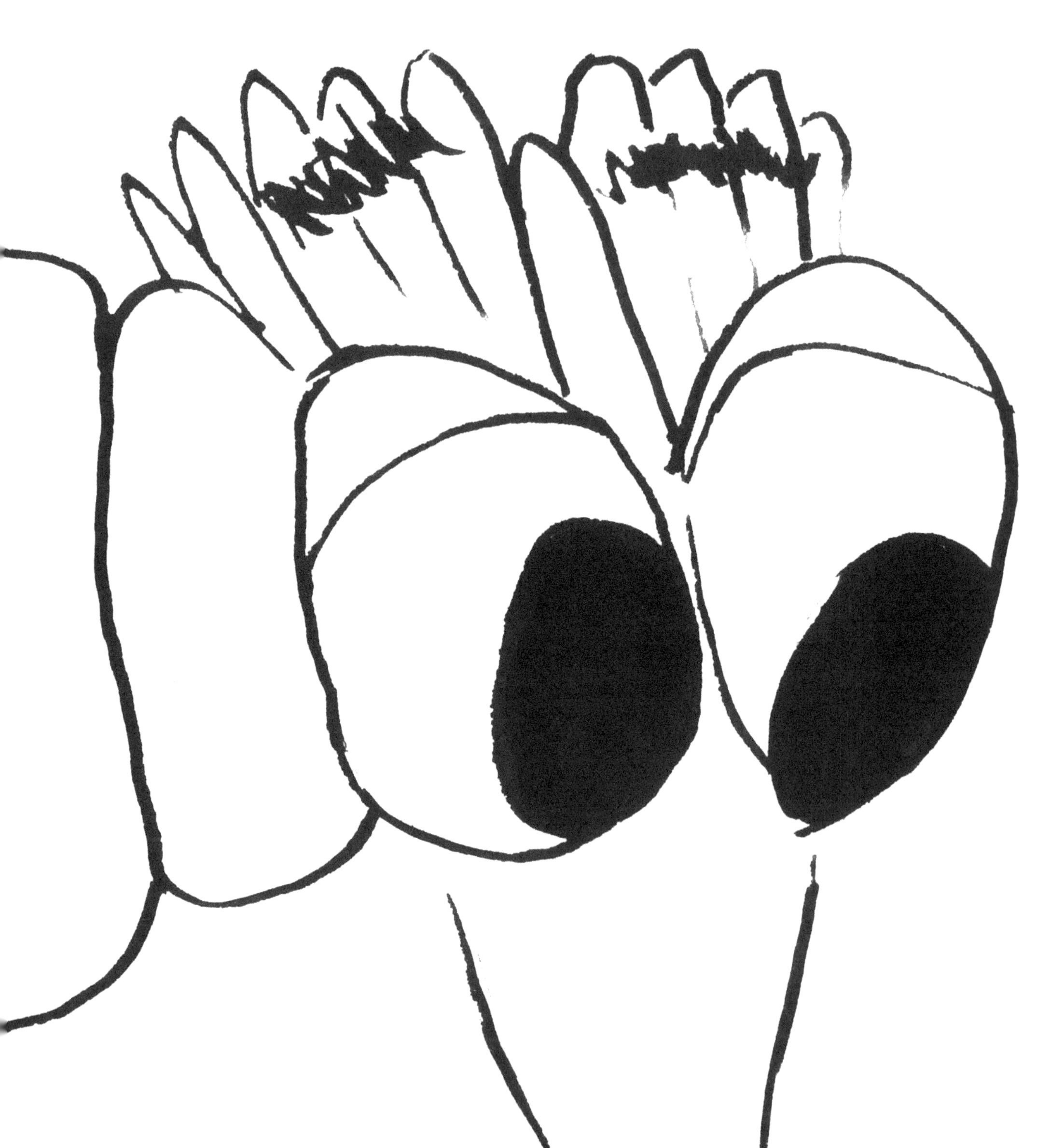

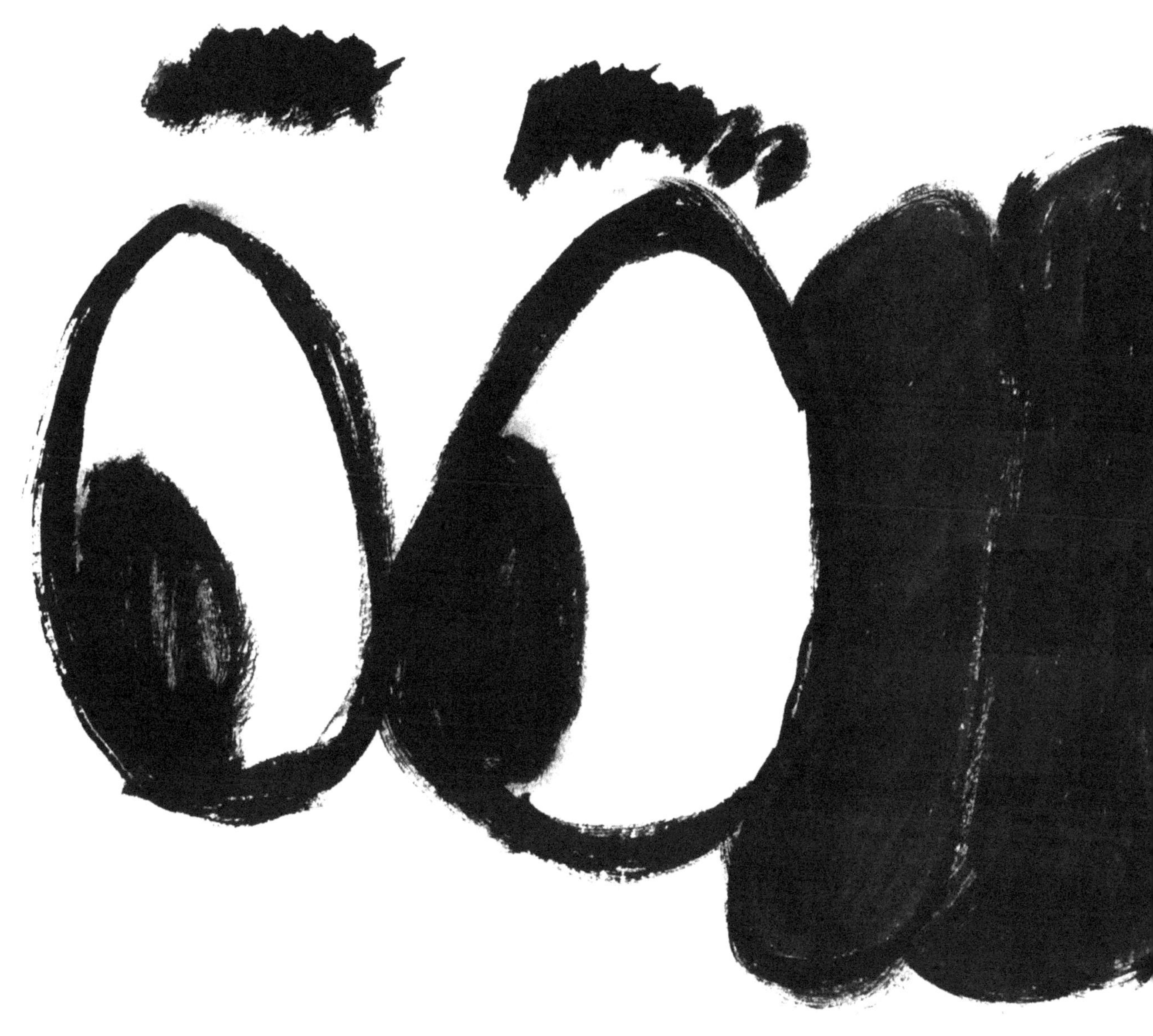

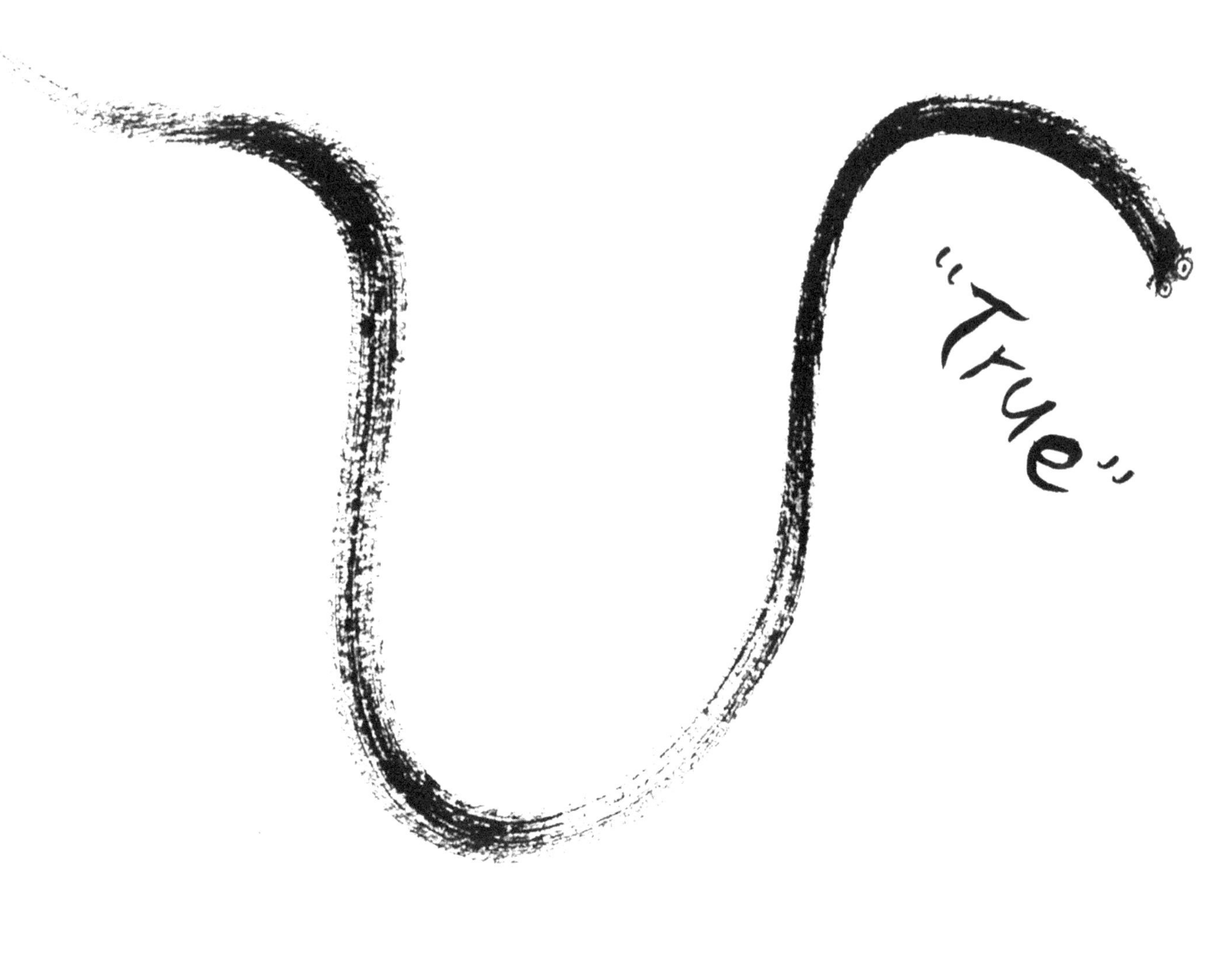
"True"

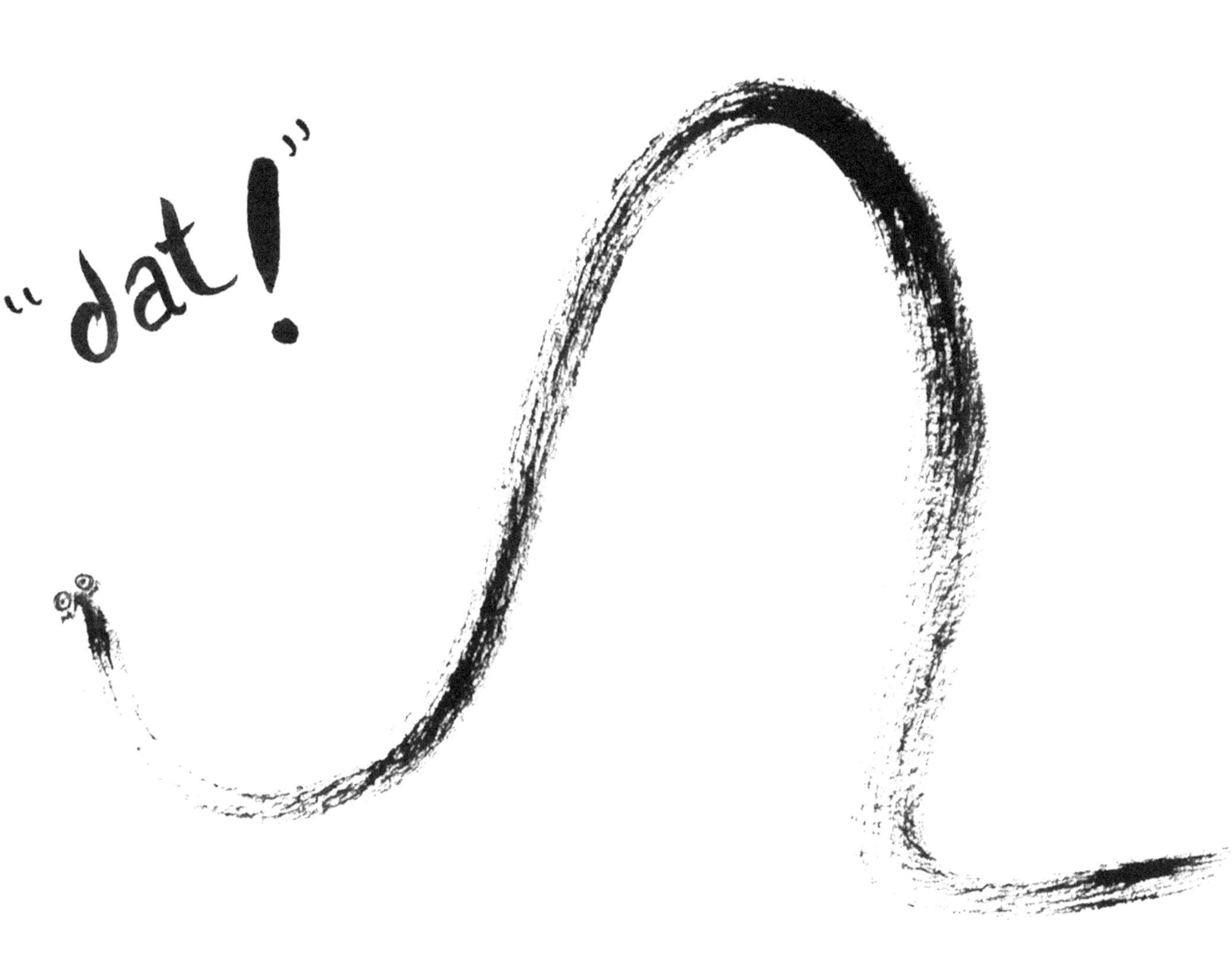
"dat!"

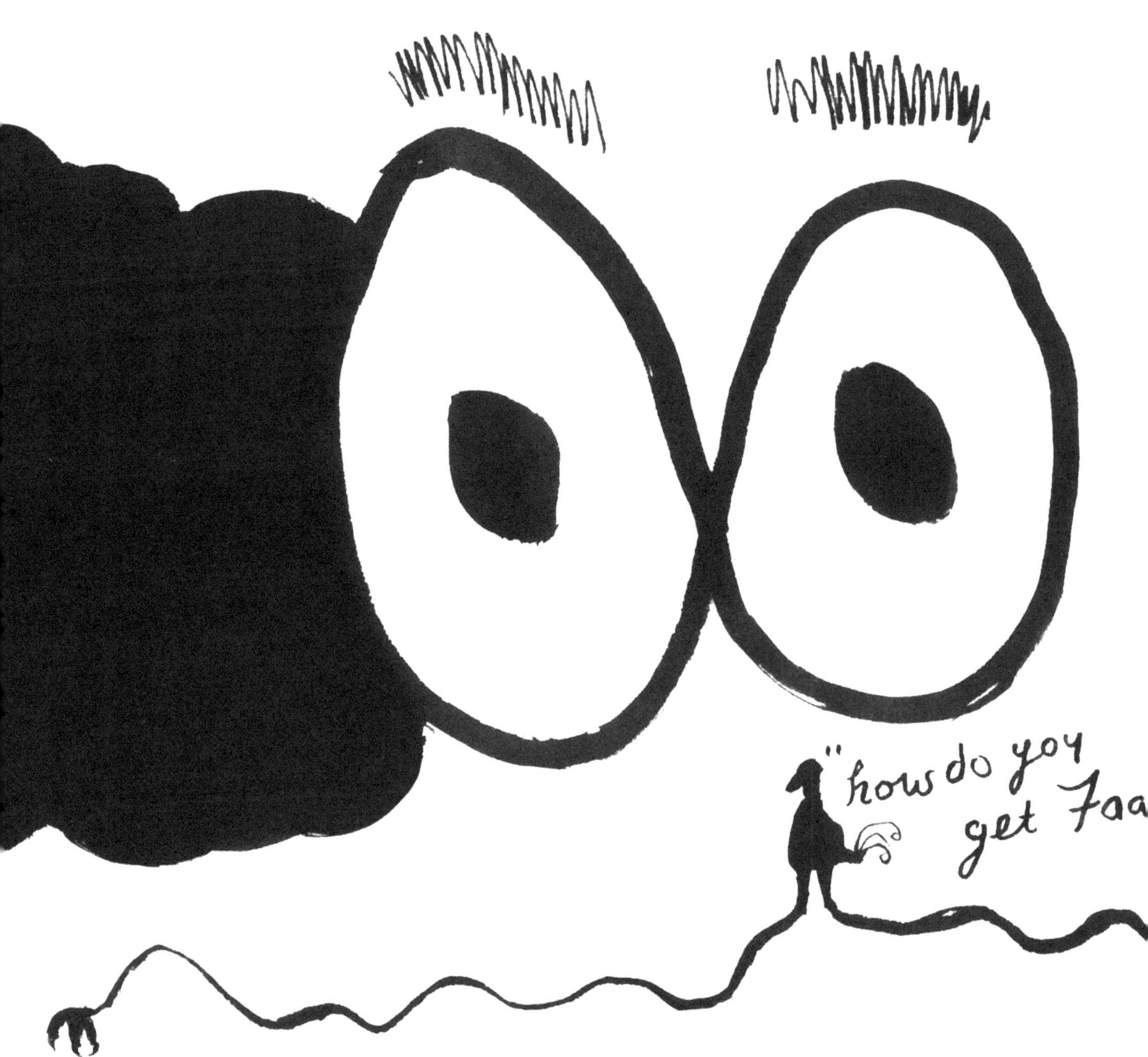
"how do you
get faa

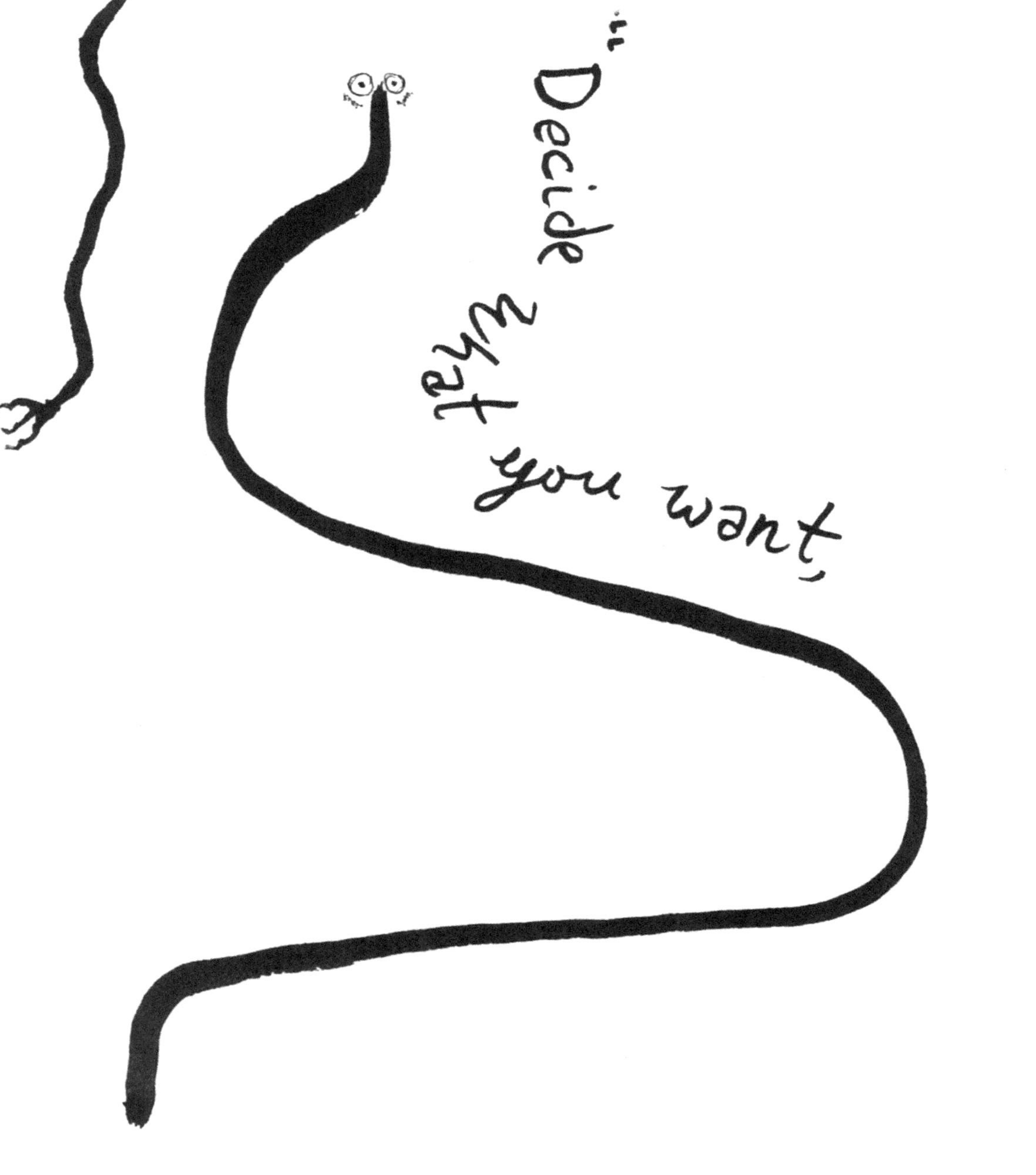
"Decide what you want,

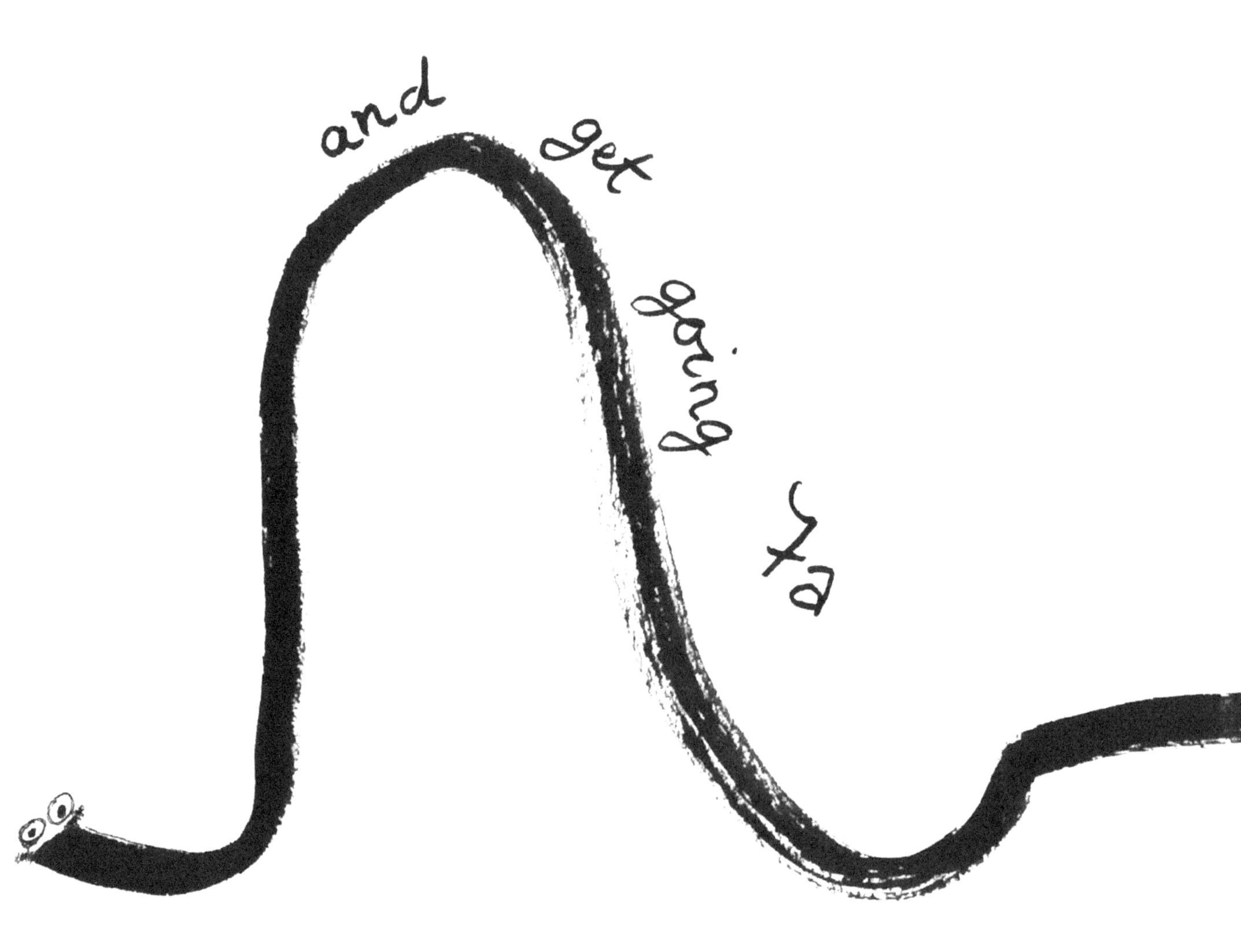

and
get
going
ta

7aa

7aaa

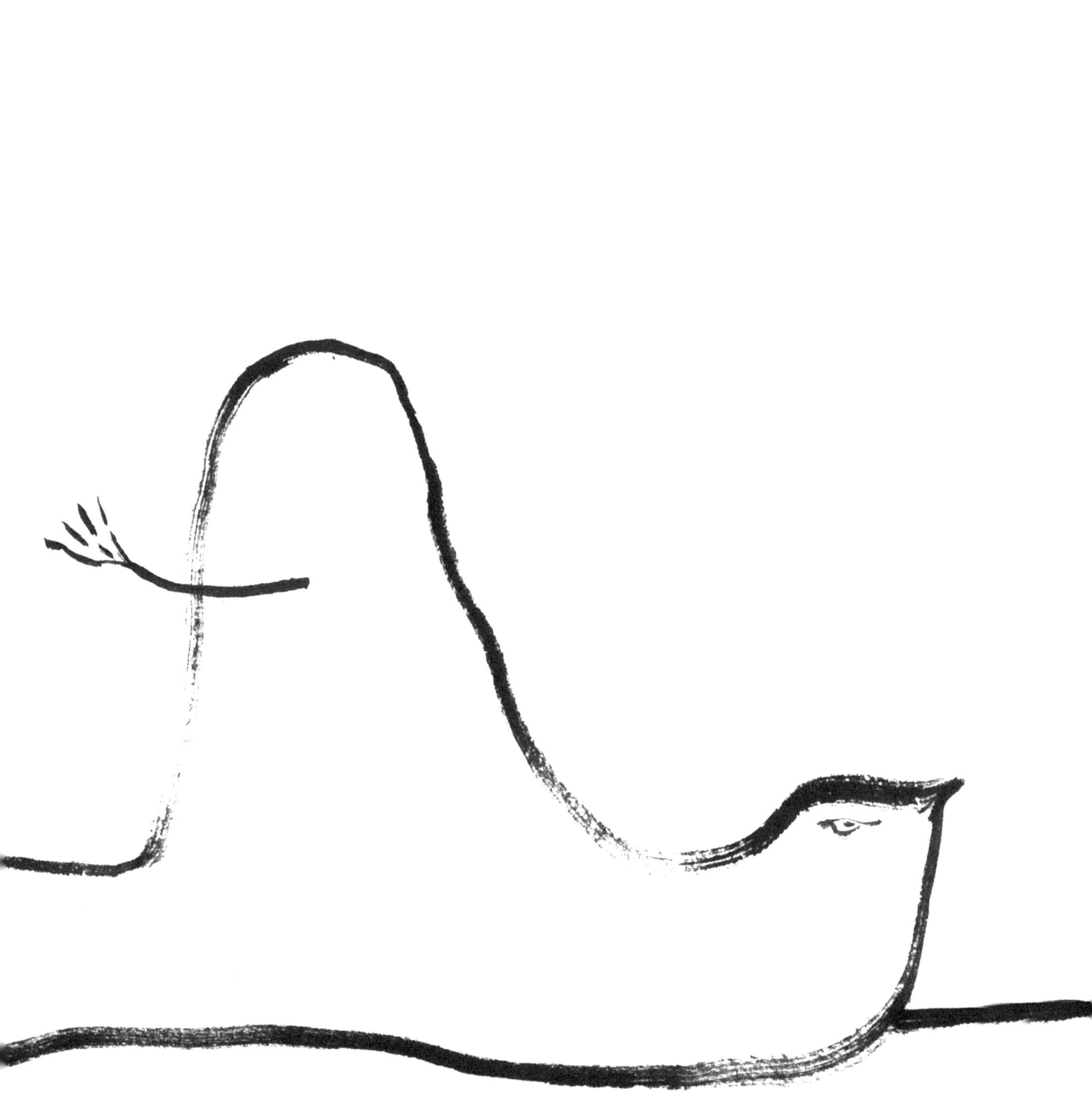

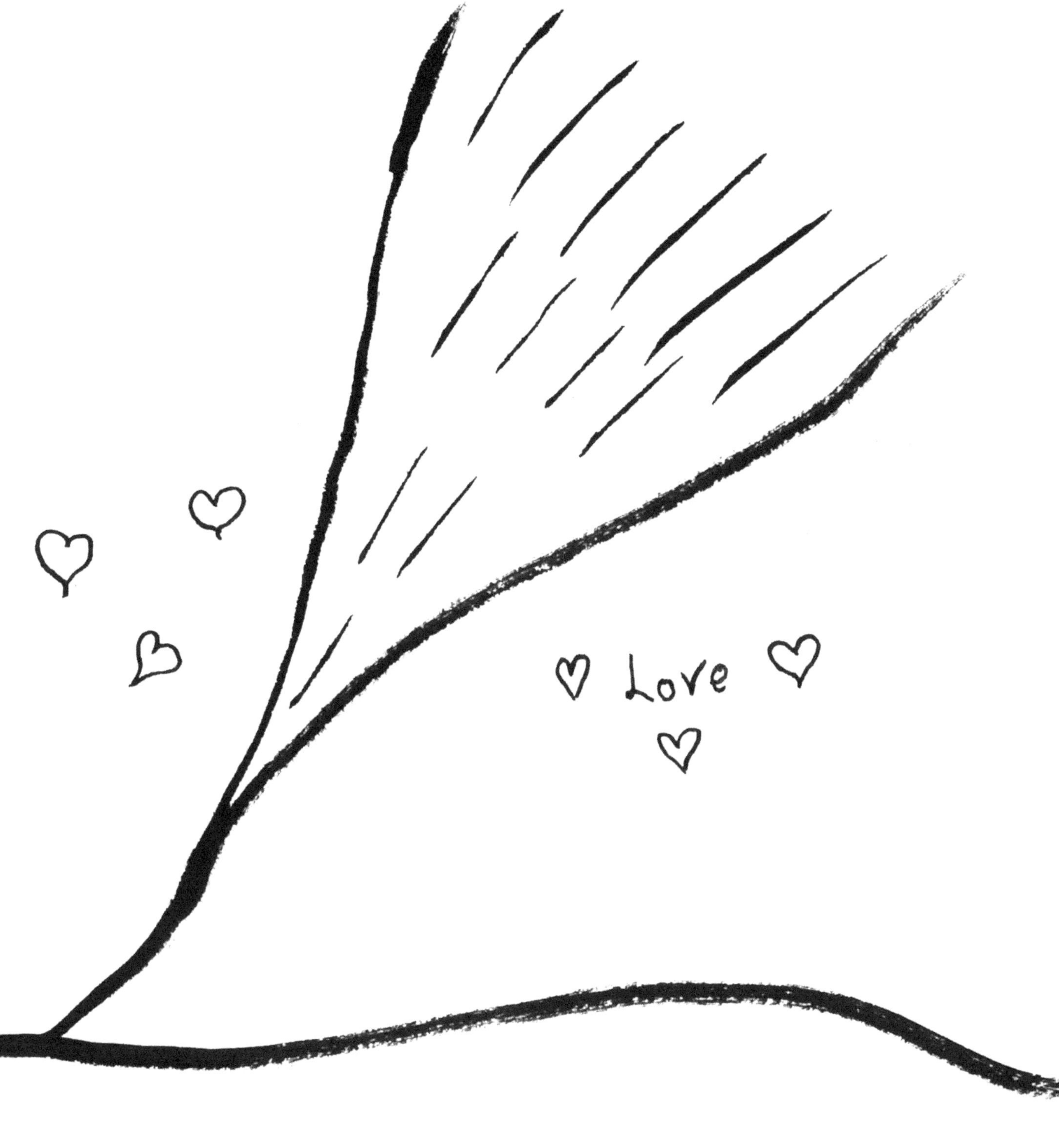
Love

" i love feathers
i love feathers "

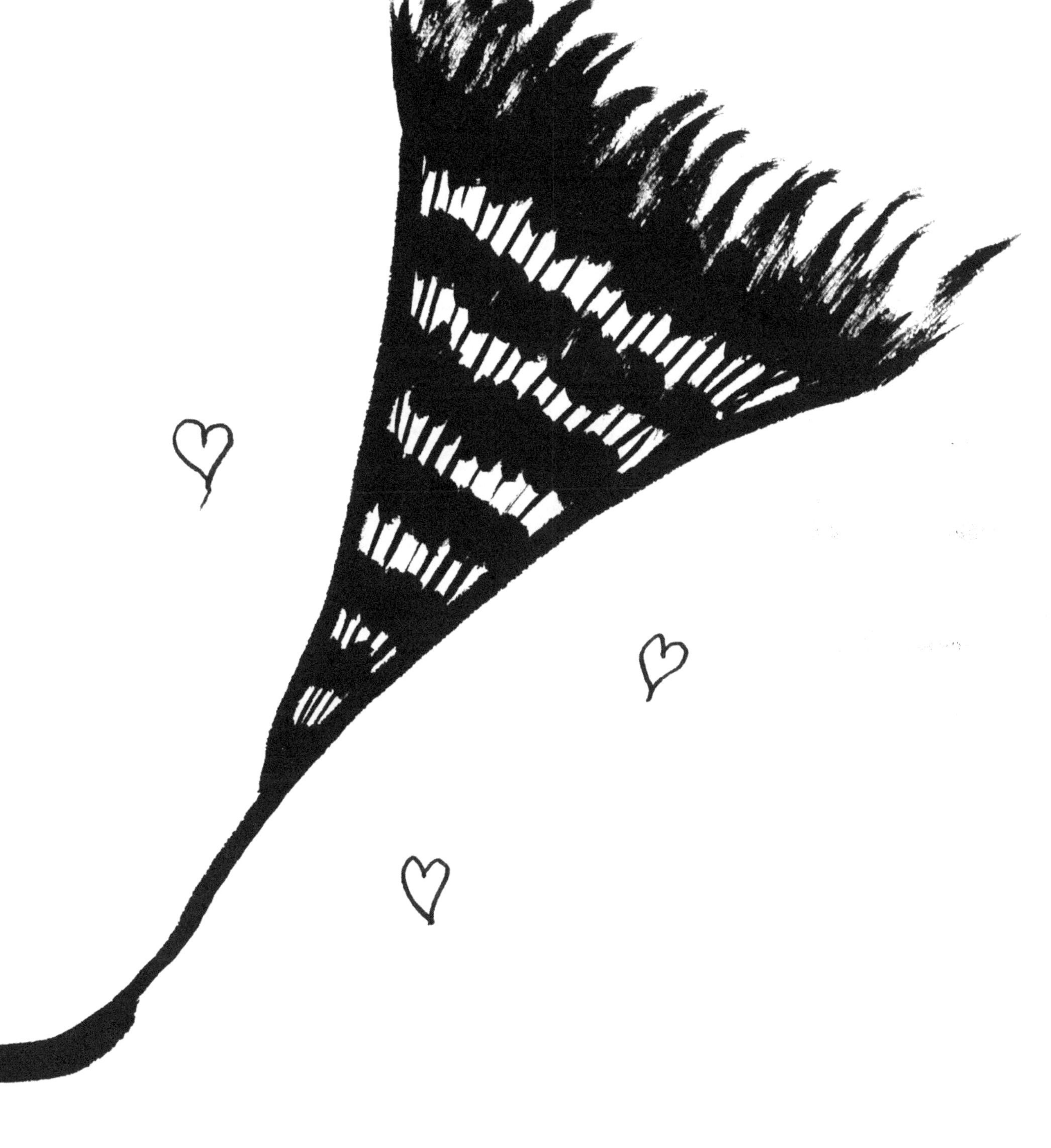

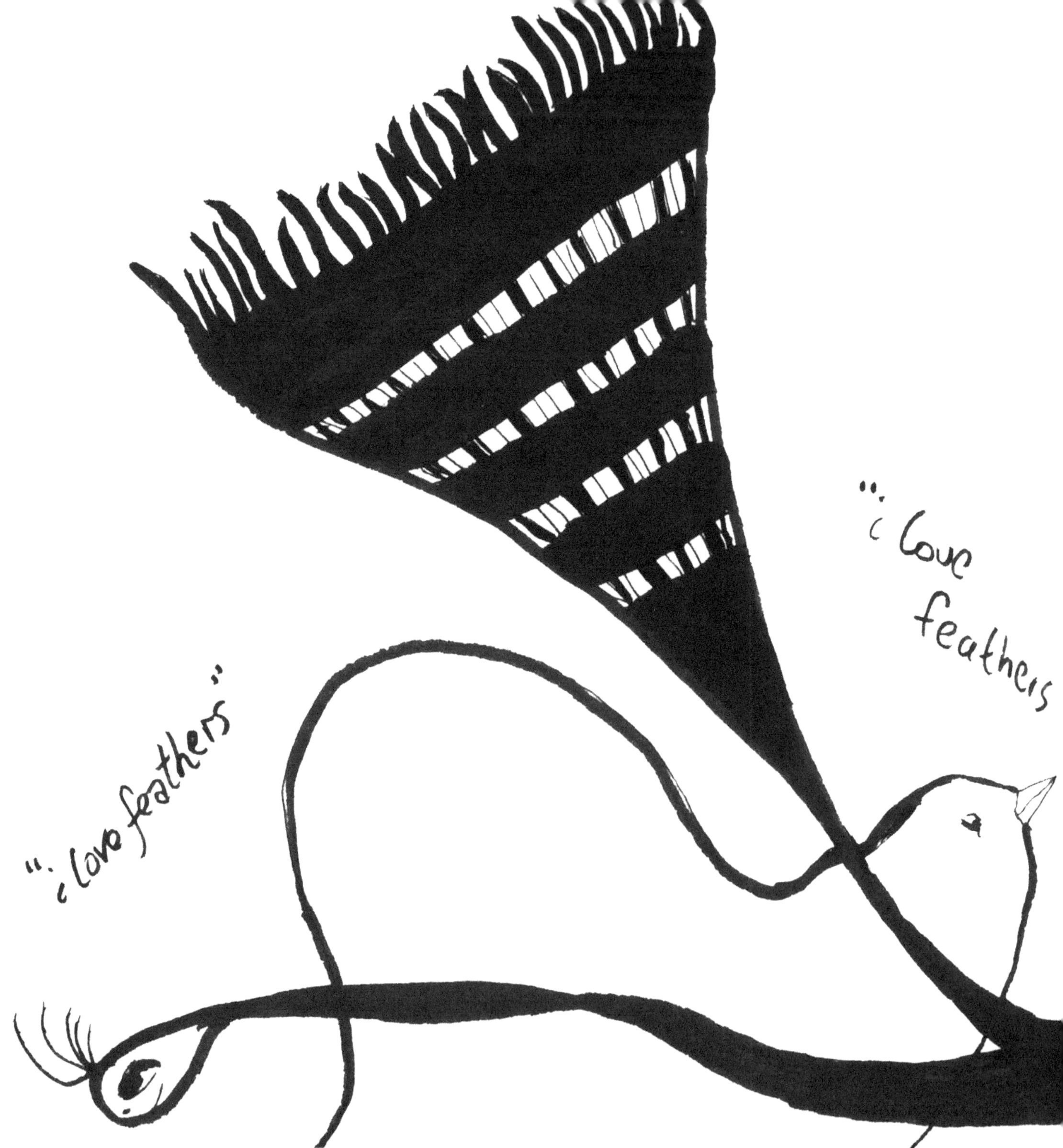
"¿ love feathers"
"¿ love feathers"

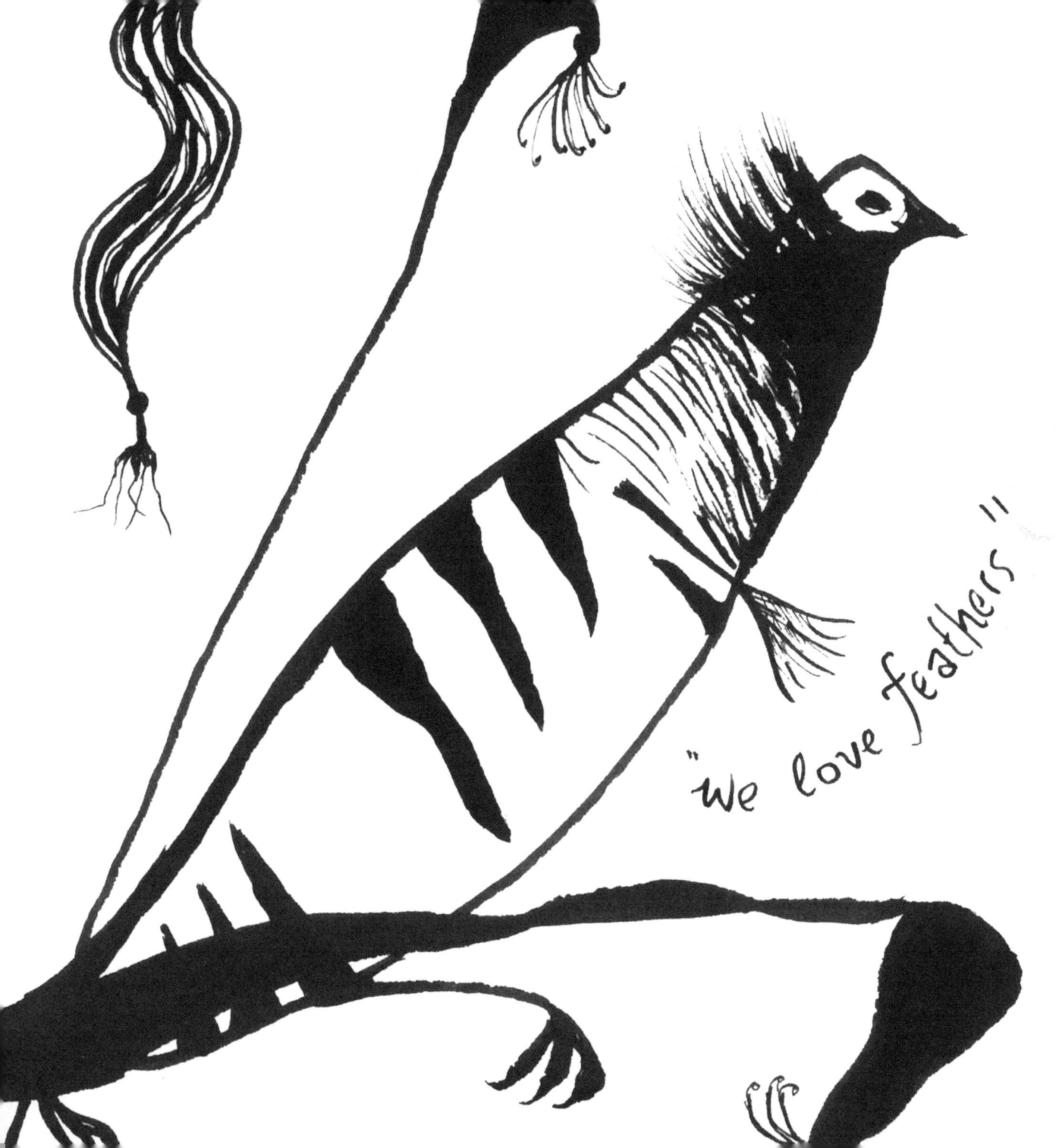
"we love feathers"

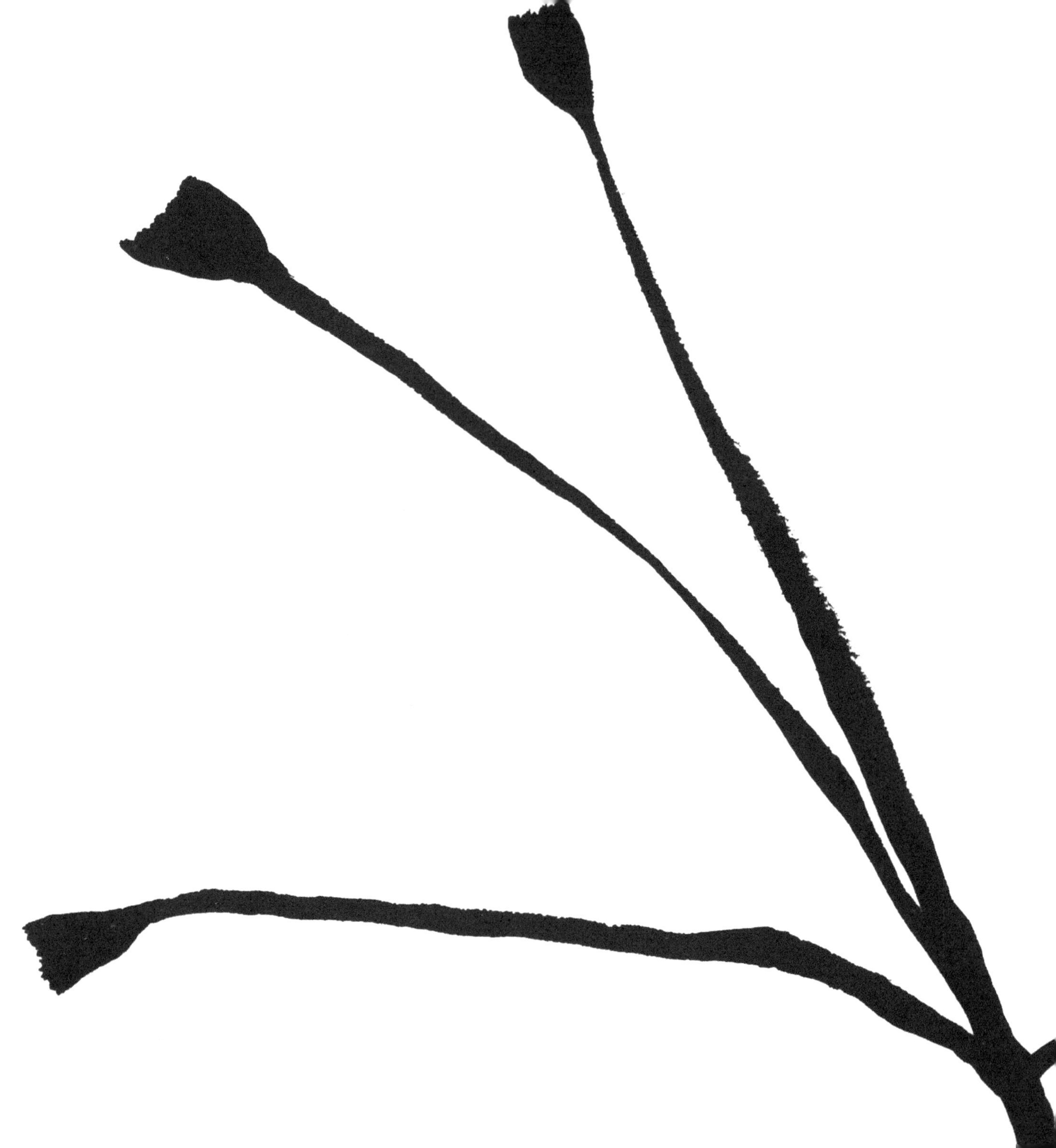

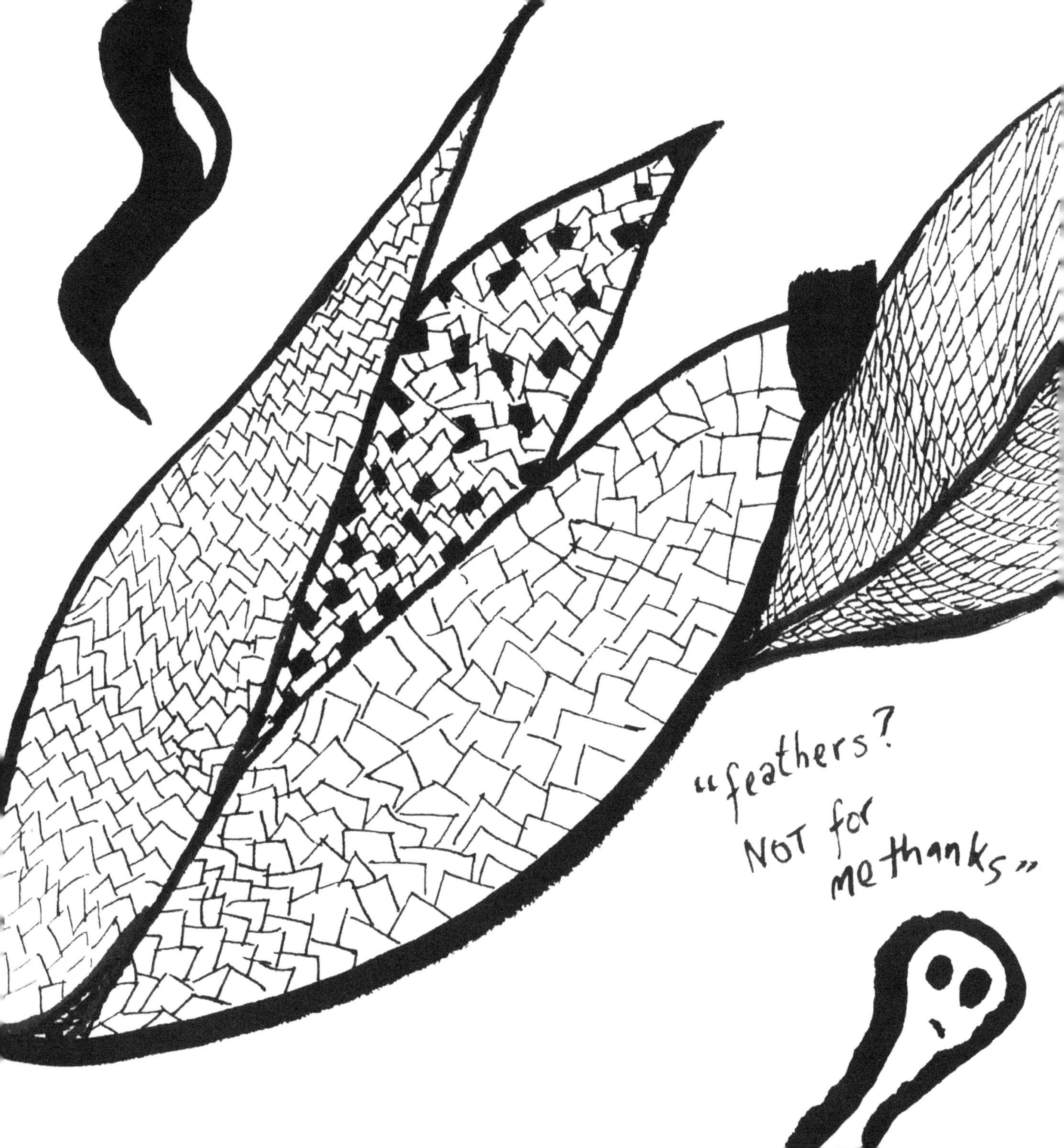
"feathers?
NOT for
me thanks"

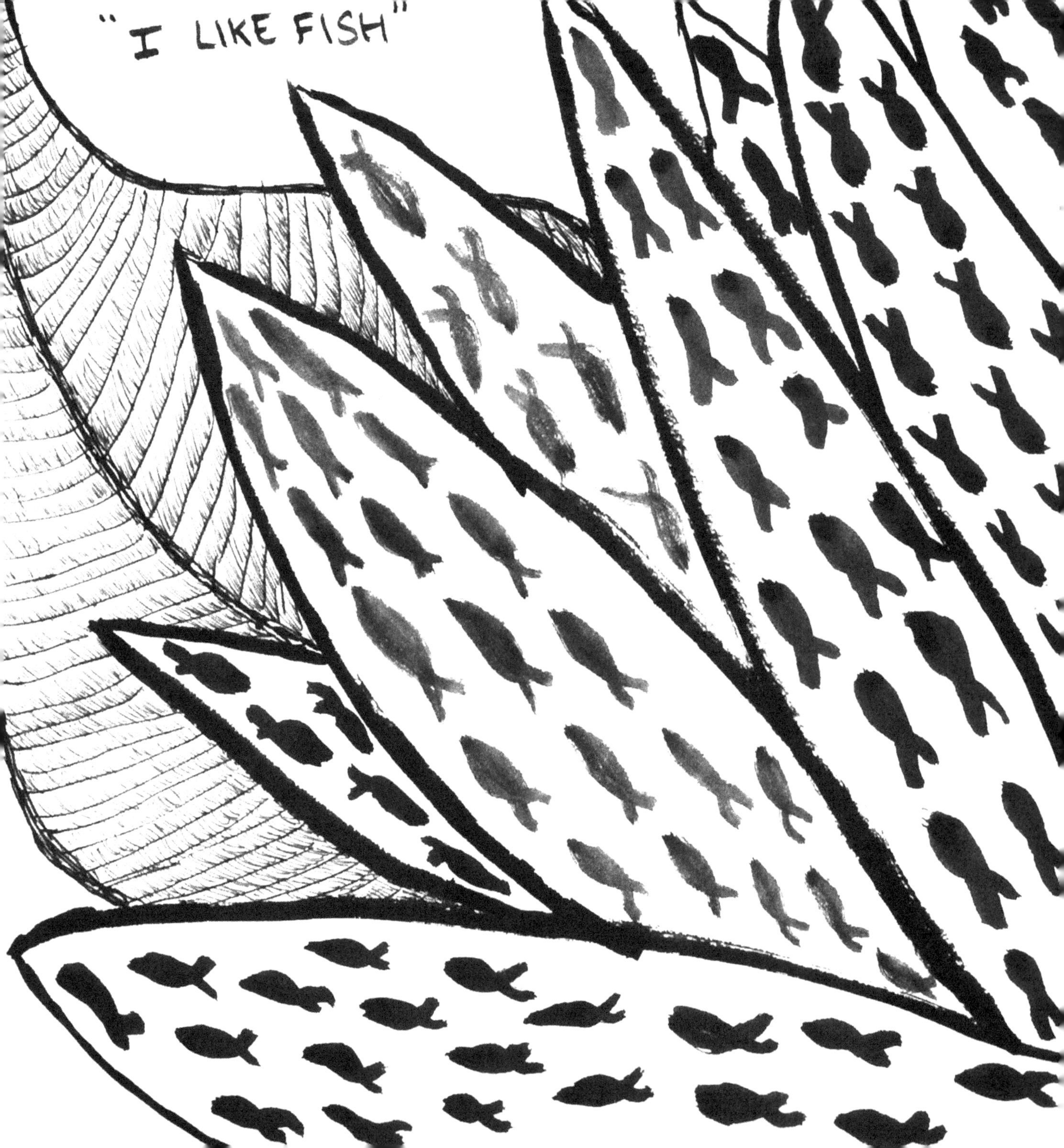
"I LIKE FISH"

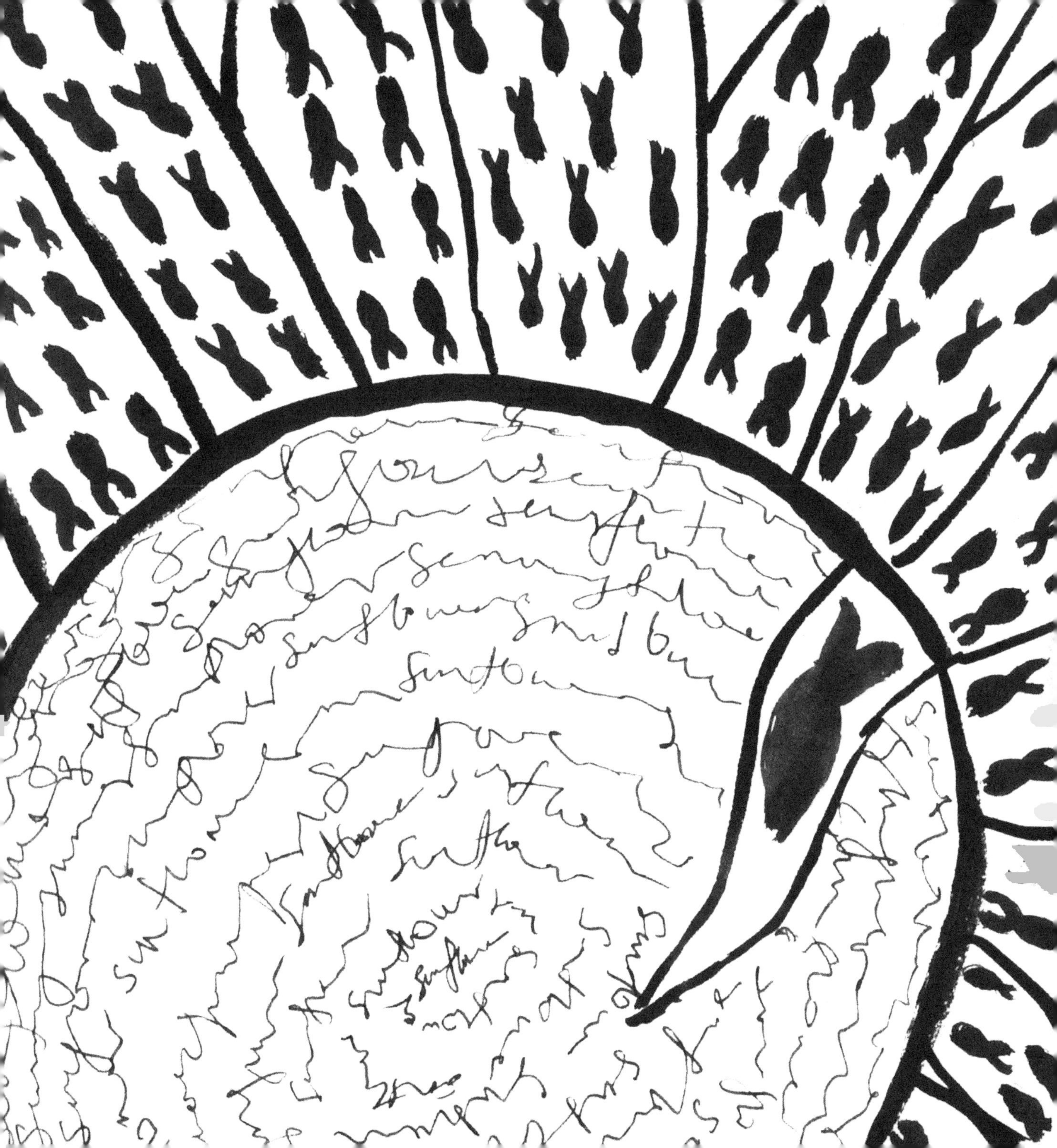

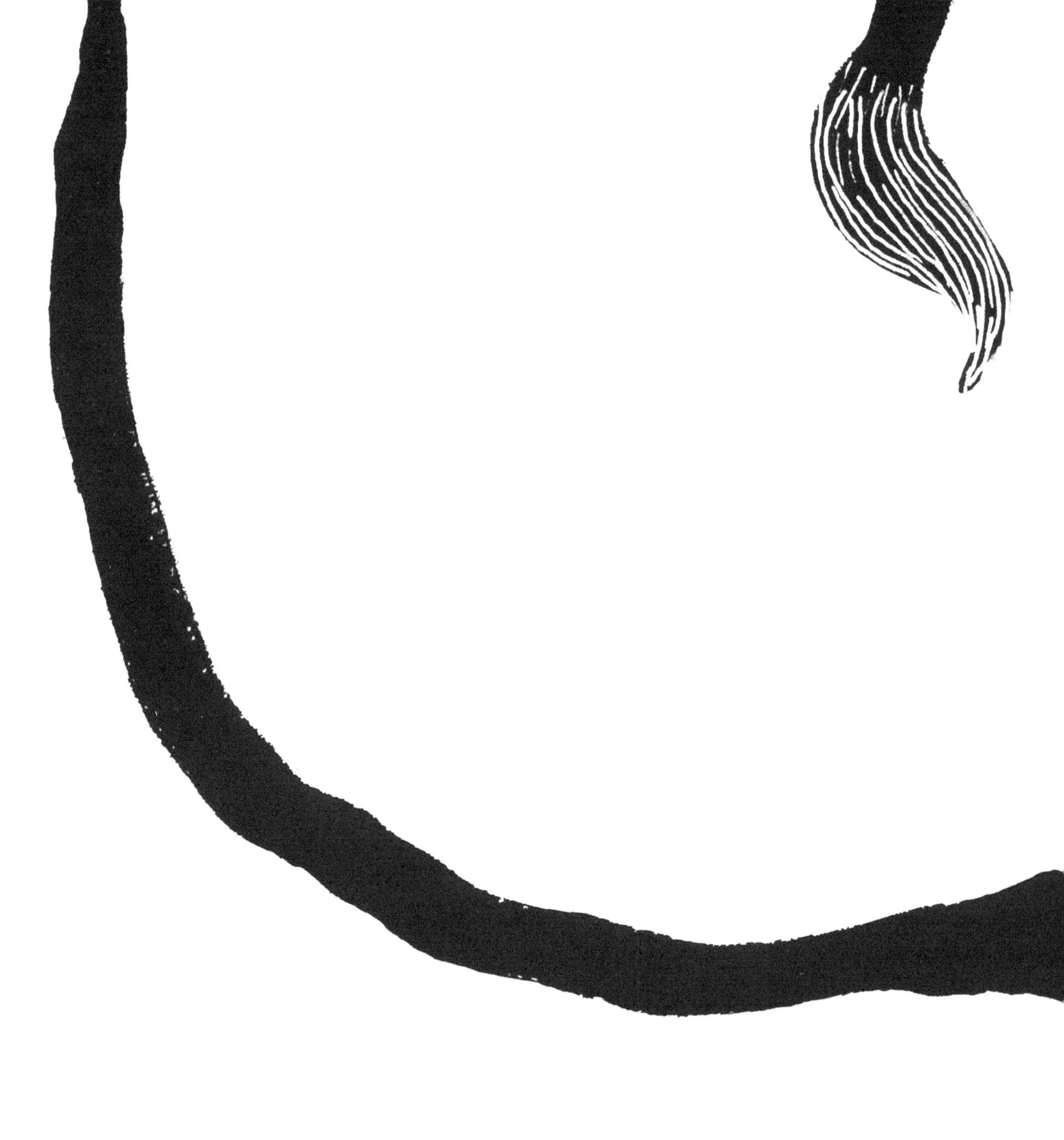

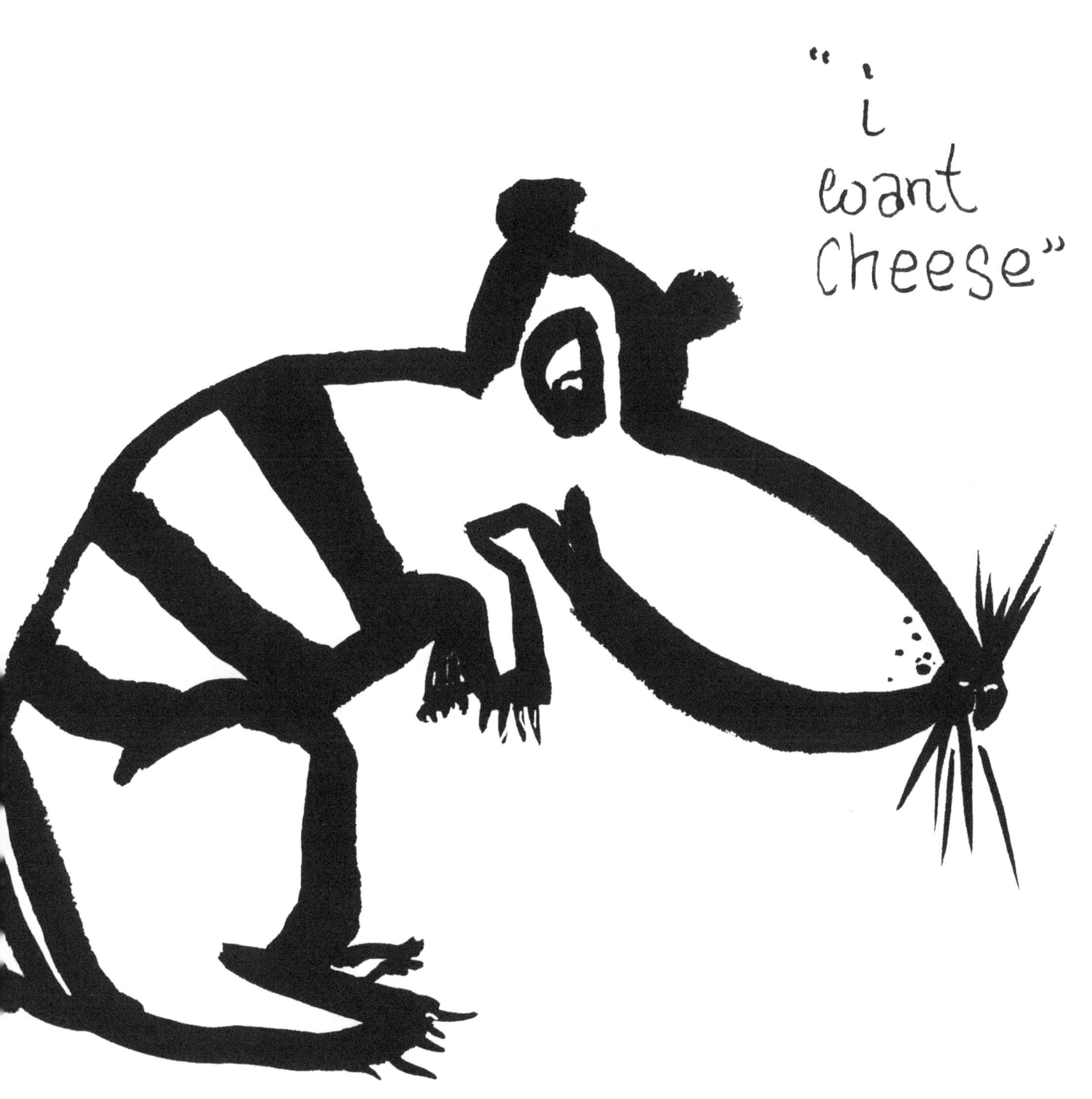

"i
want
cheese"

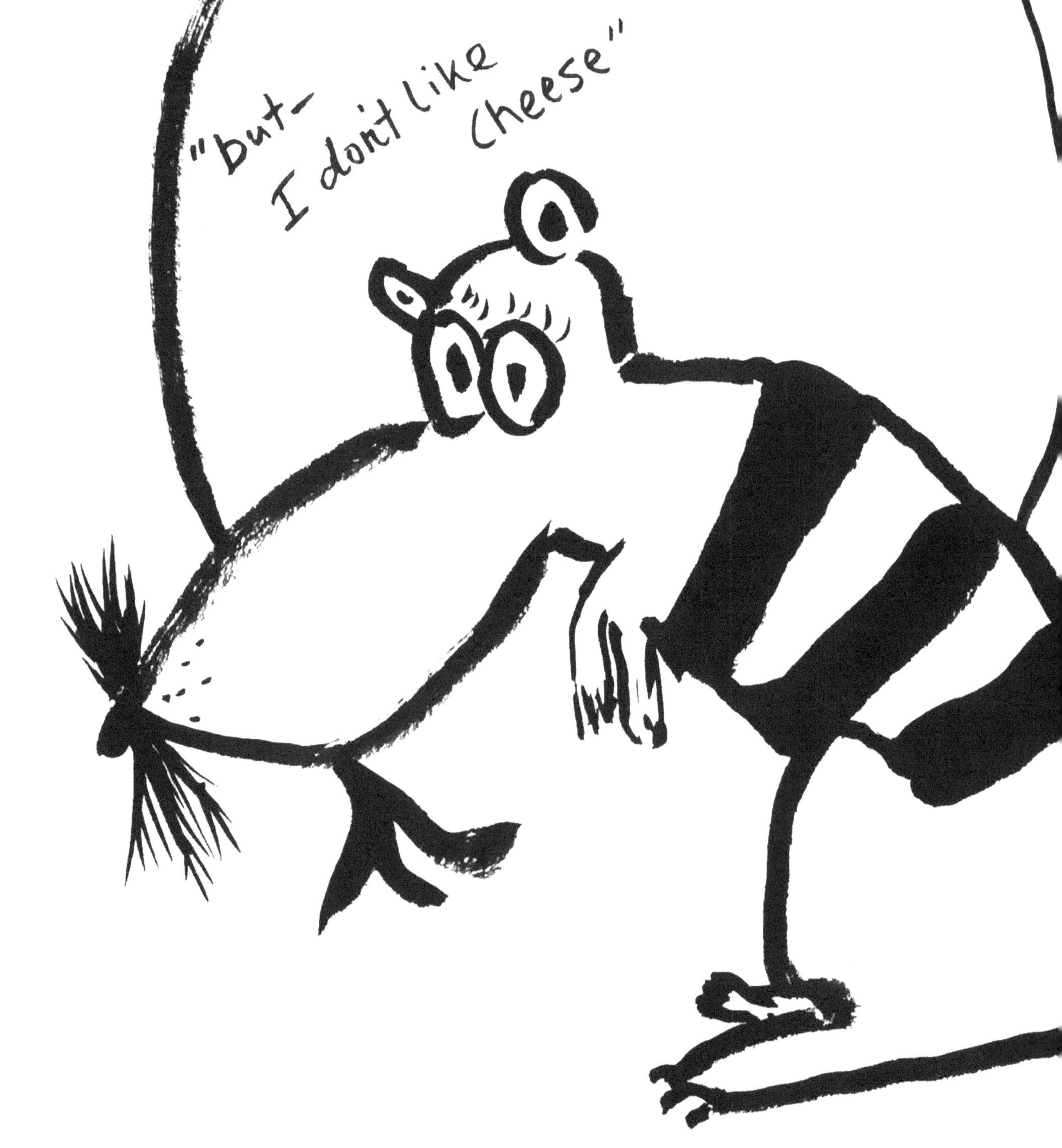

"but-
I don't like cheese"

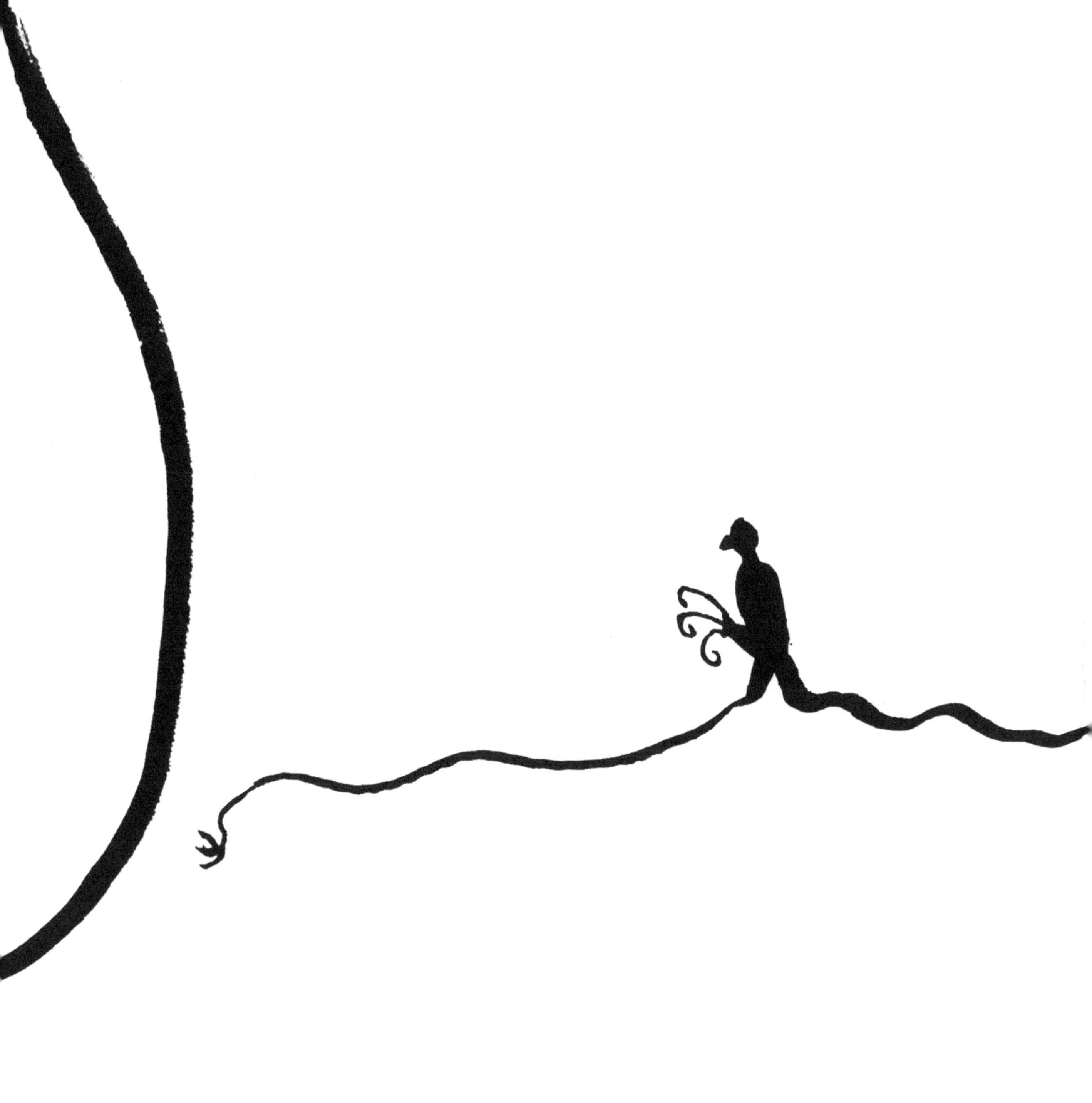

the home
of ˜Faada?

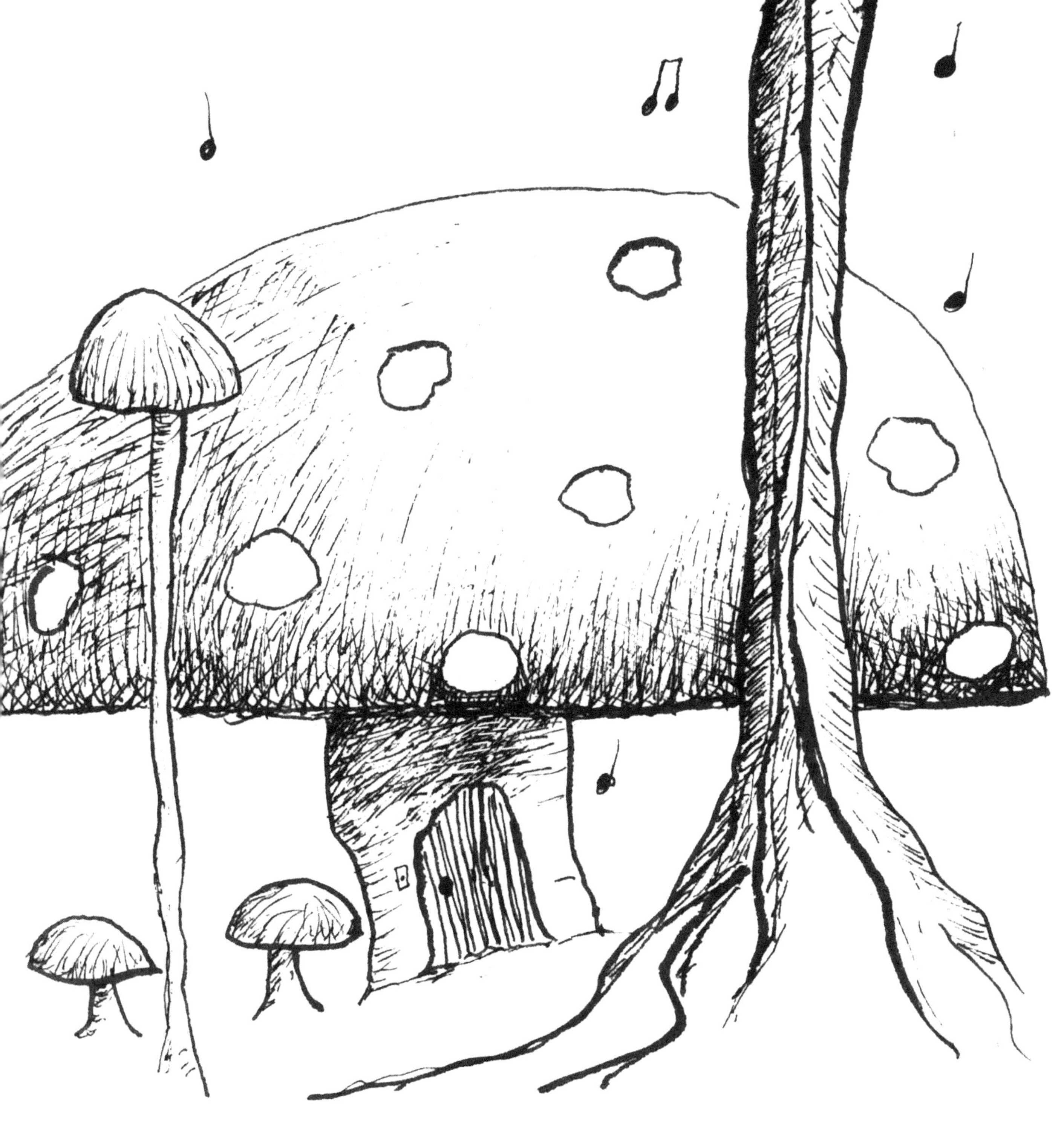

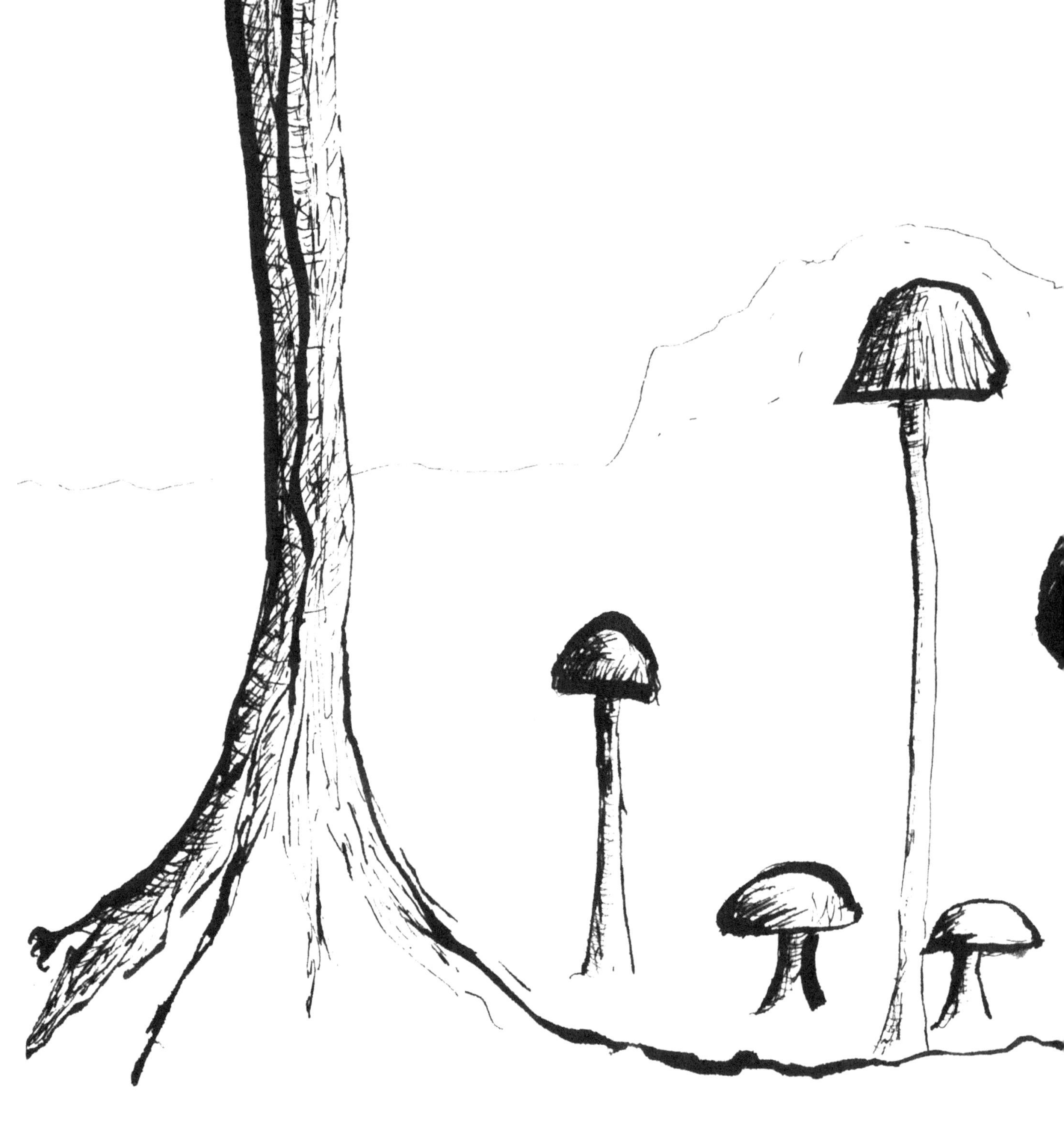

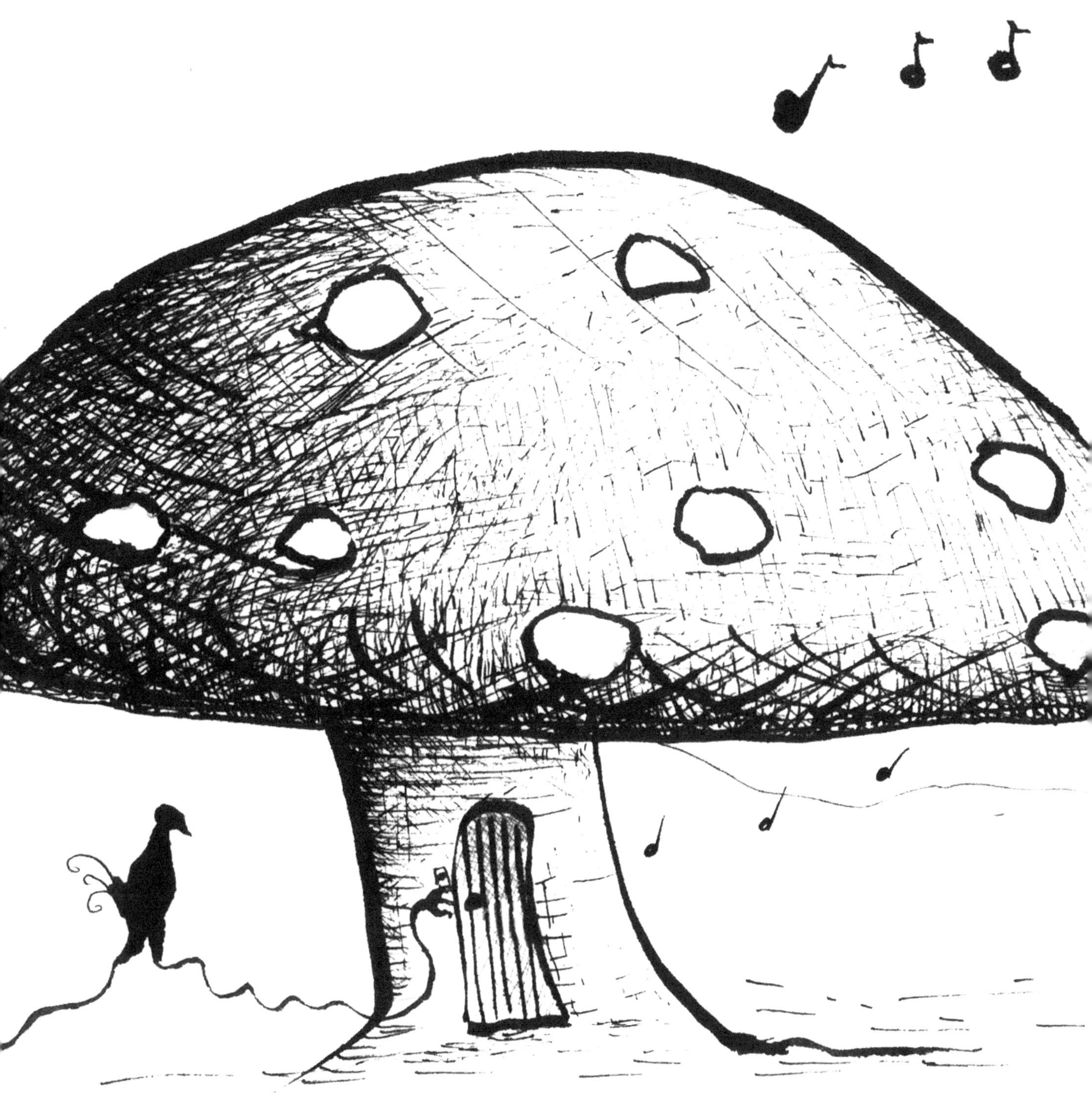

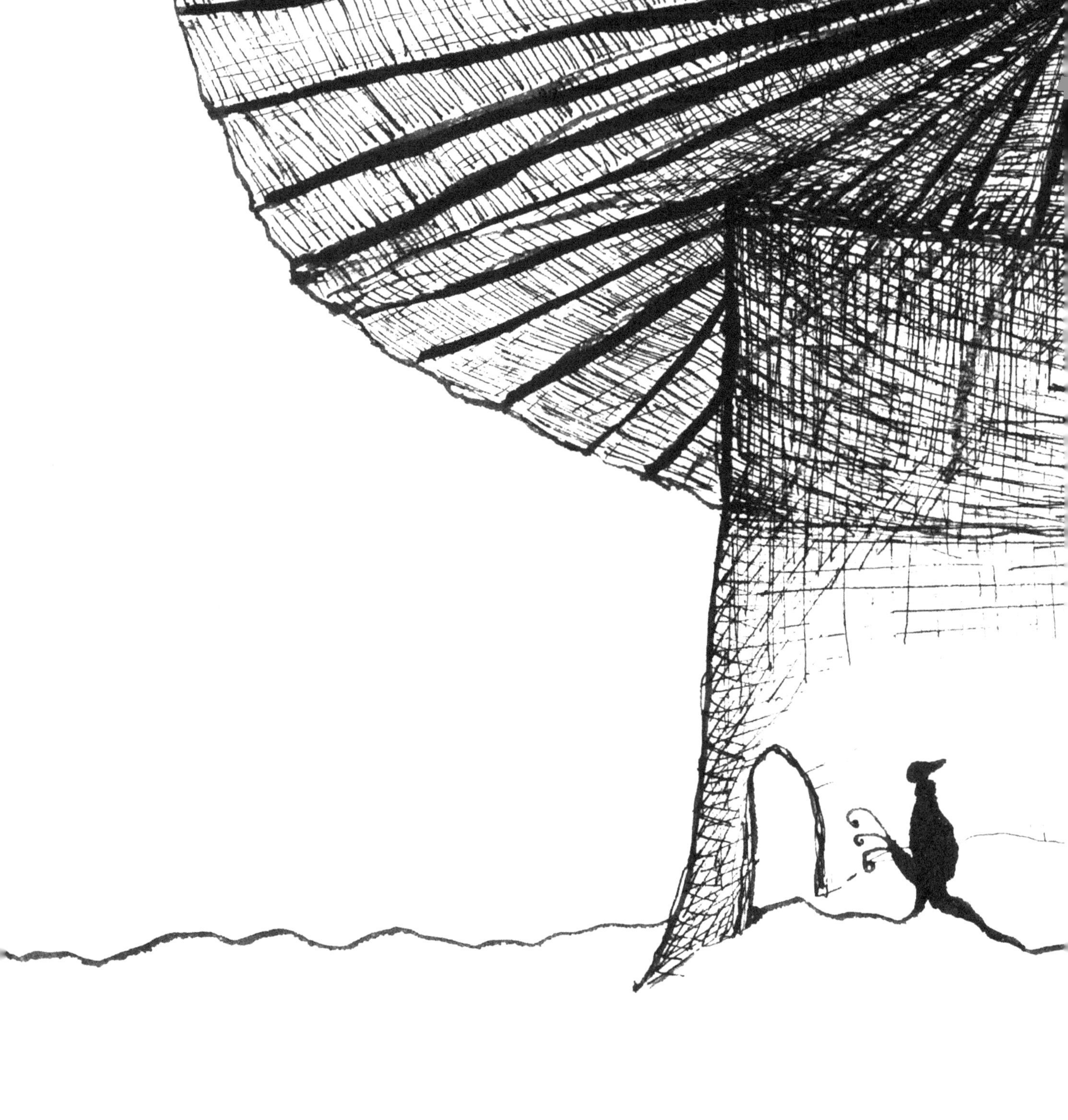

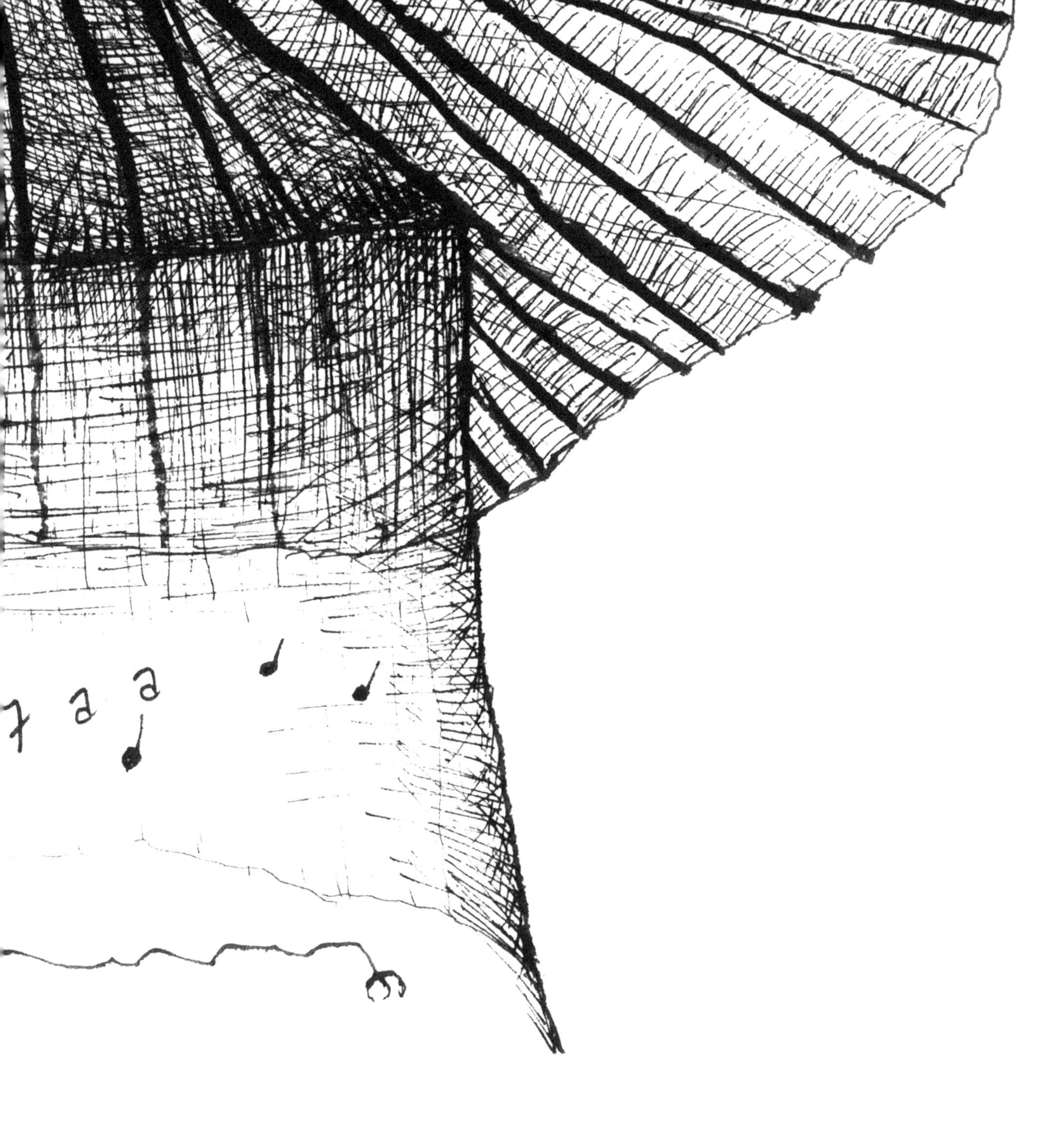

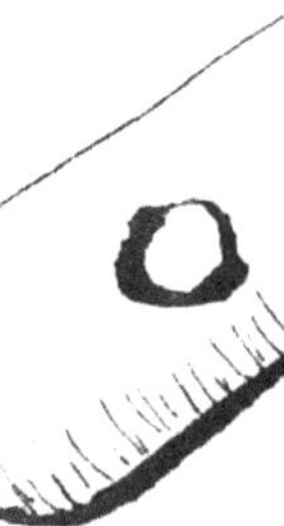
how do I
get going
7aa?"

"everyone has a
different tune.

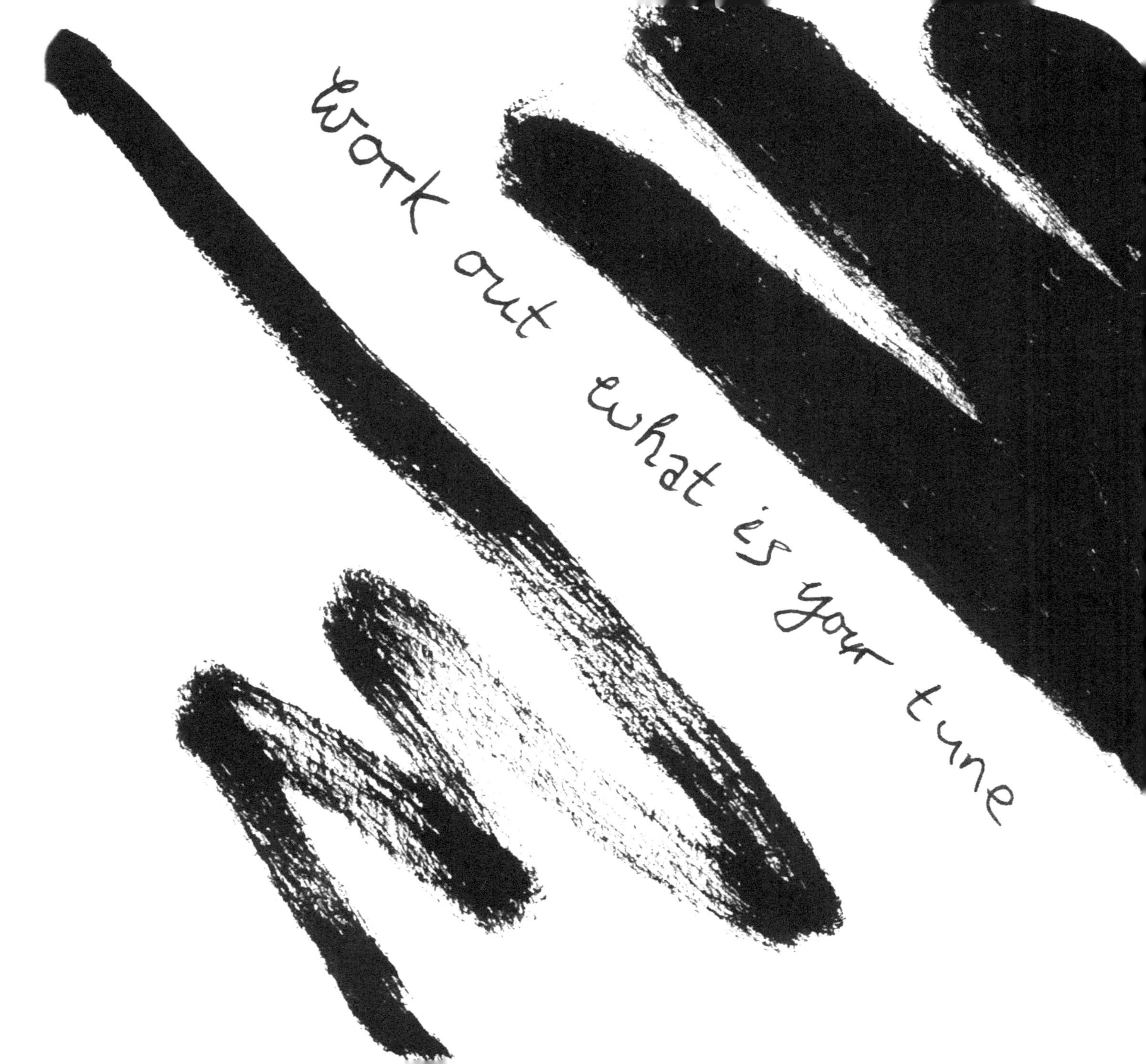
work out   what is your tune

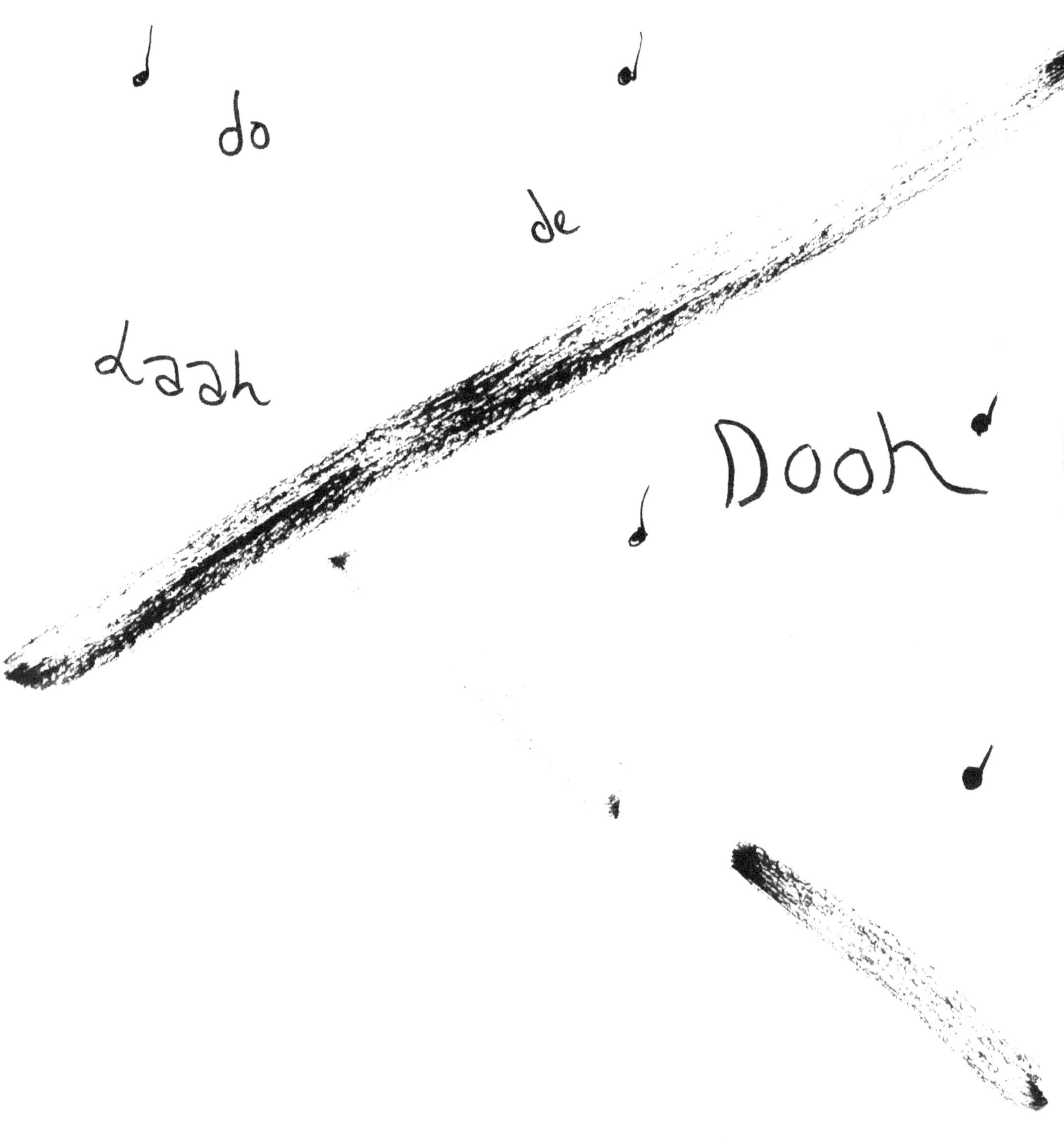
do
de
Laah
Dooh

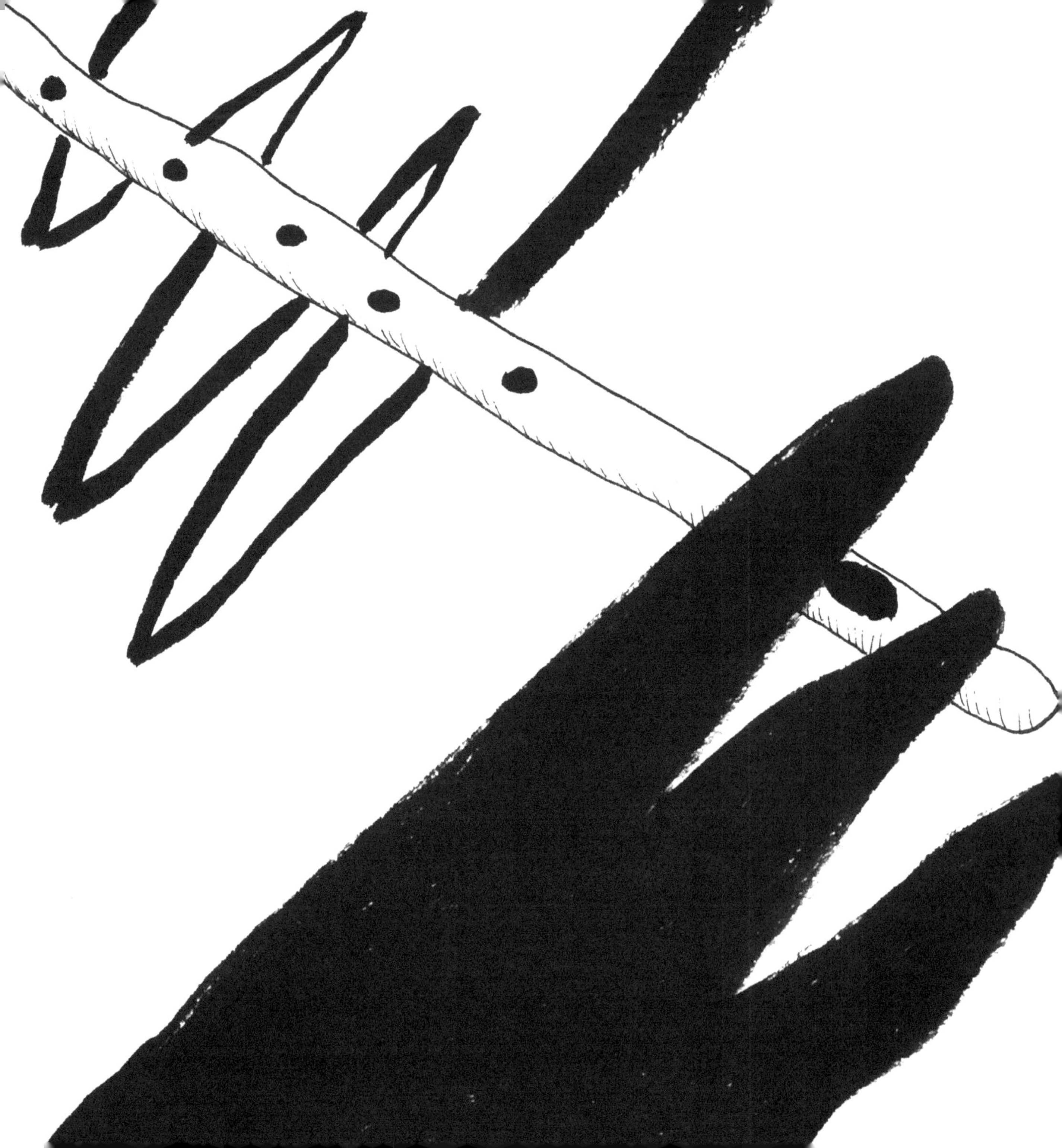

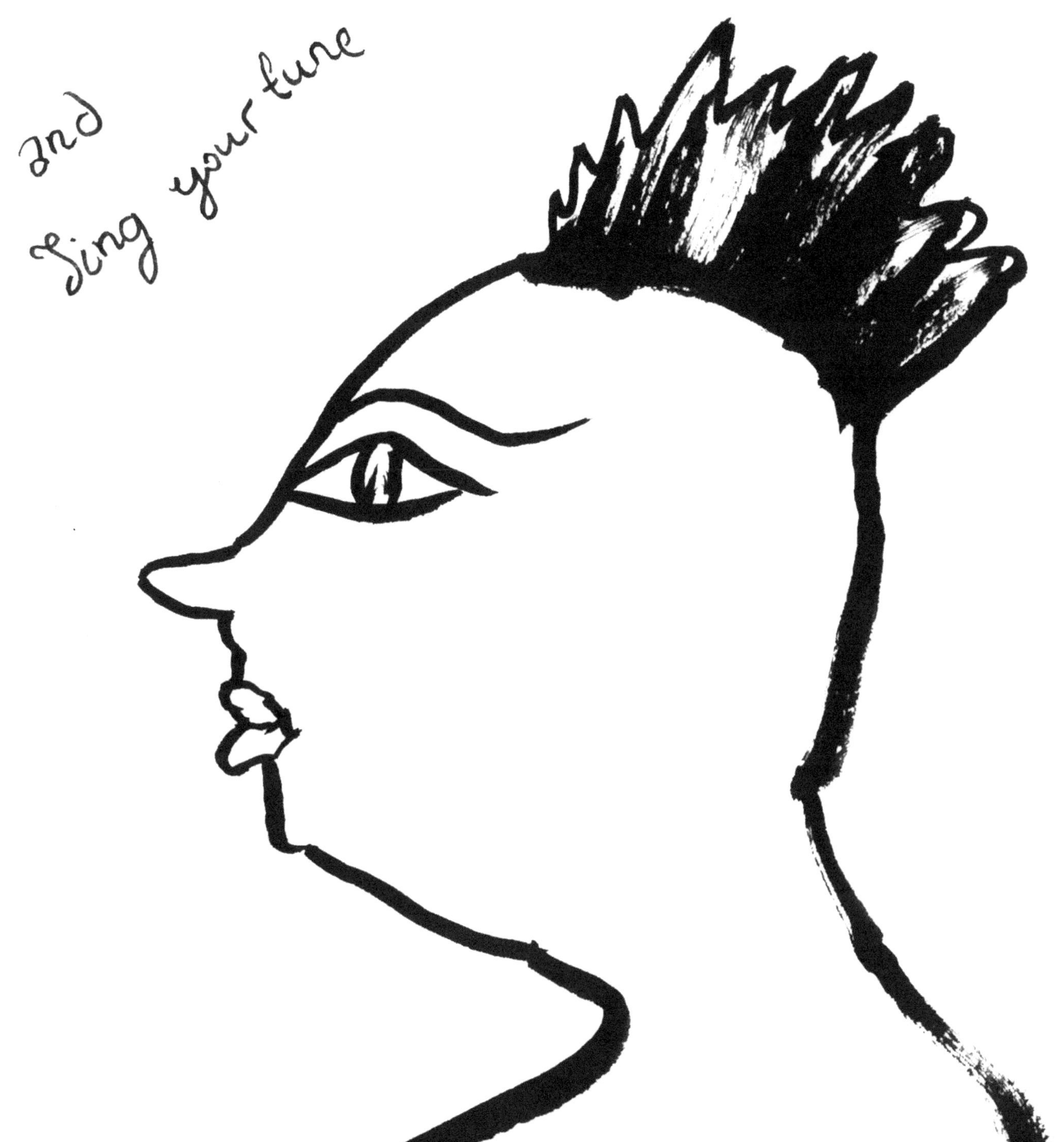
2nd
Sing your tune

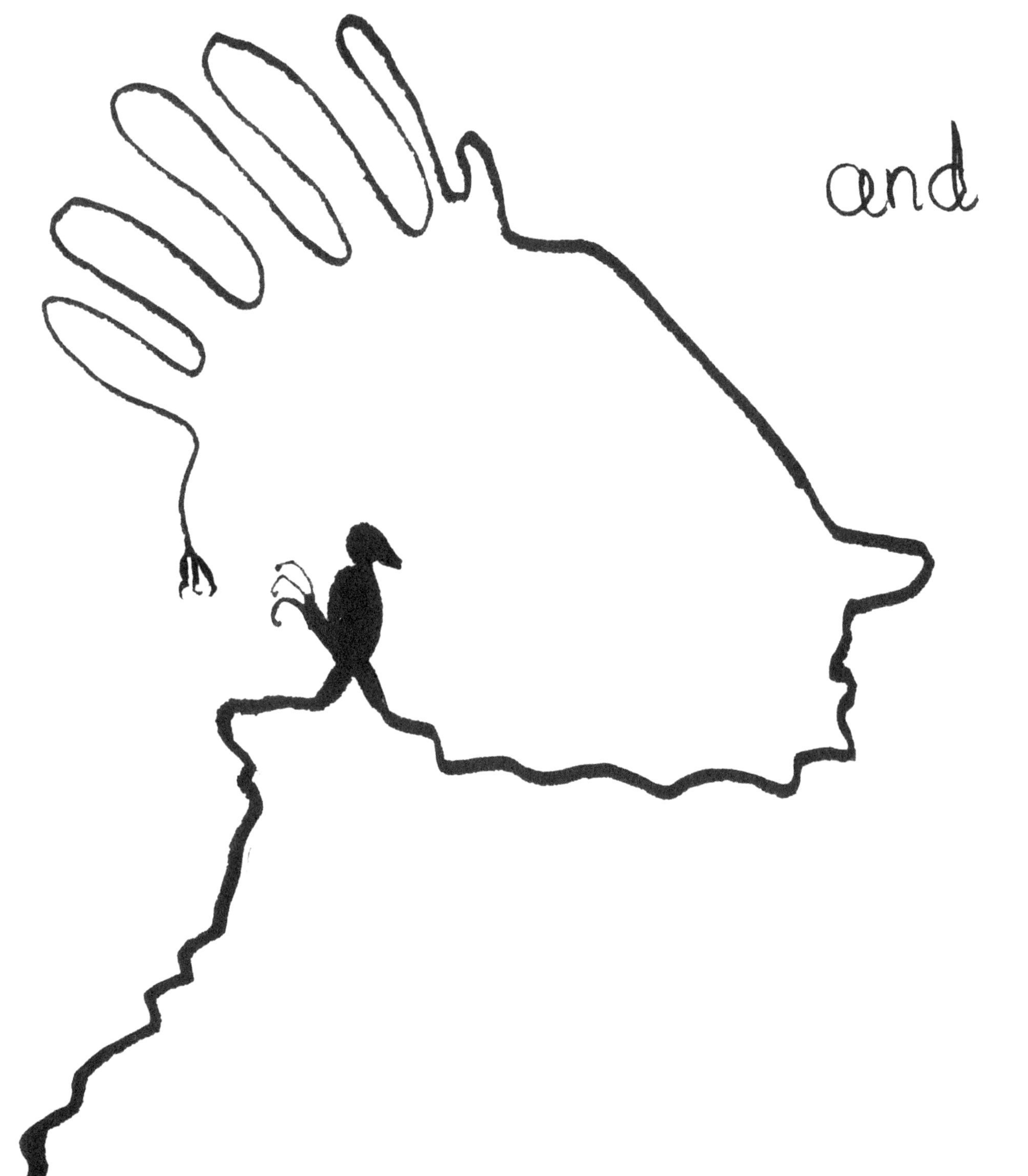
and

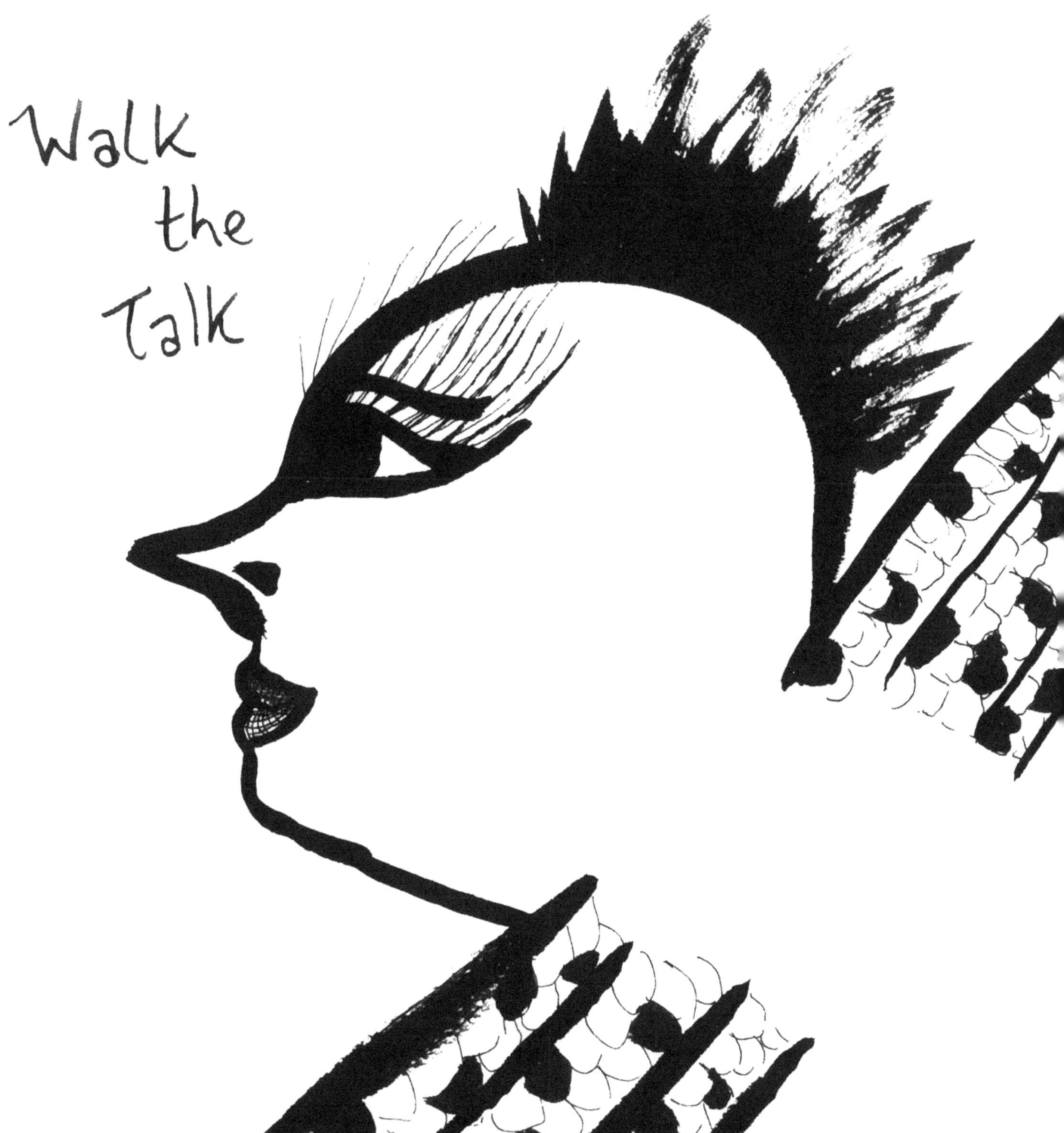
Walk the
Talk

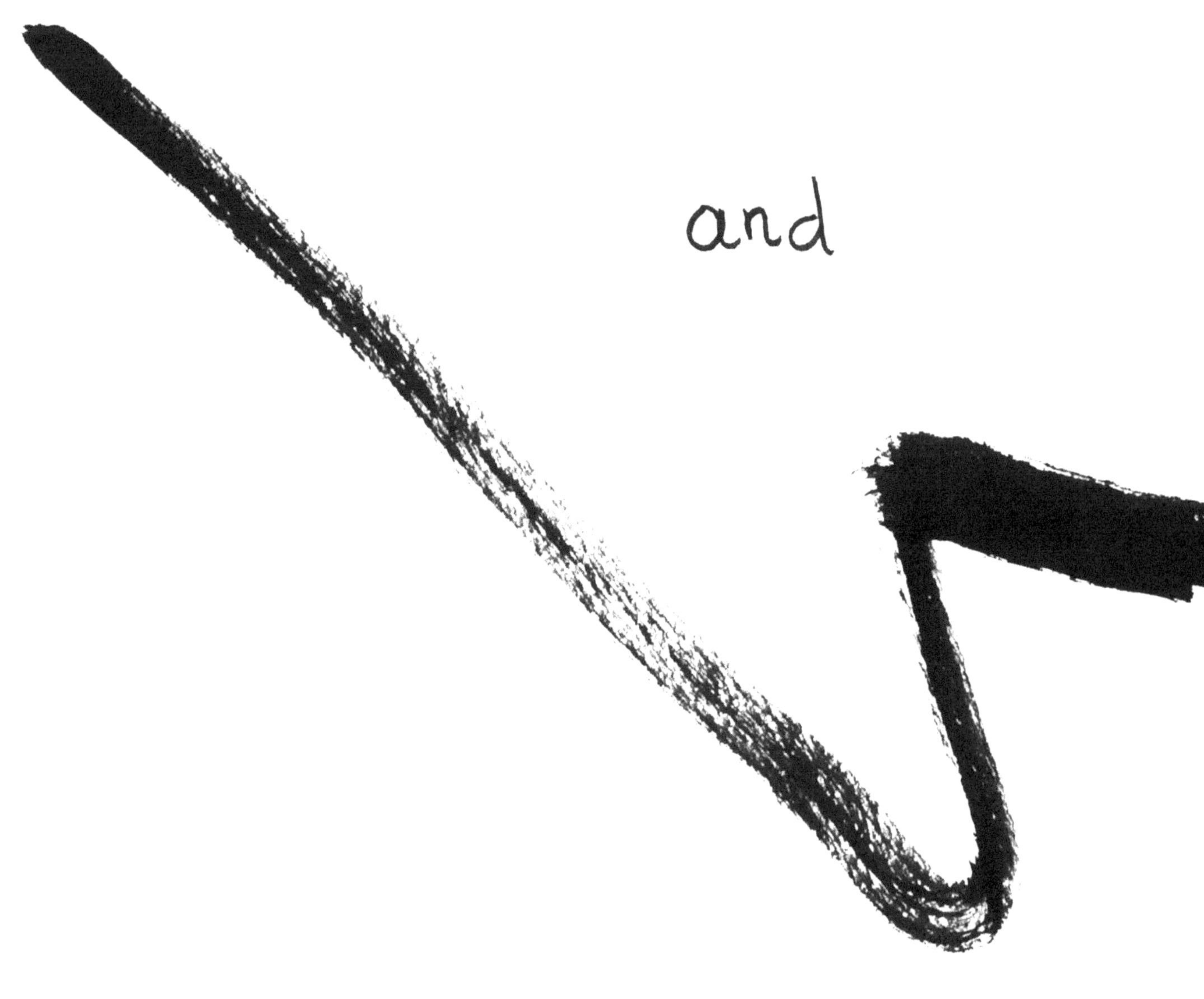
and

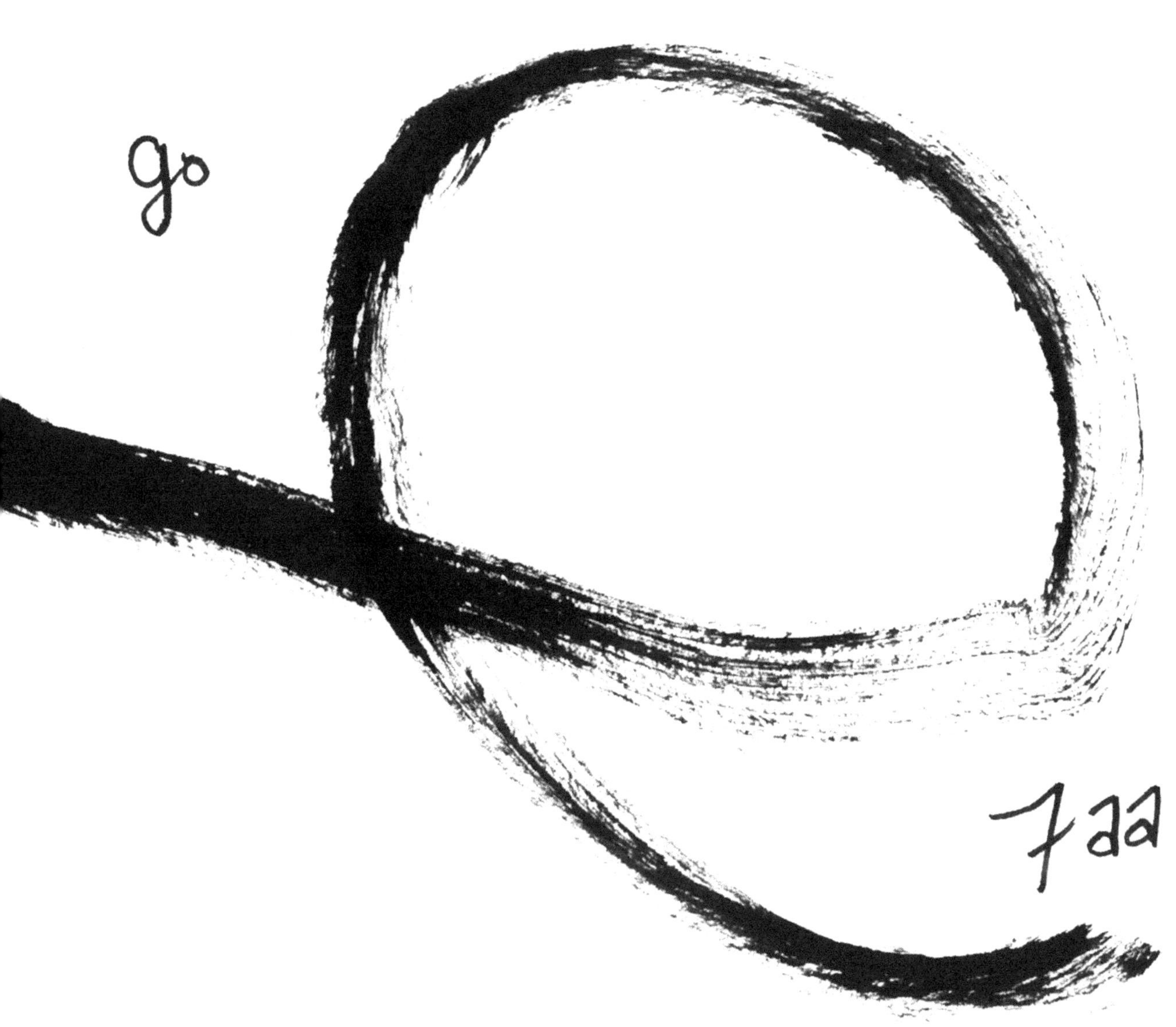

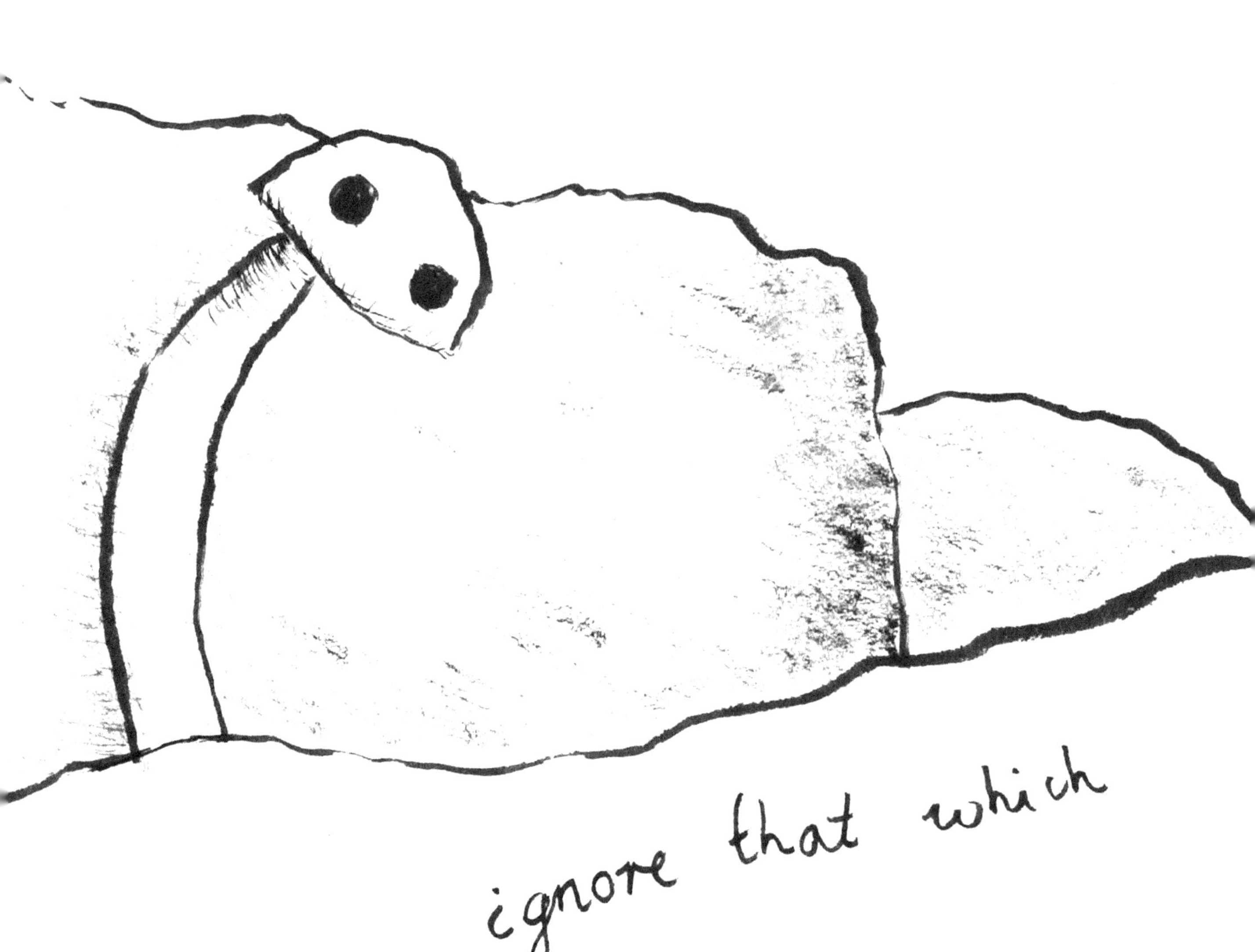

ignore that which

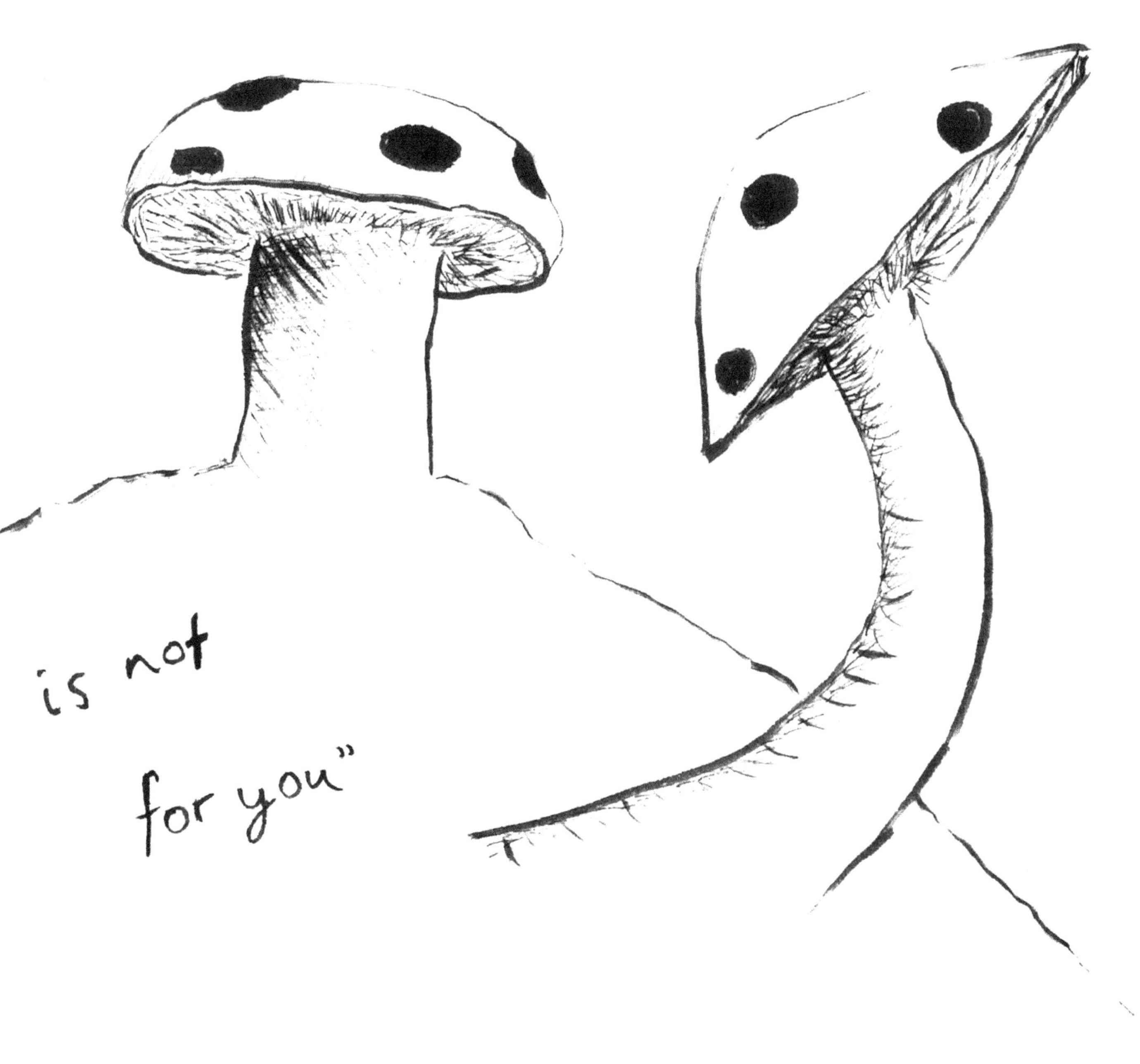
is not
for you"

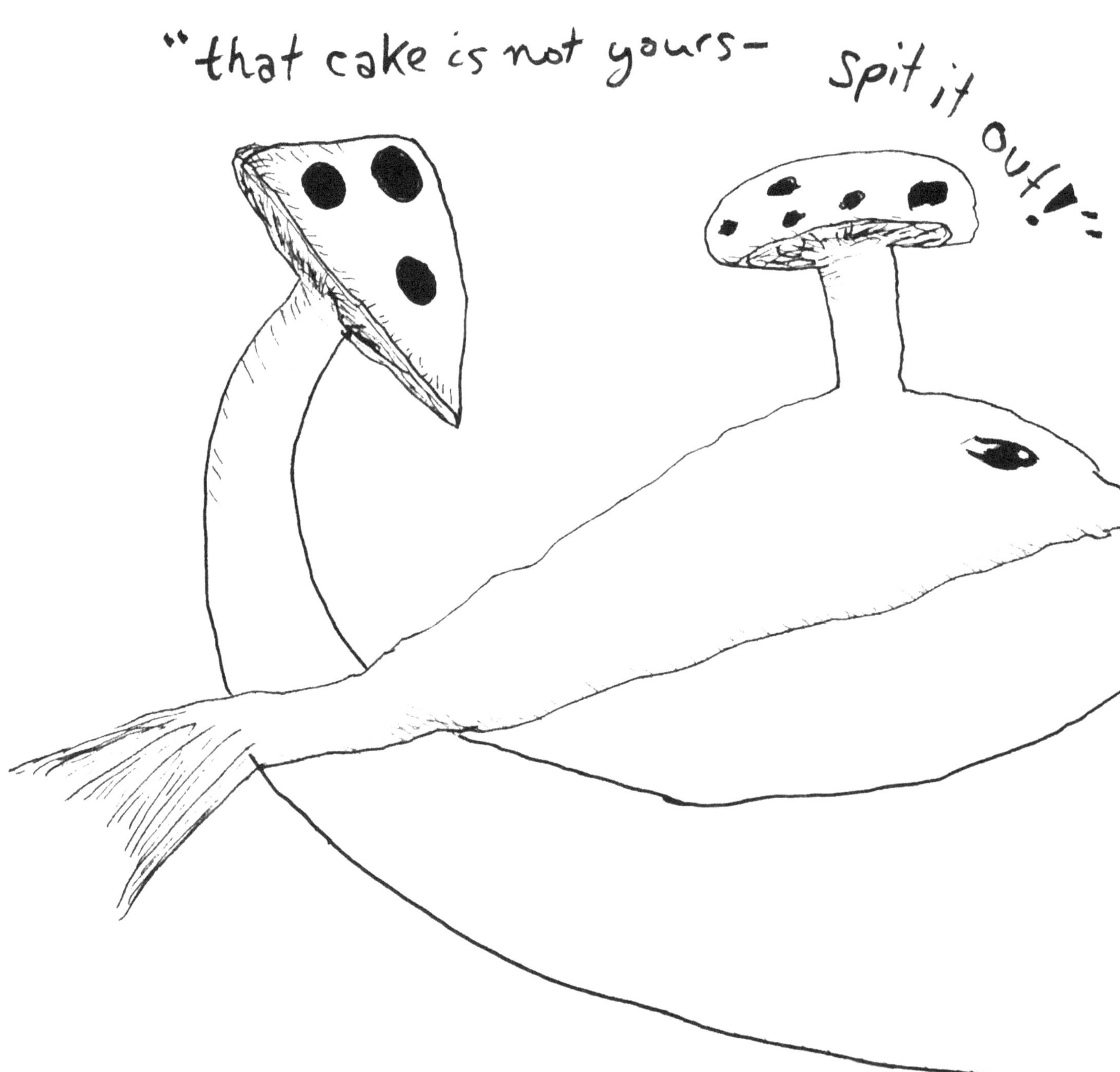
"that cake is not yours—
spit it out!"

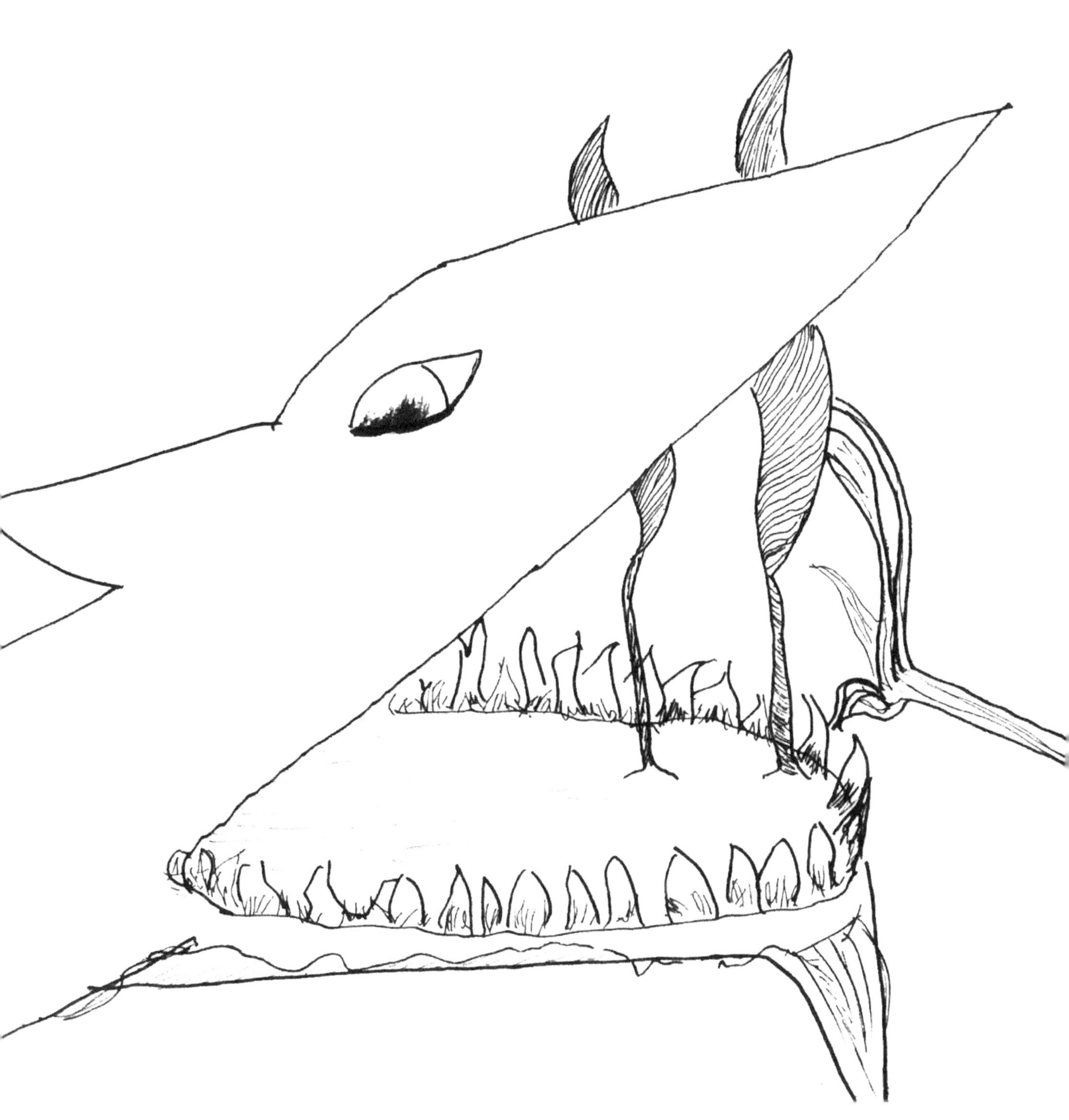

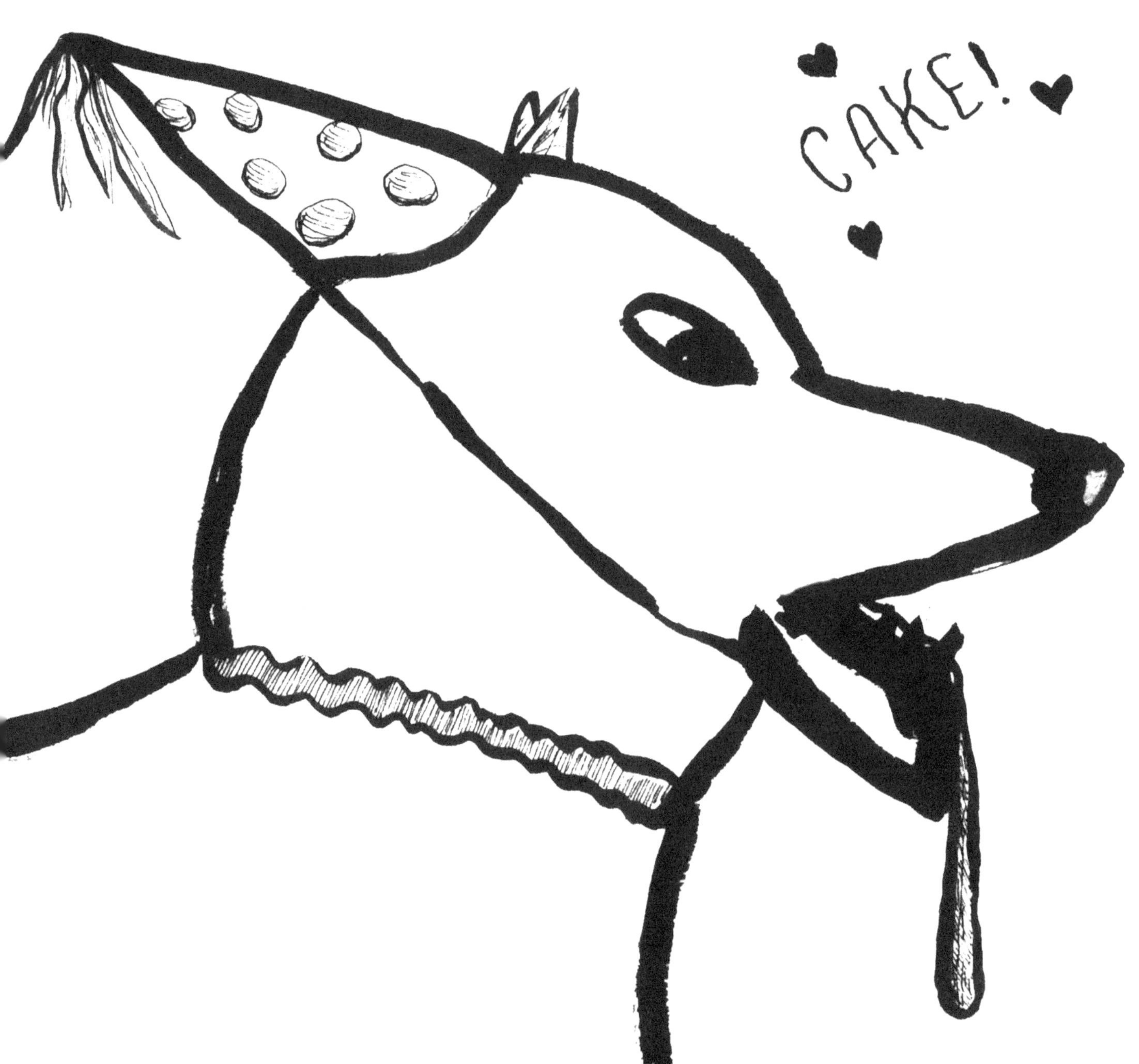
CAKE!

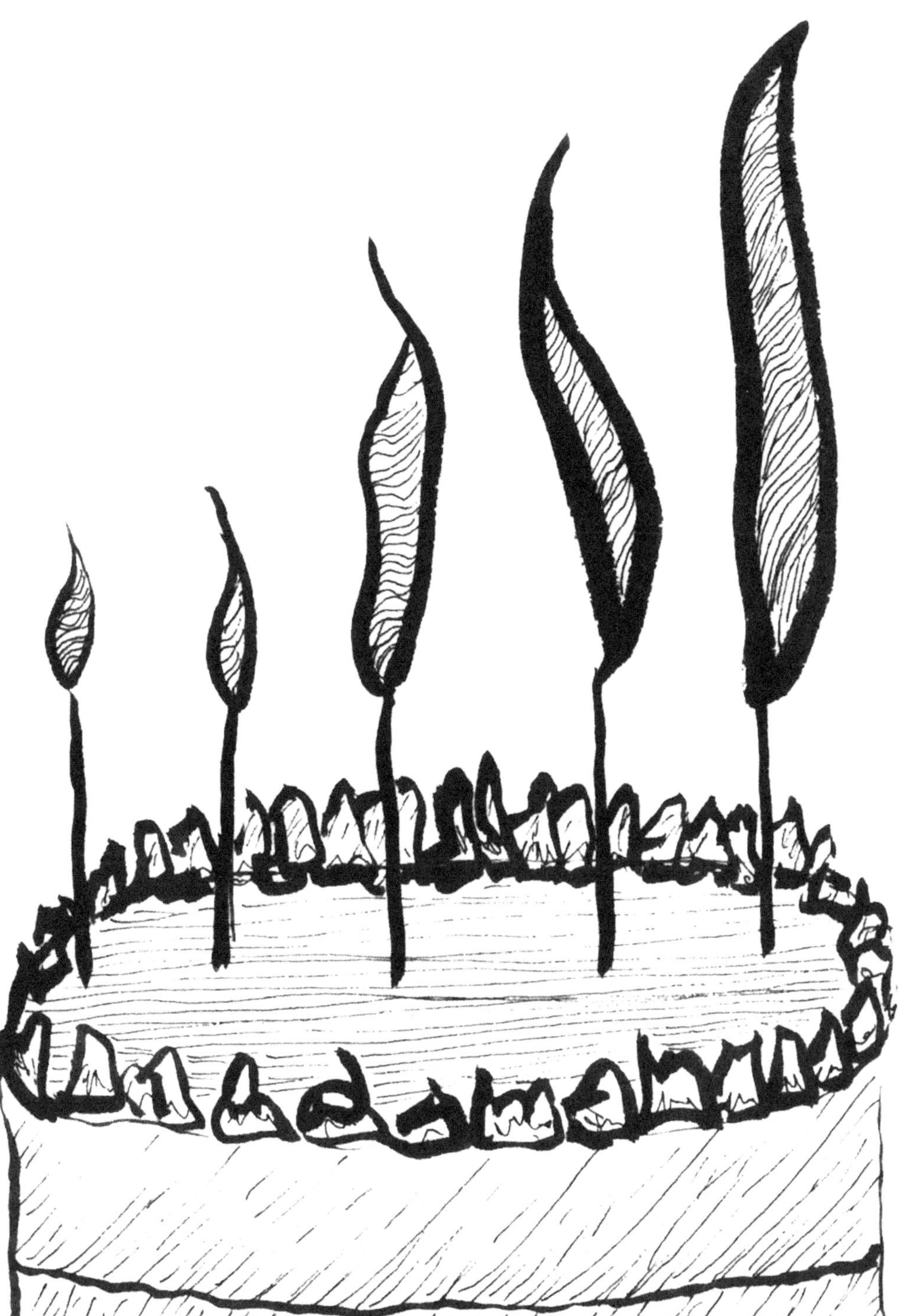

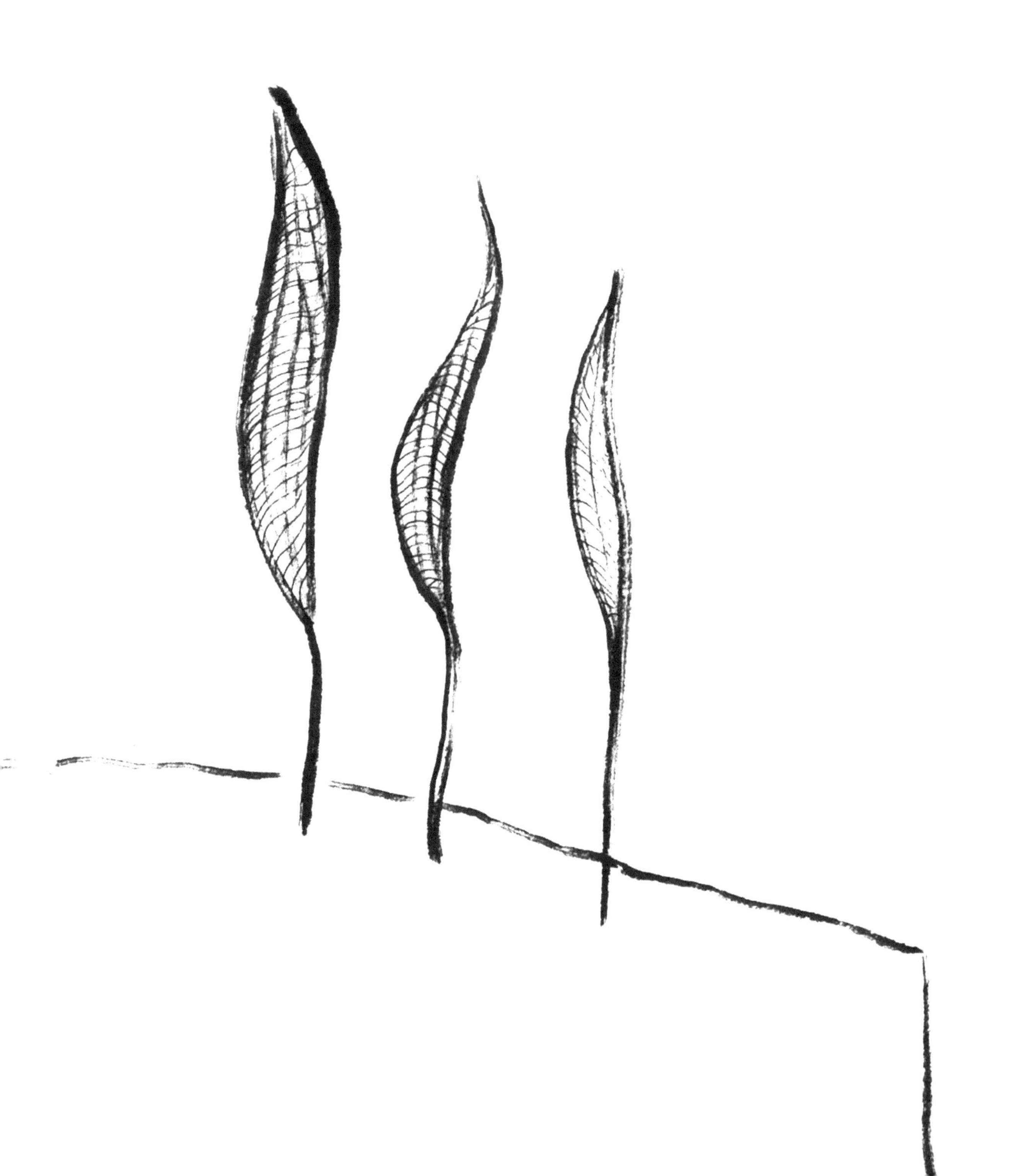

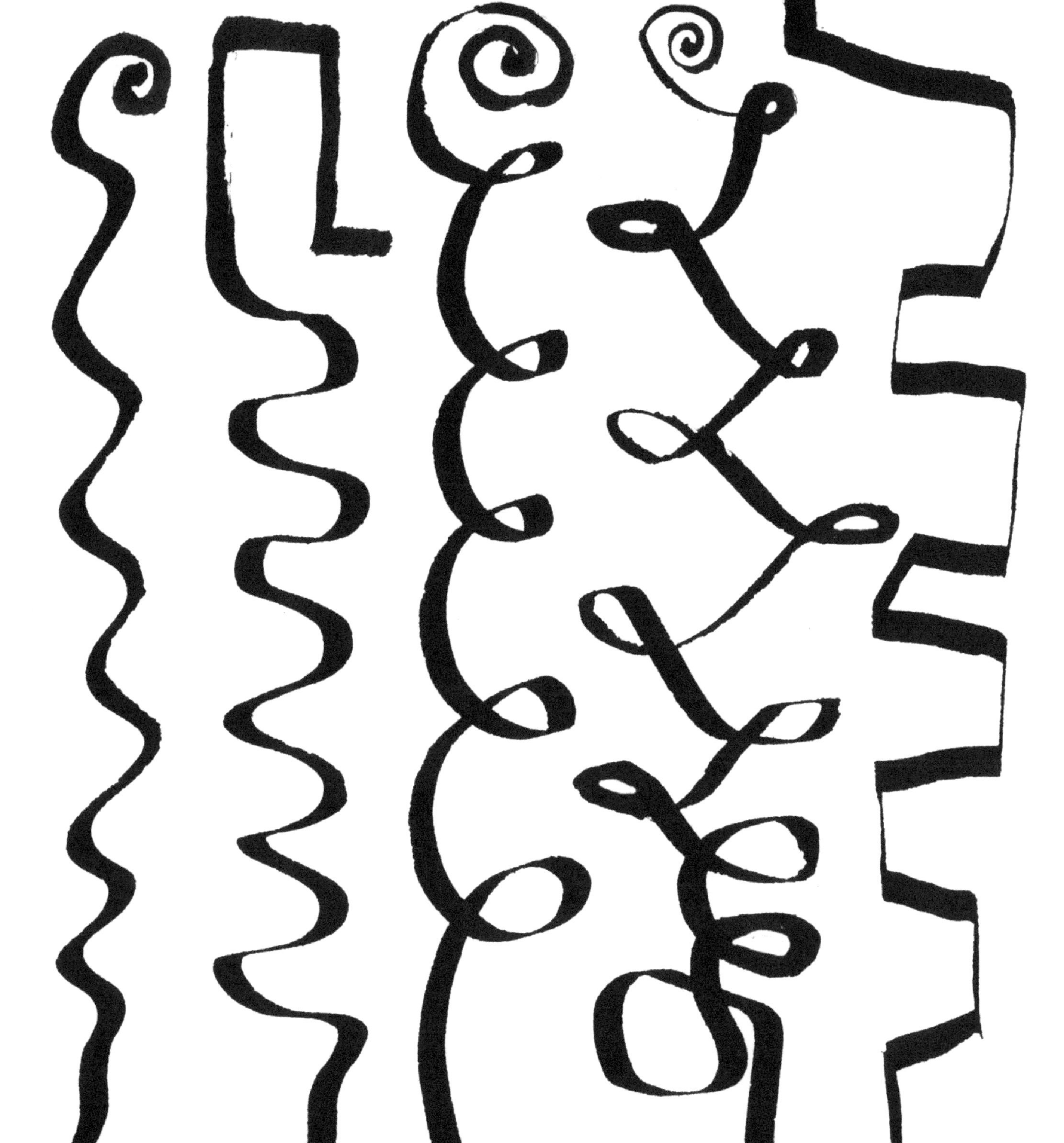

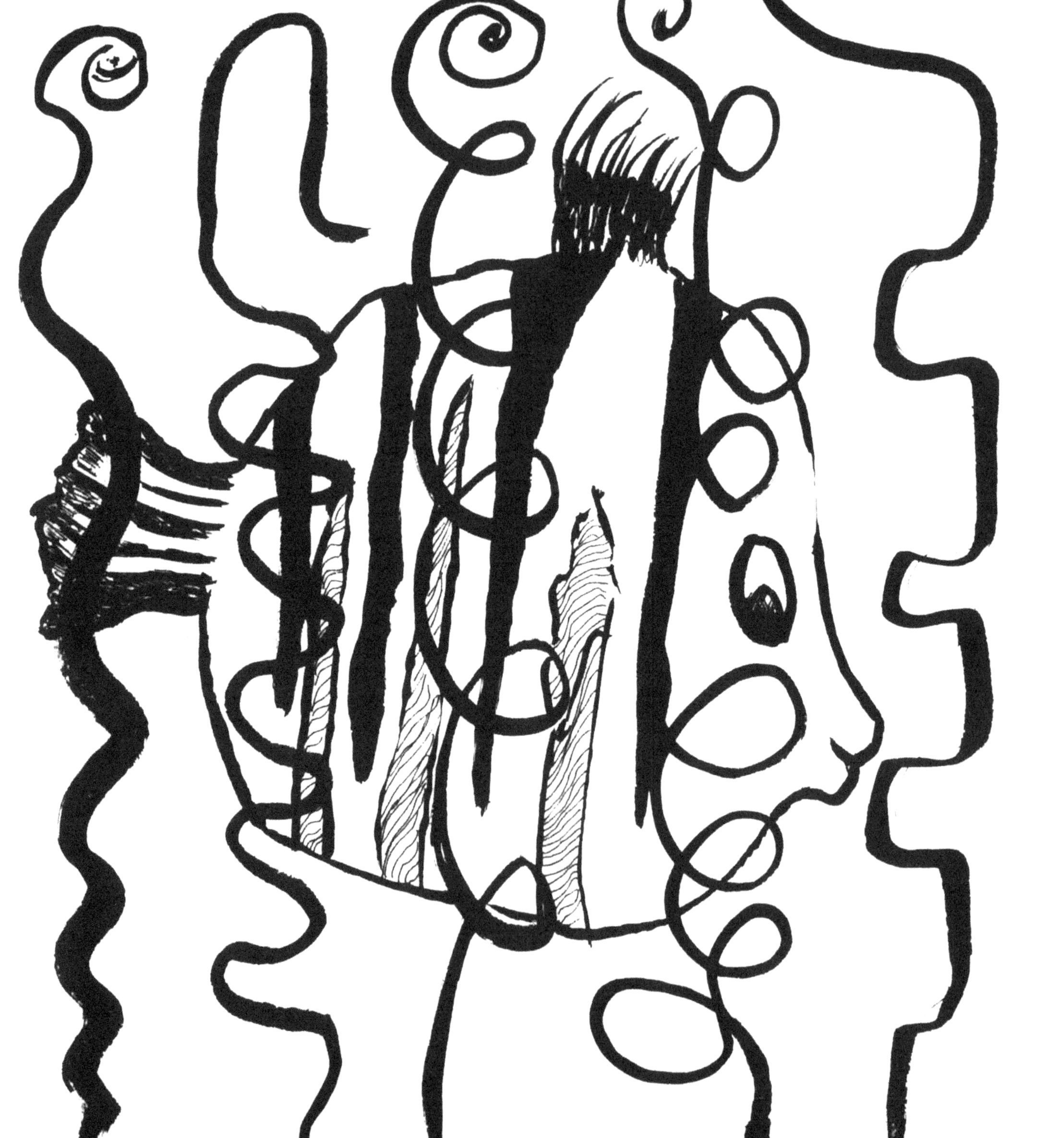

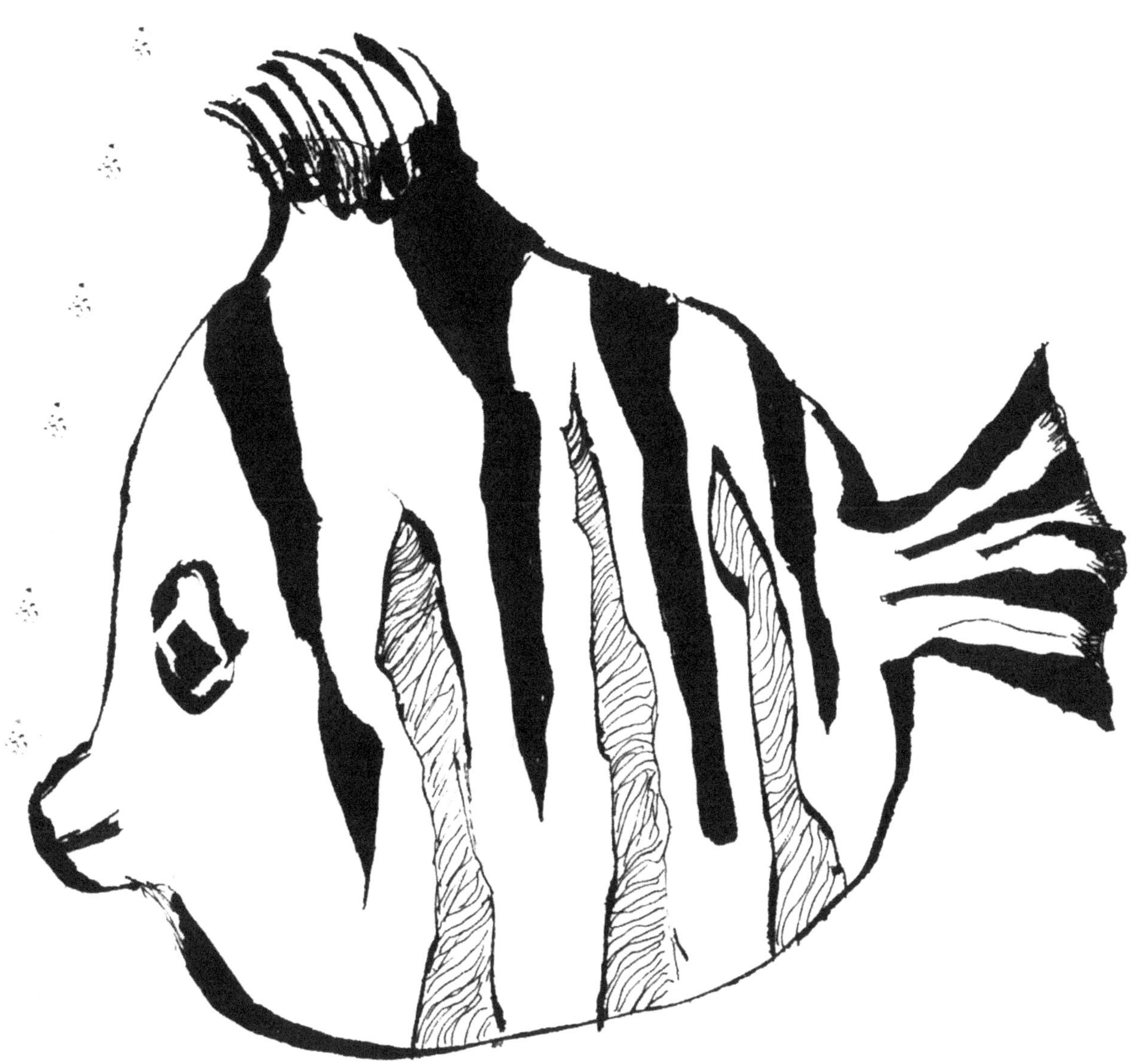

"i love sunflowers,
    i miss my sunflower"

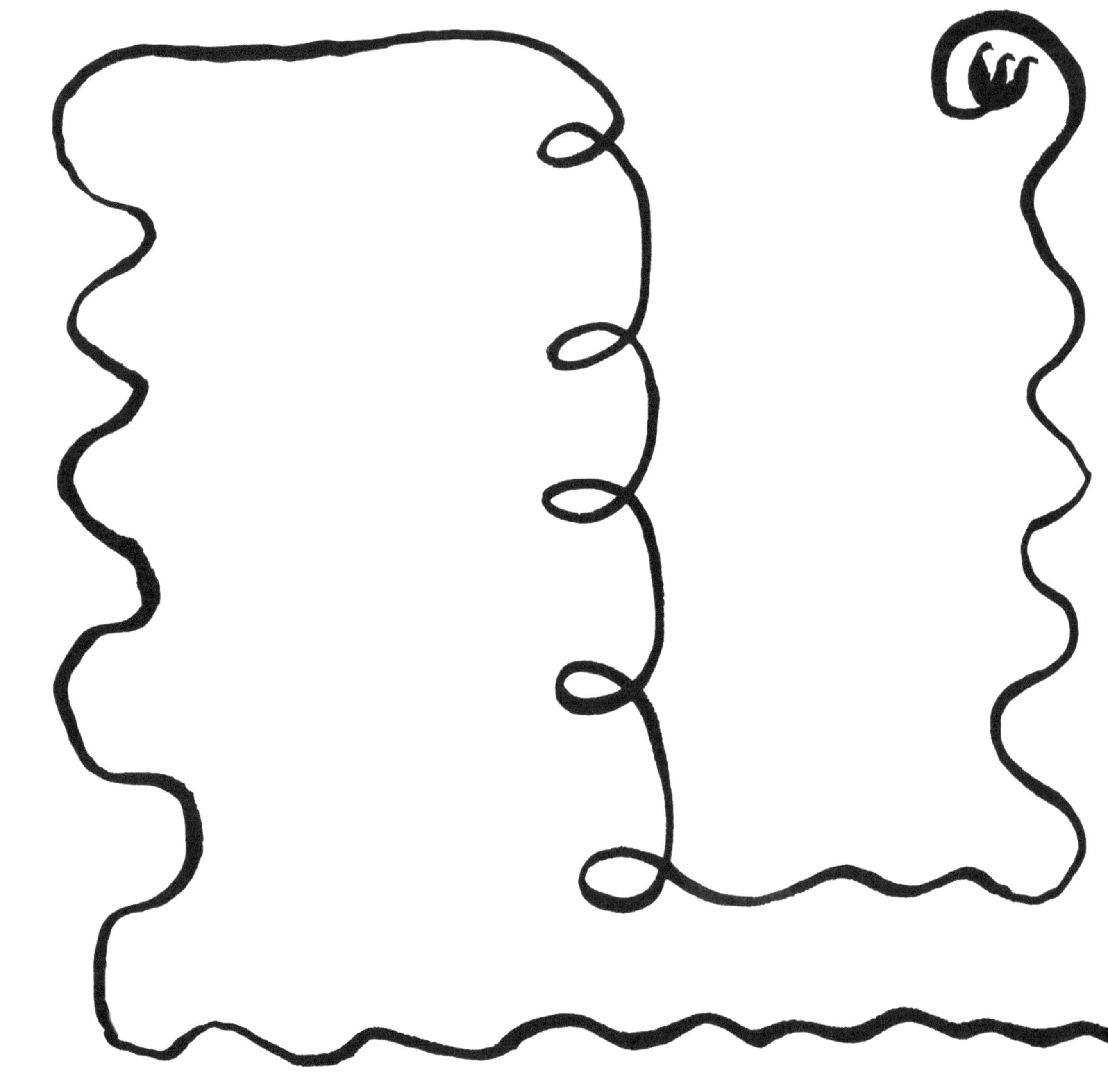

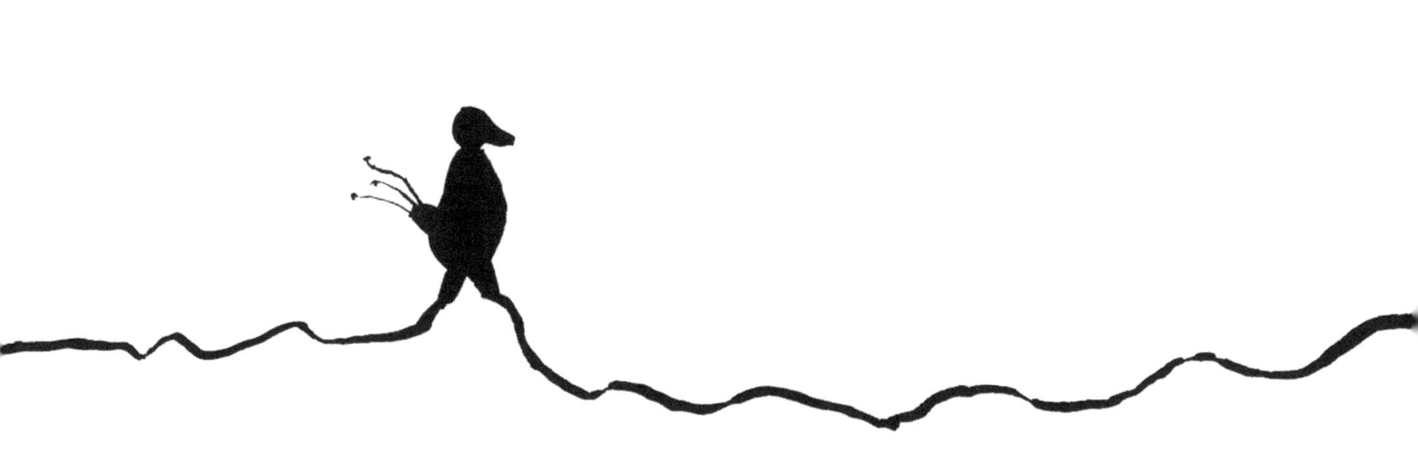

"WHAT _is_ IT that you want?

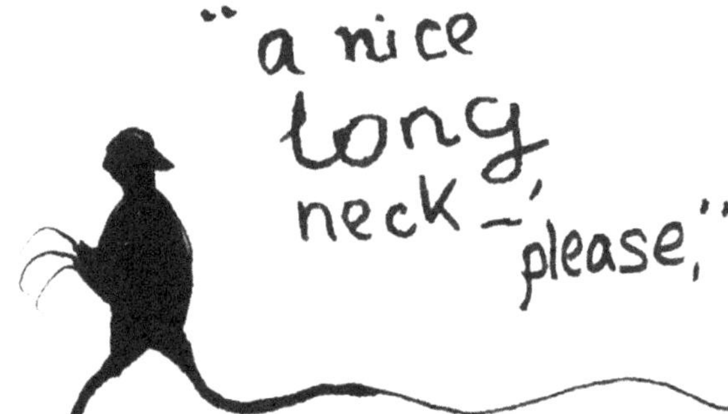

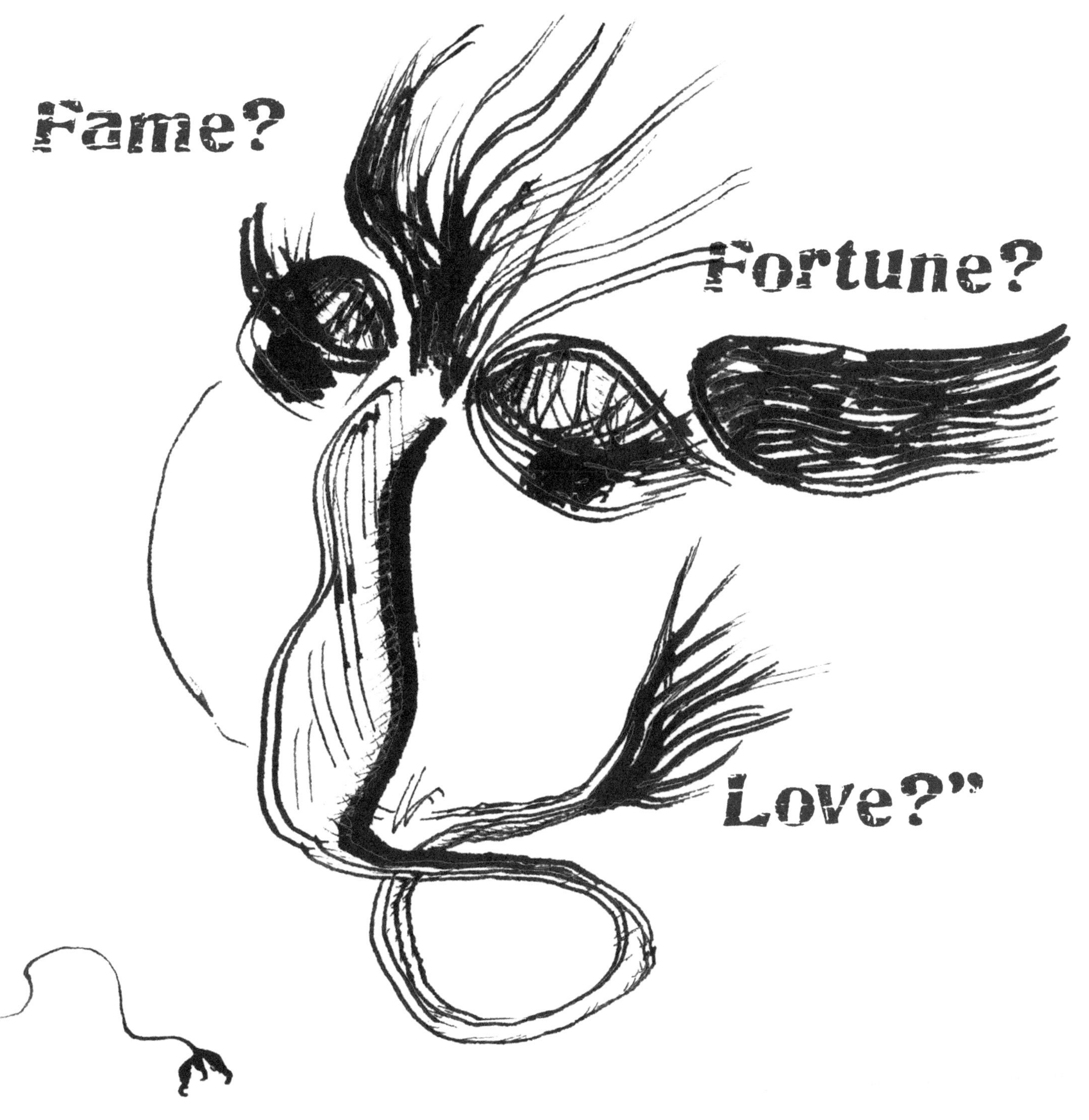

Fame?
Fortune?
Love?"

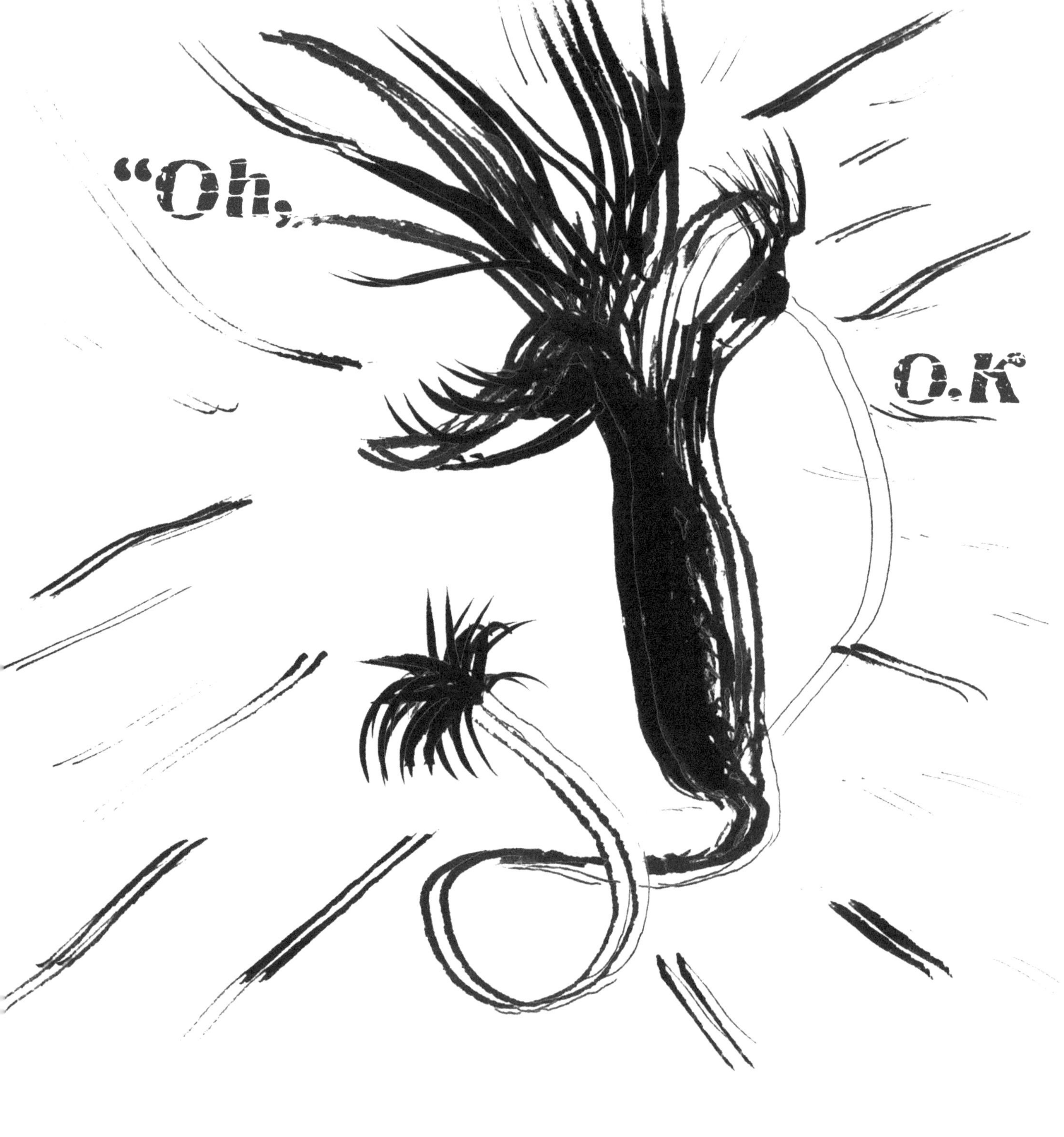

"Oh,
O.K"

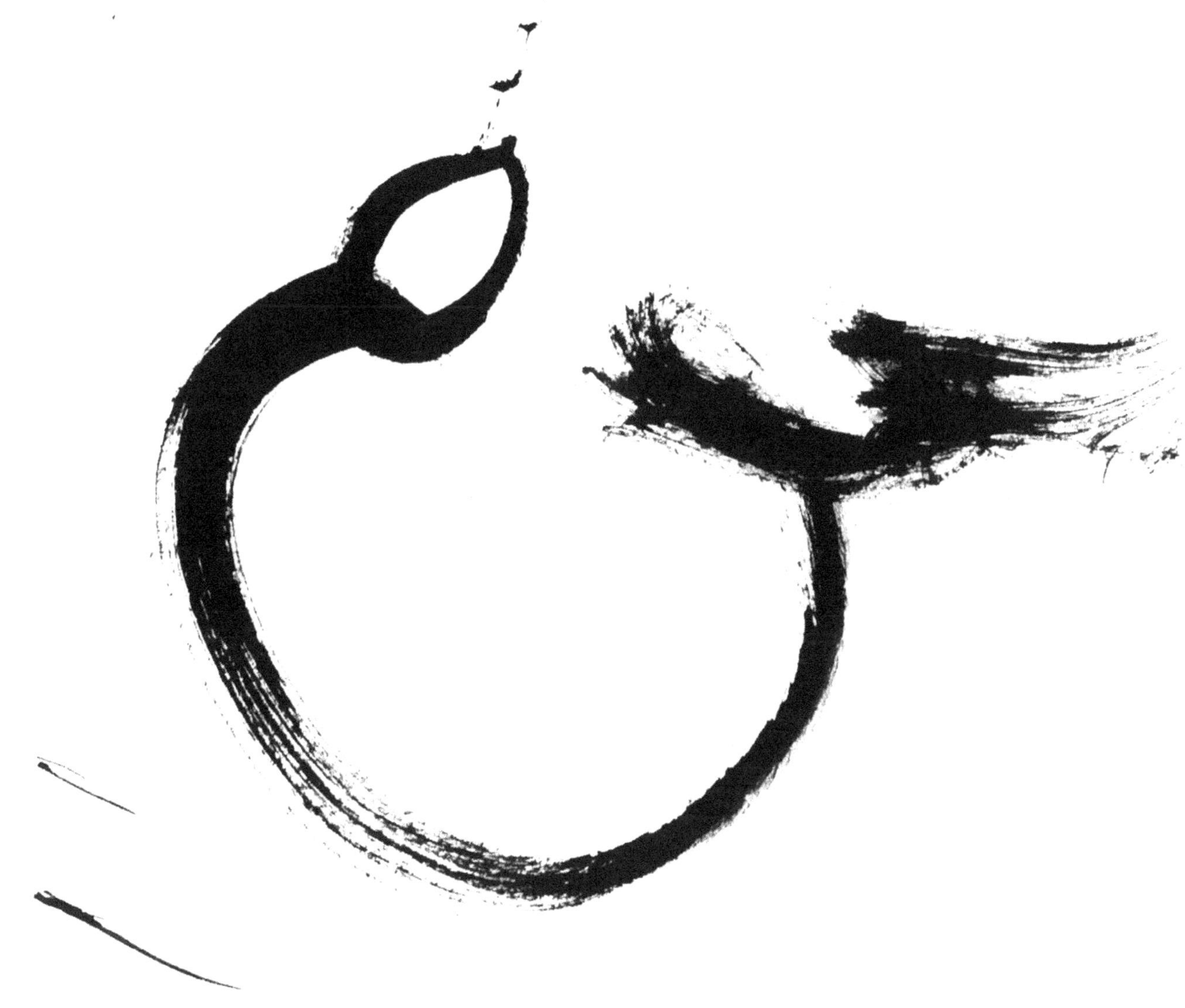
here you go

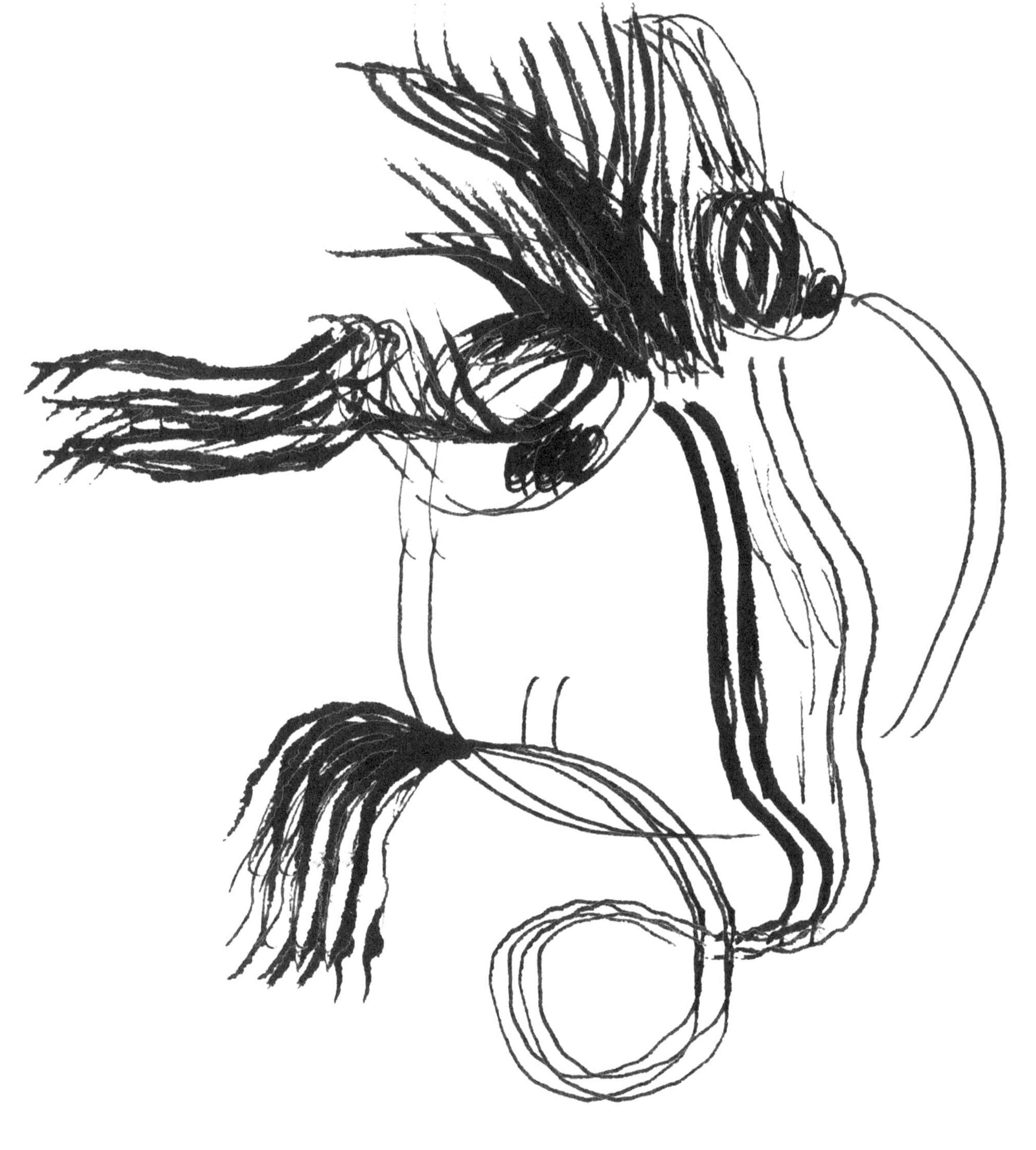

Quick, GO
you better catch it

before someone
else gets it."

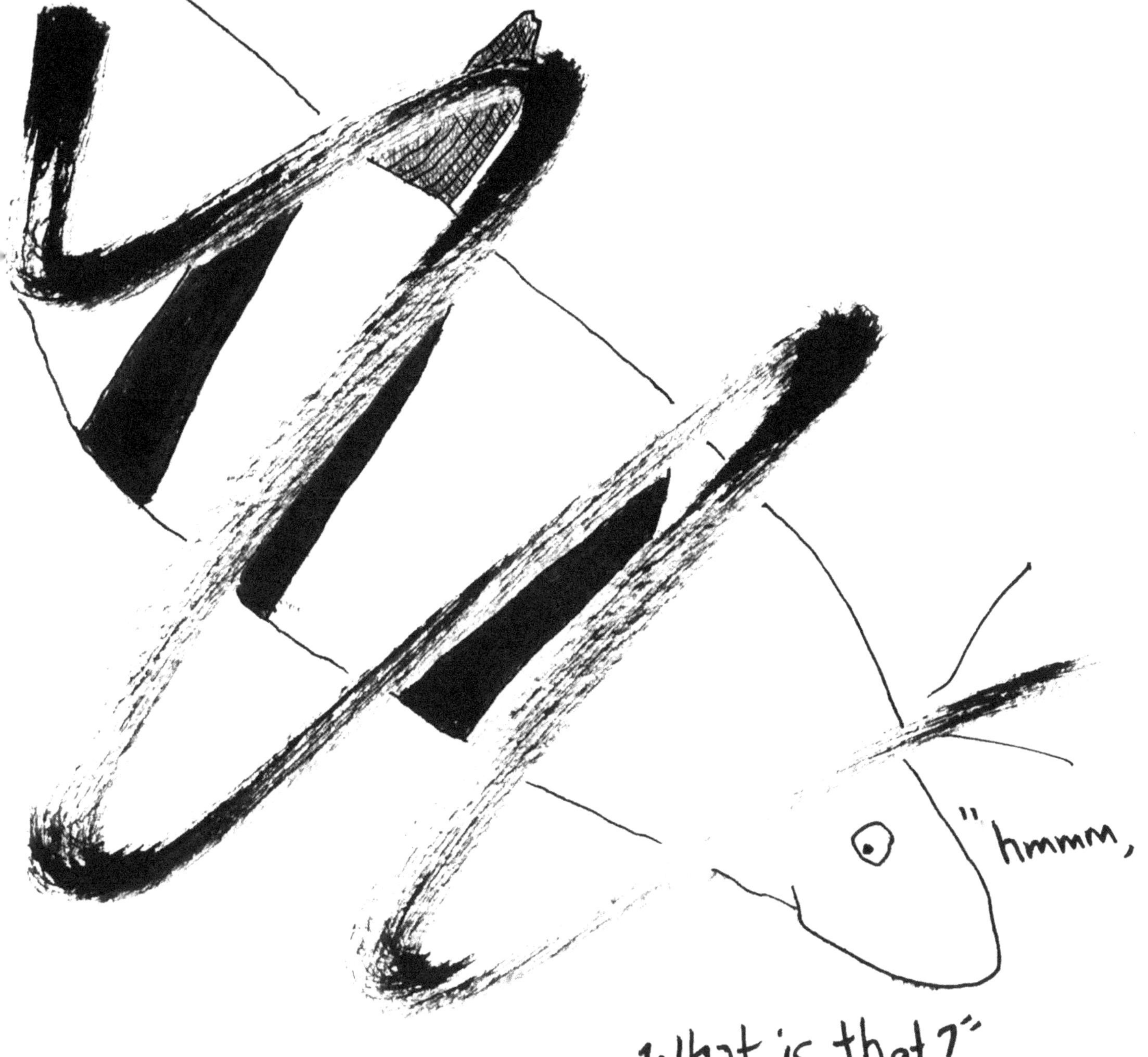
"hmmm,
what is that?"

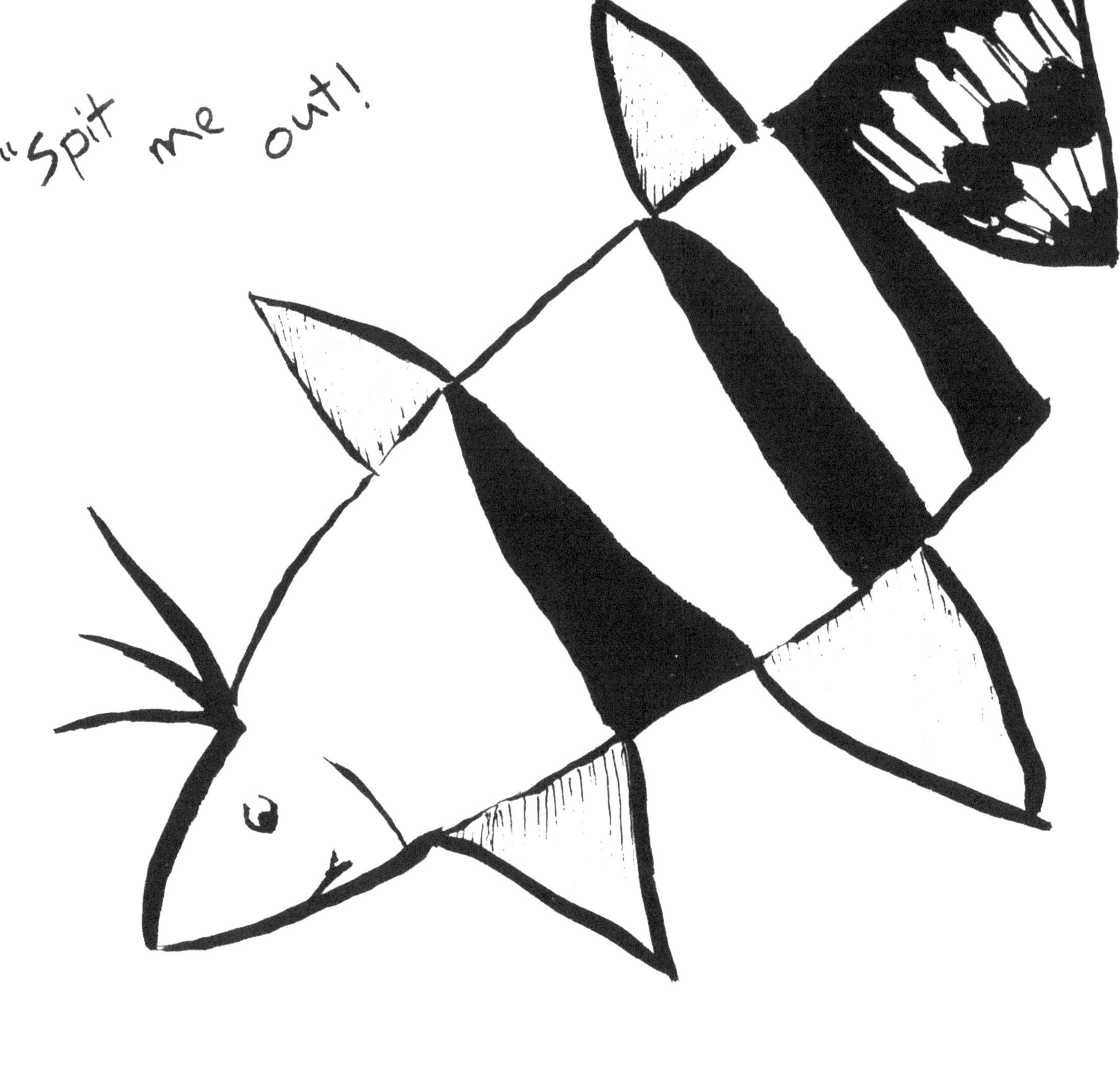
"Spit me out!

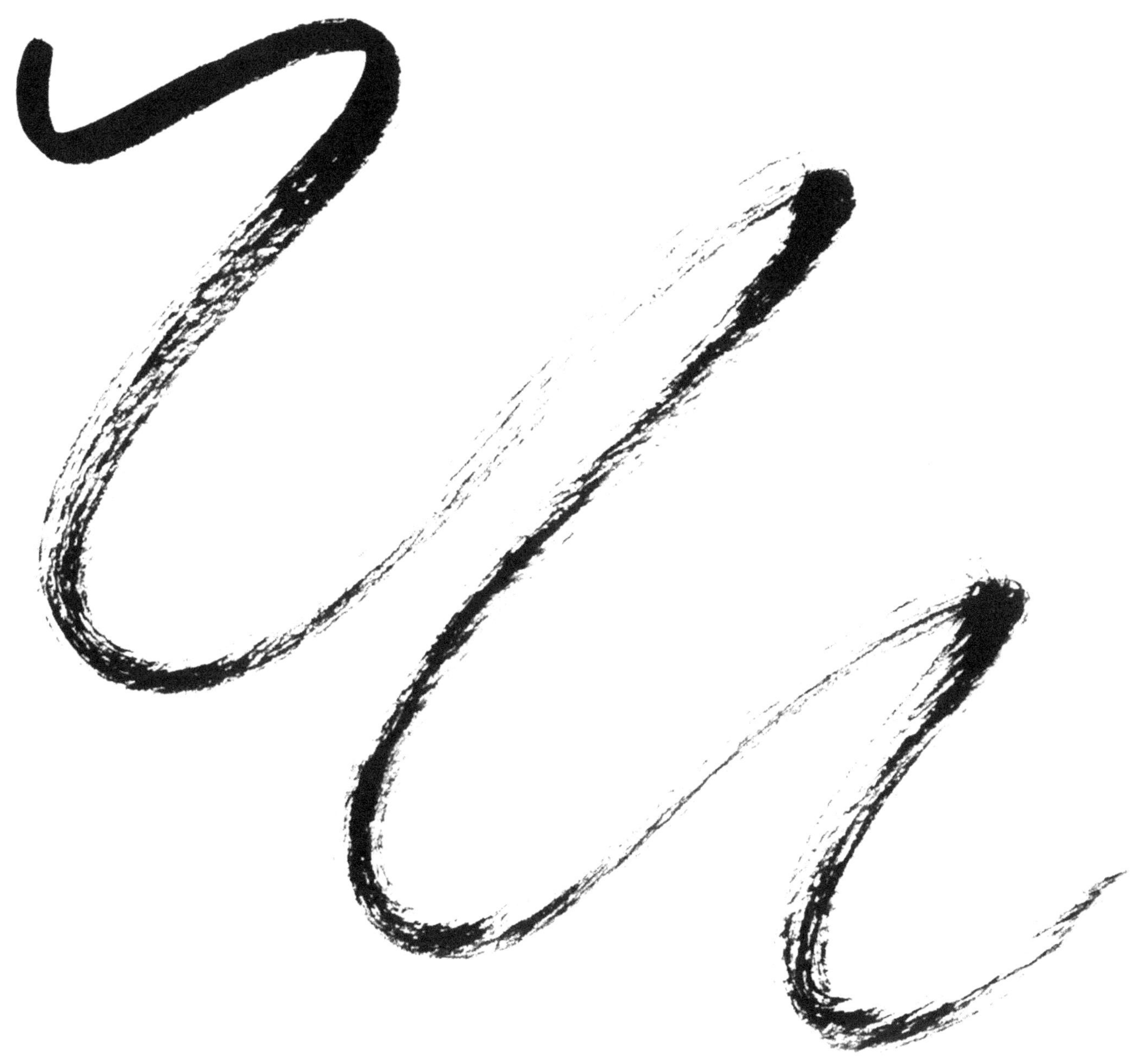

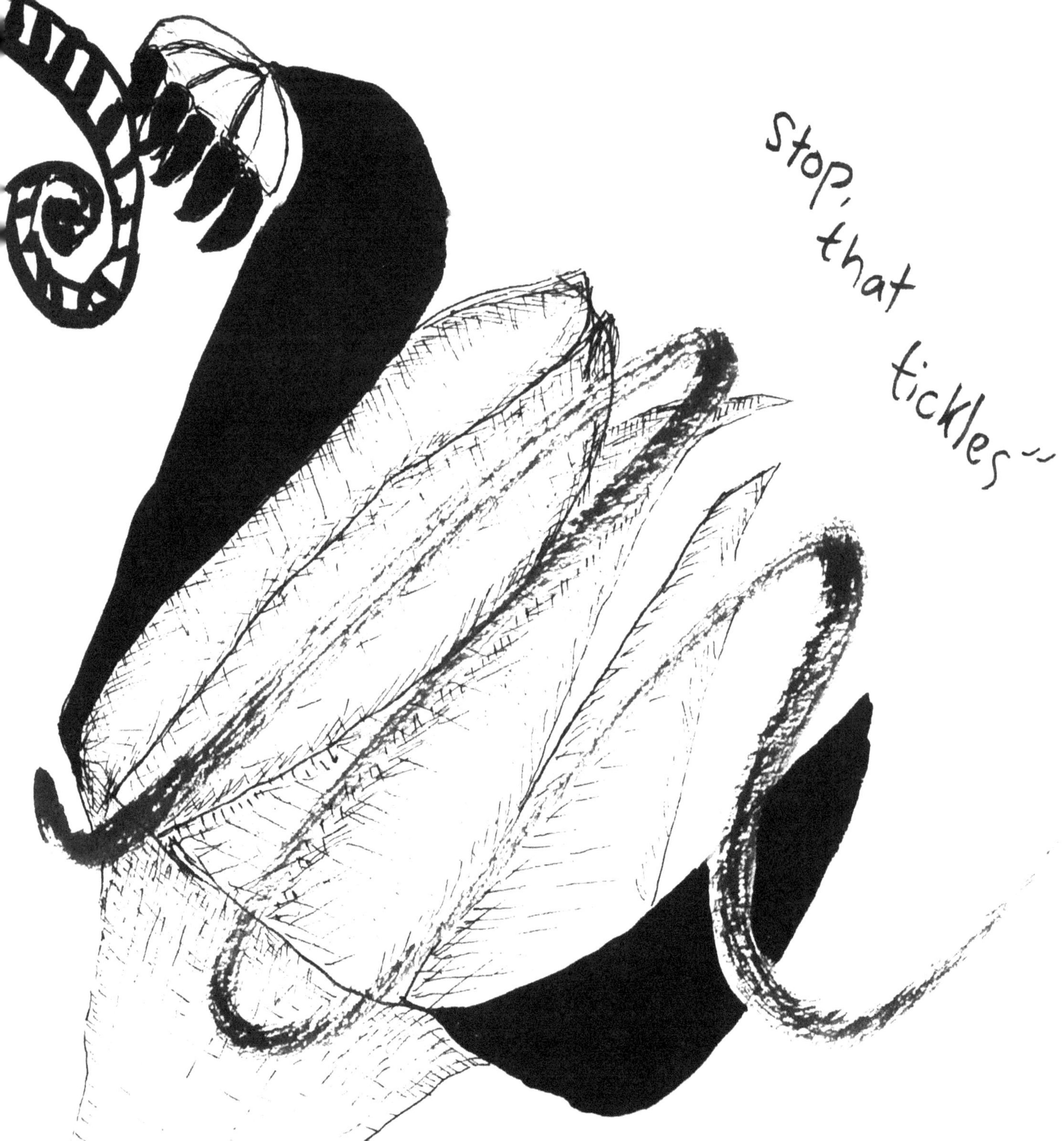

stop, that tickles~

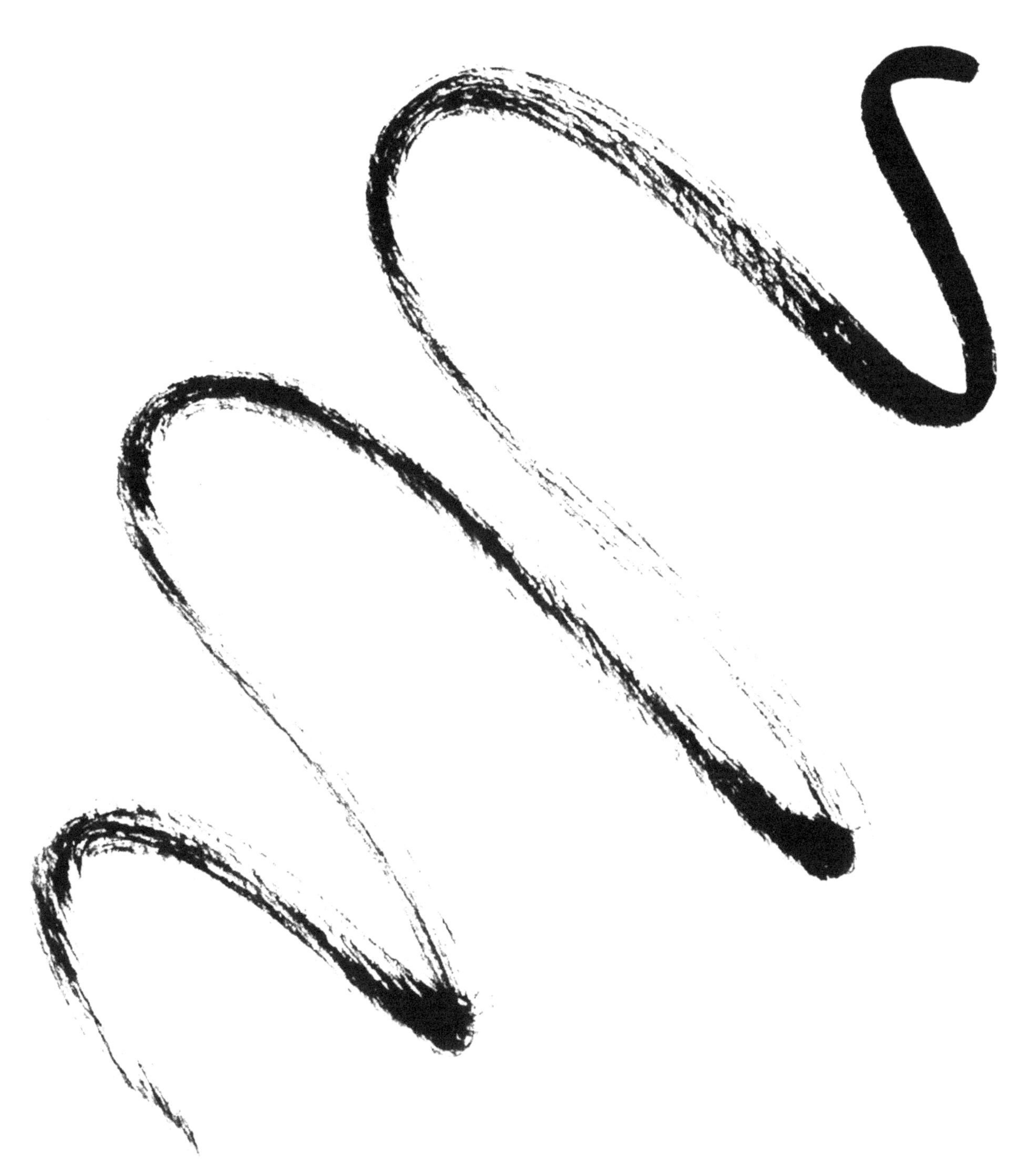

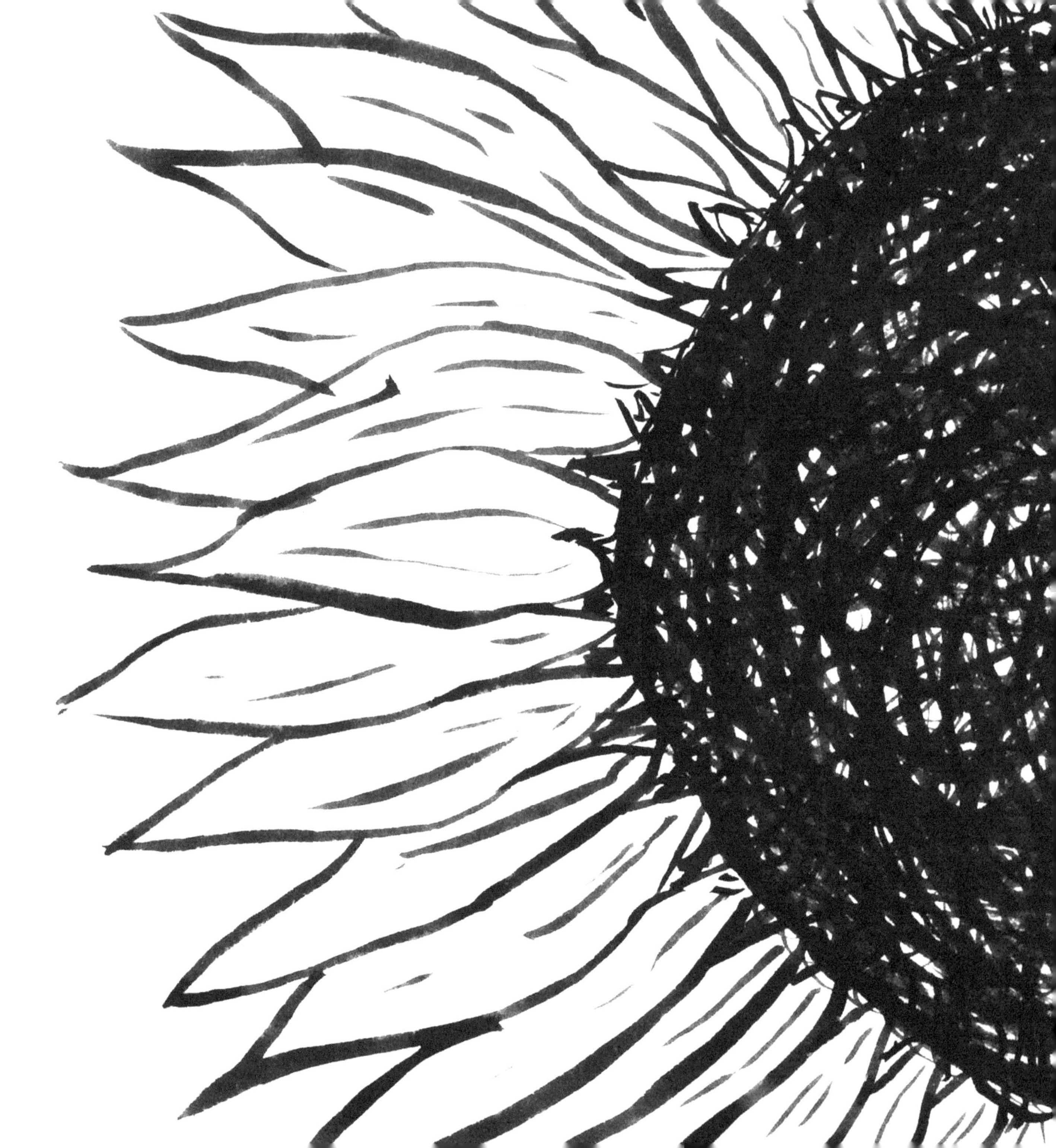

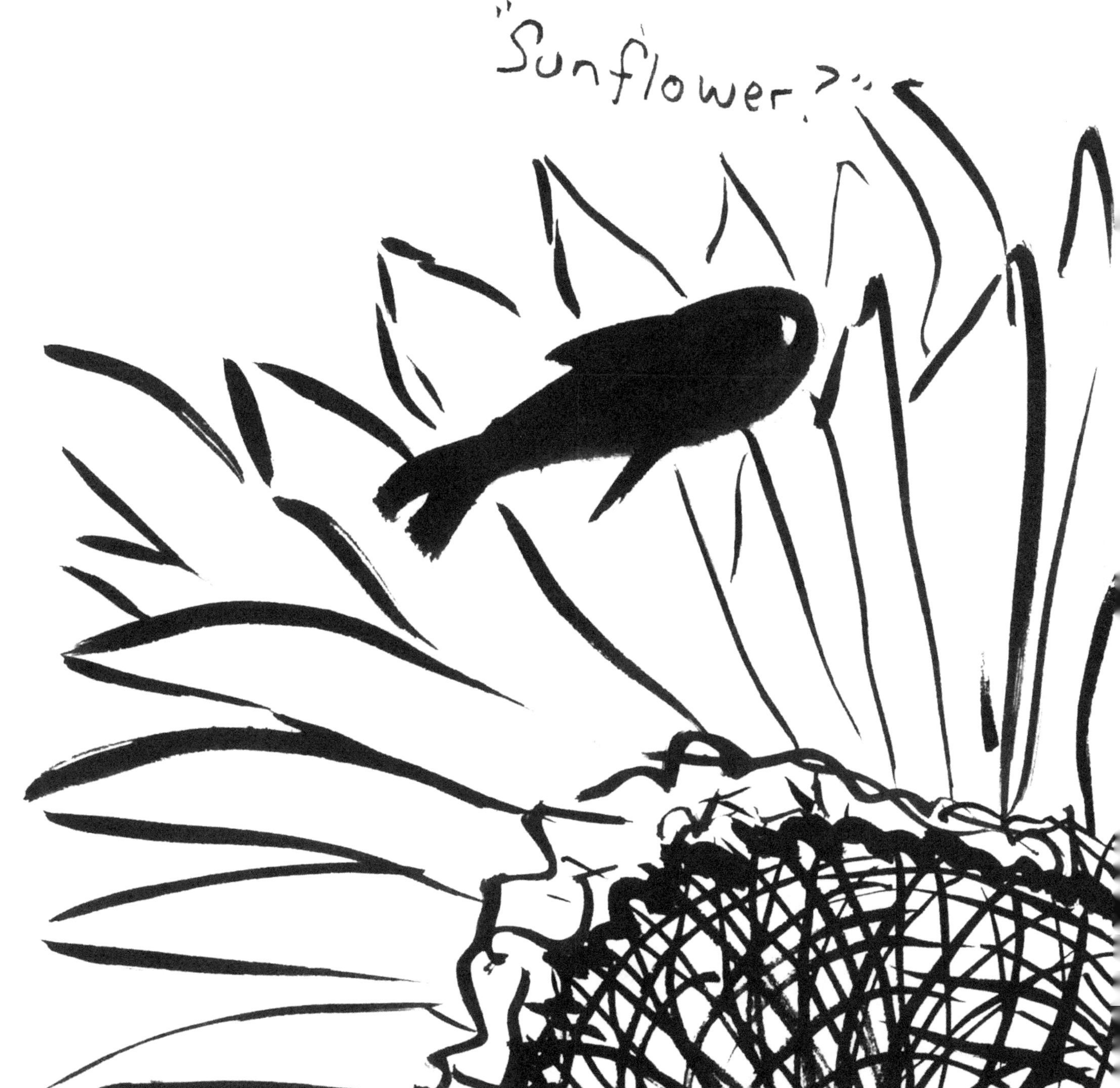
"Sunflower?"

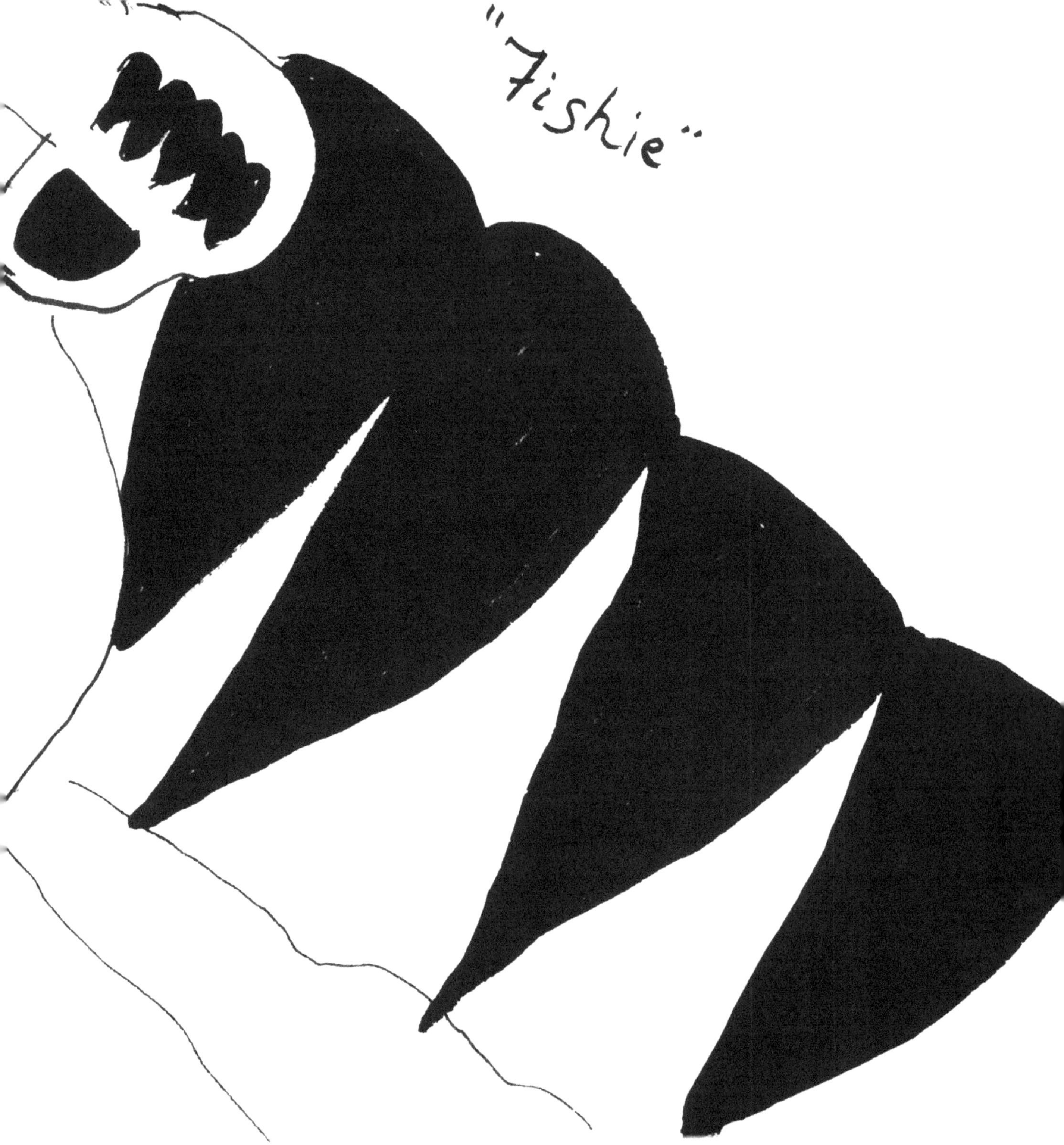
"Fishie"

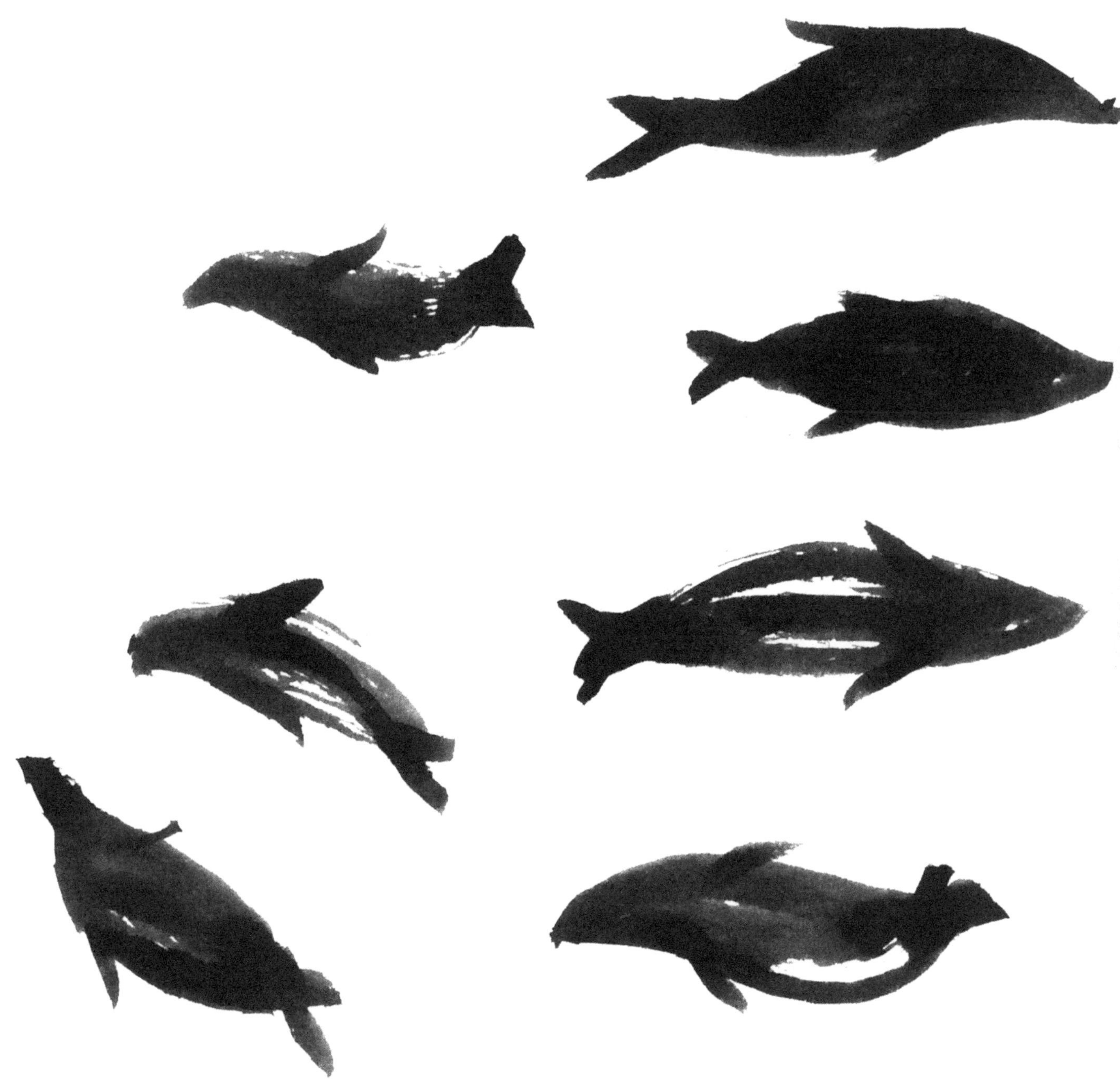

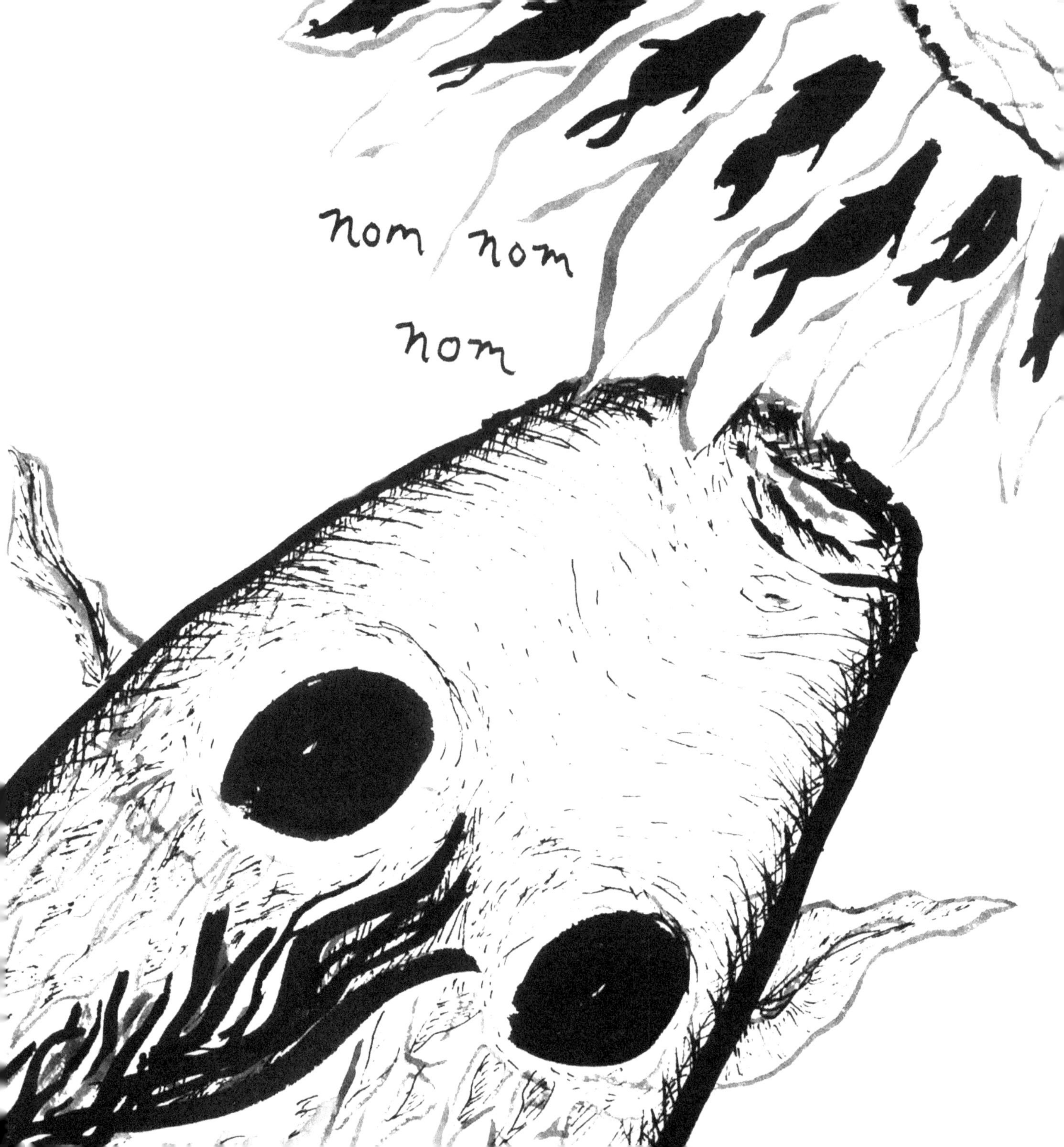
nom nom
nom

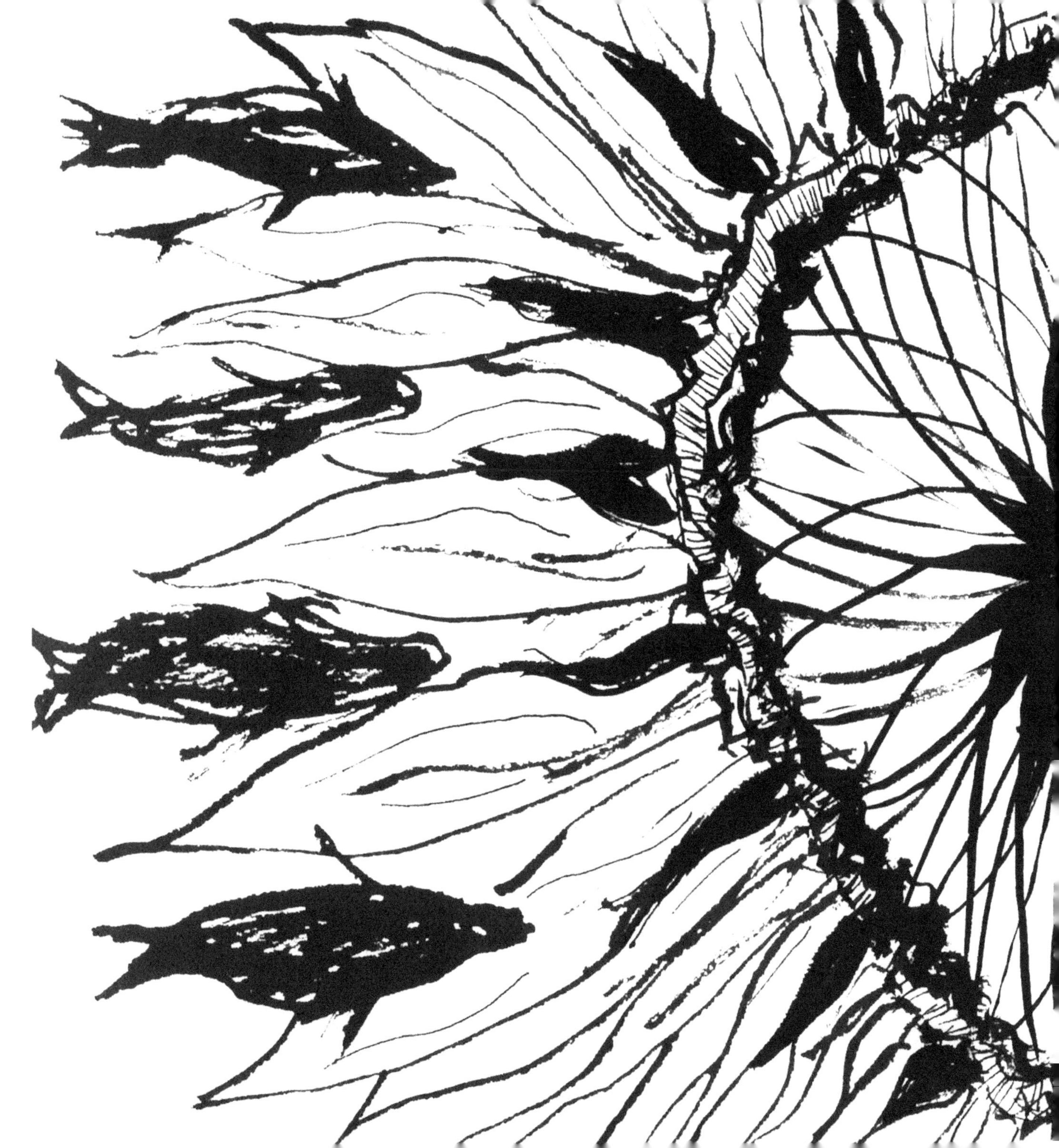

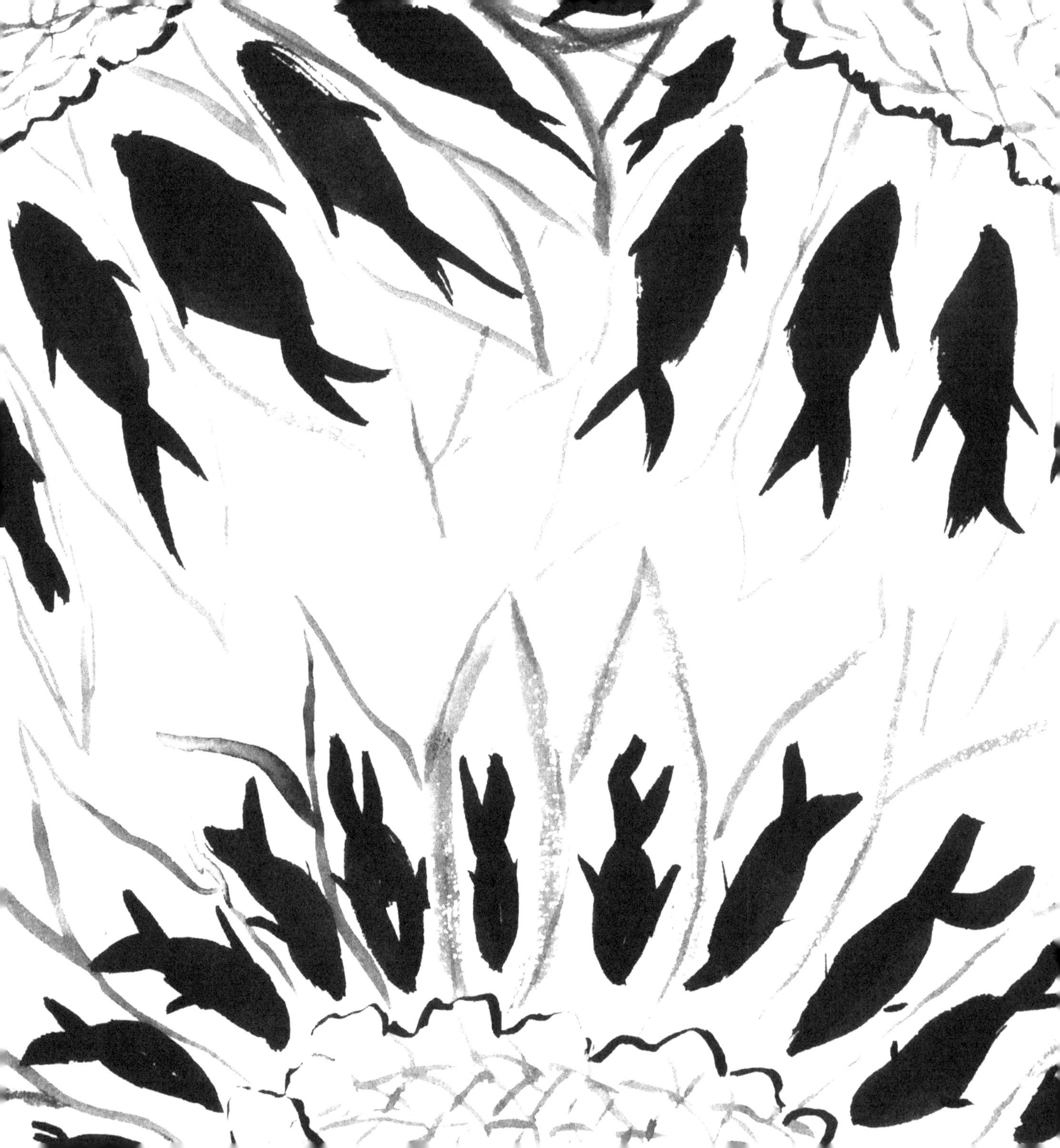

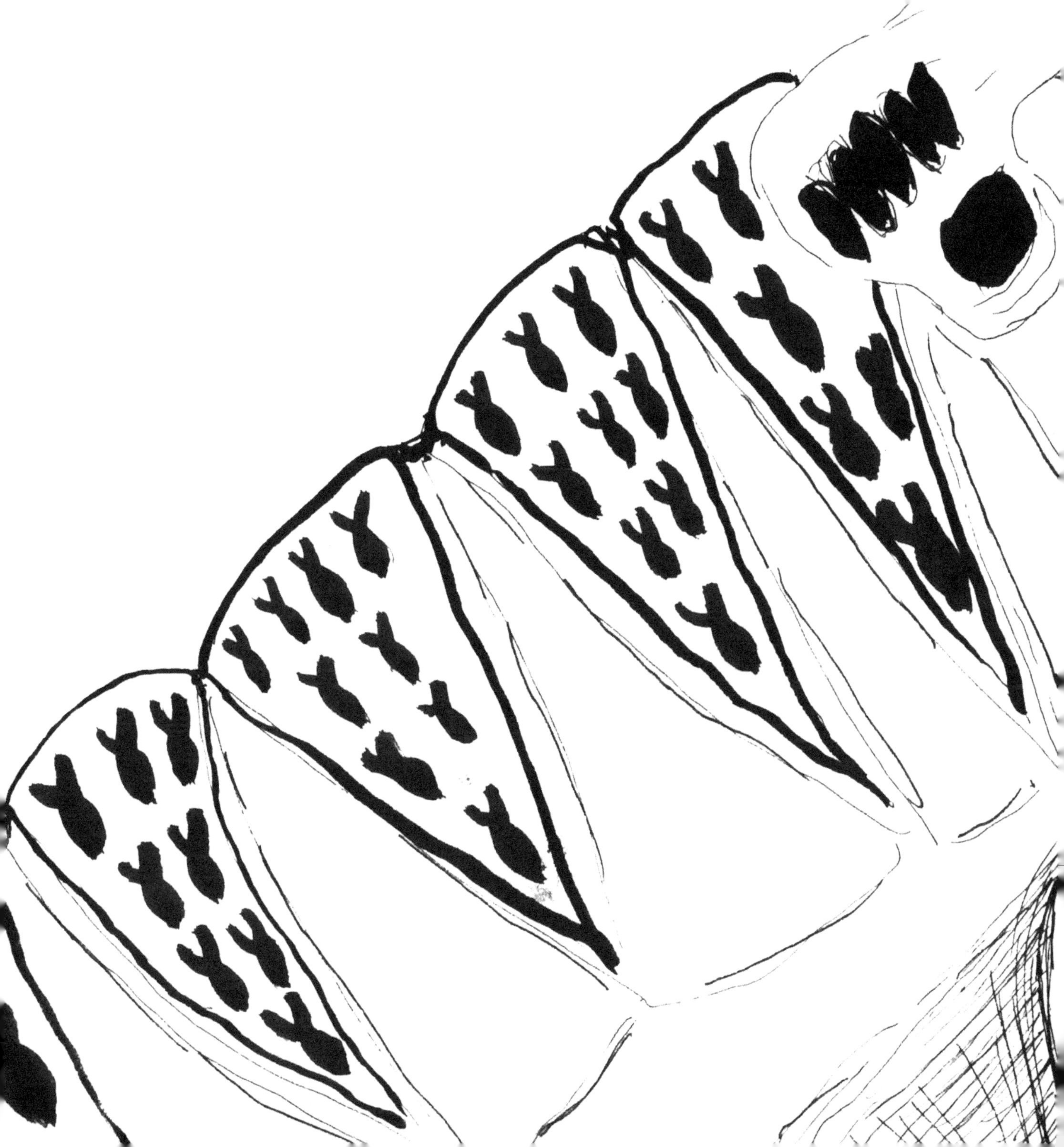

"long neck,
wait,"

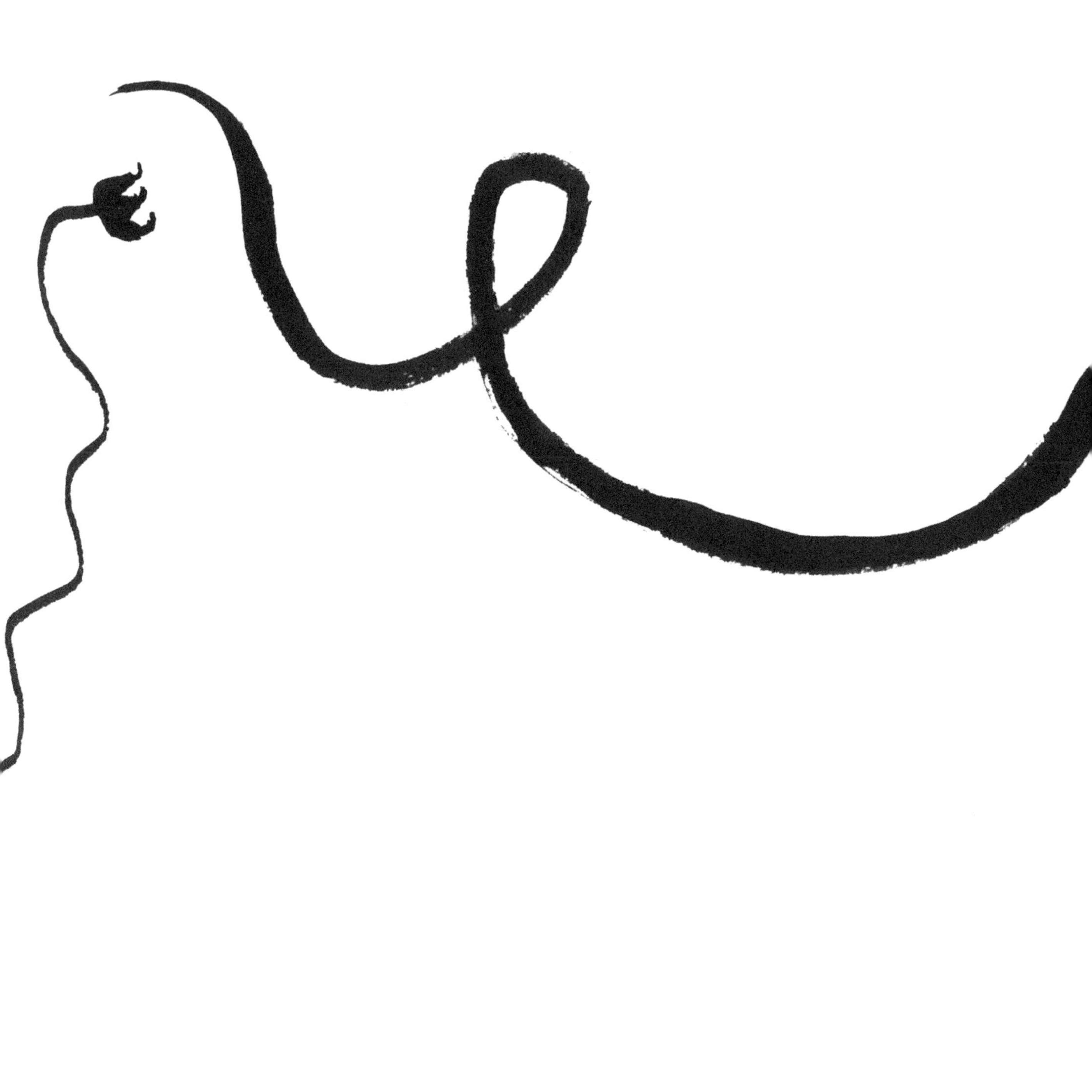

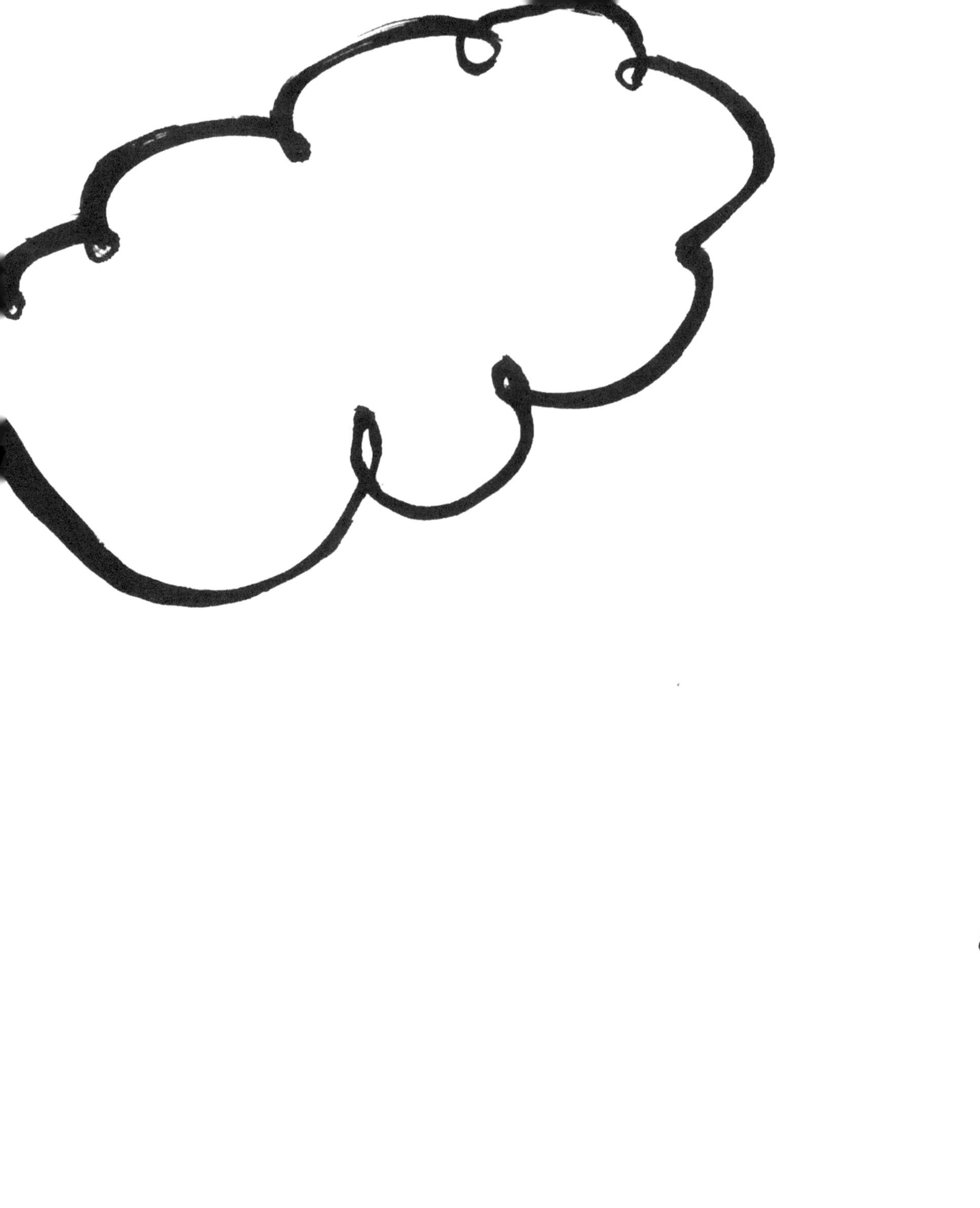

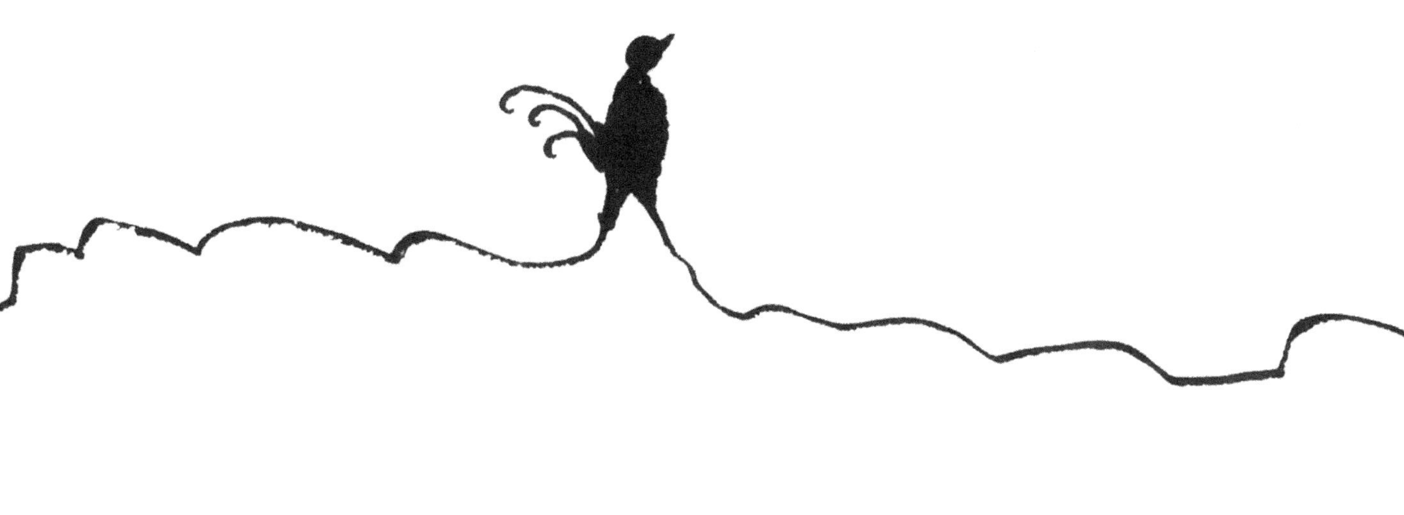

Where on...
neck
did you go?

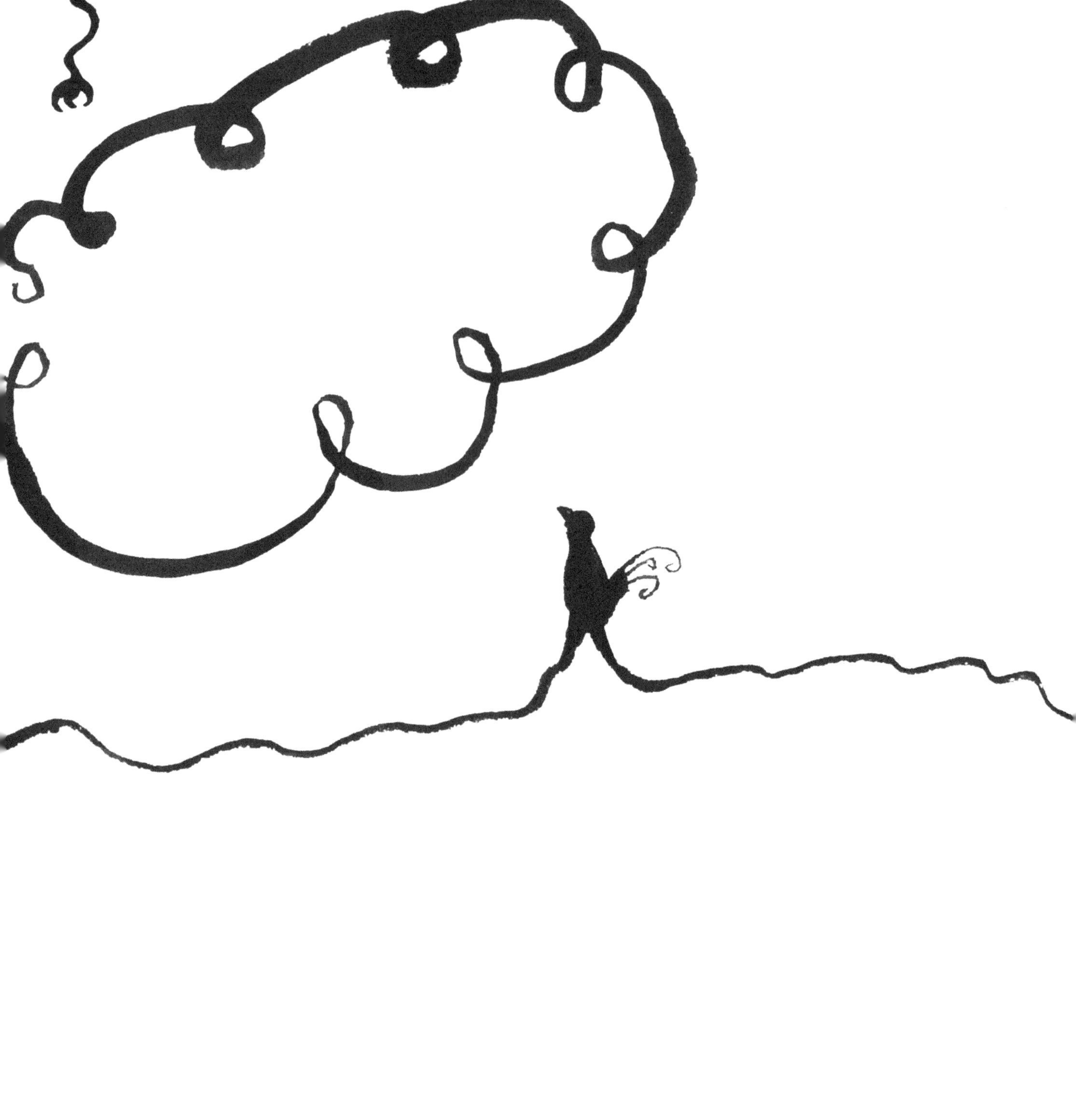

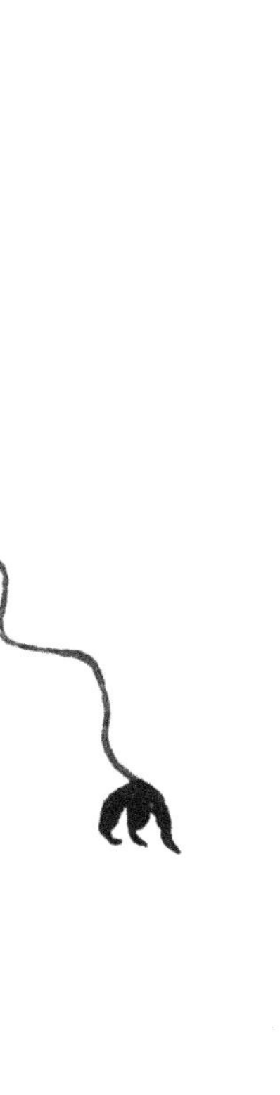

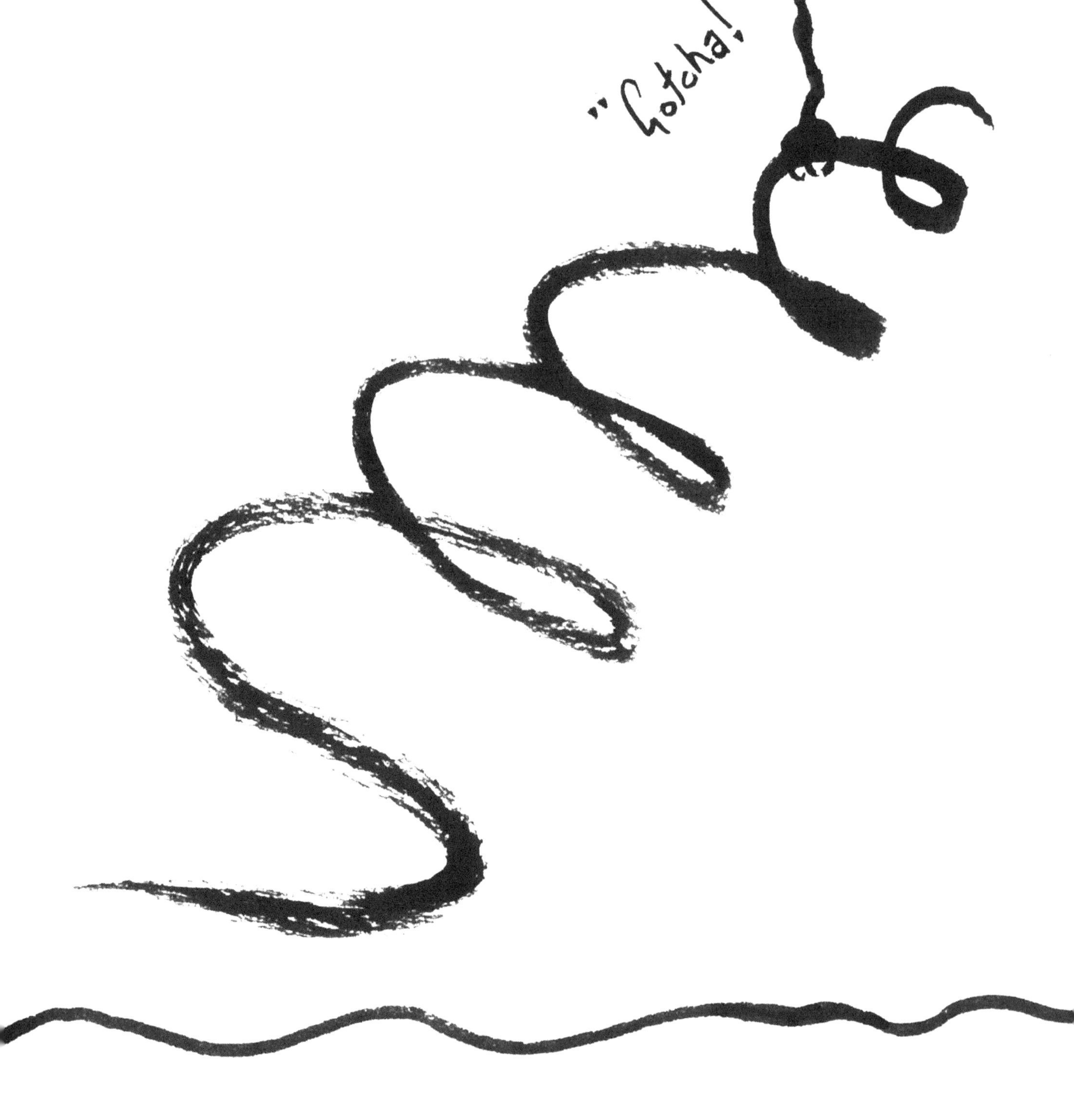
"Gotcha!

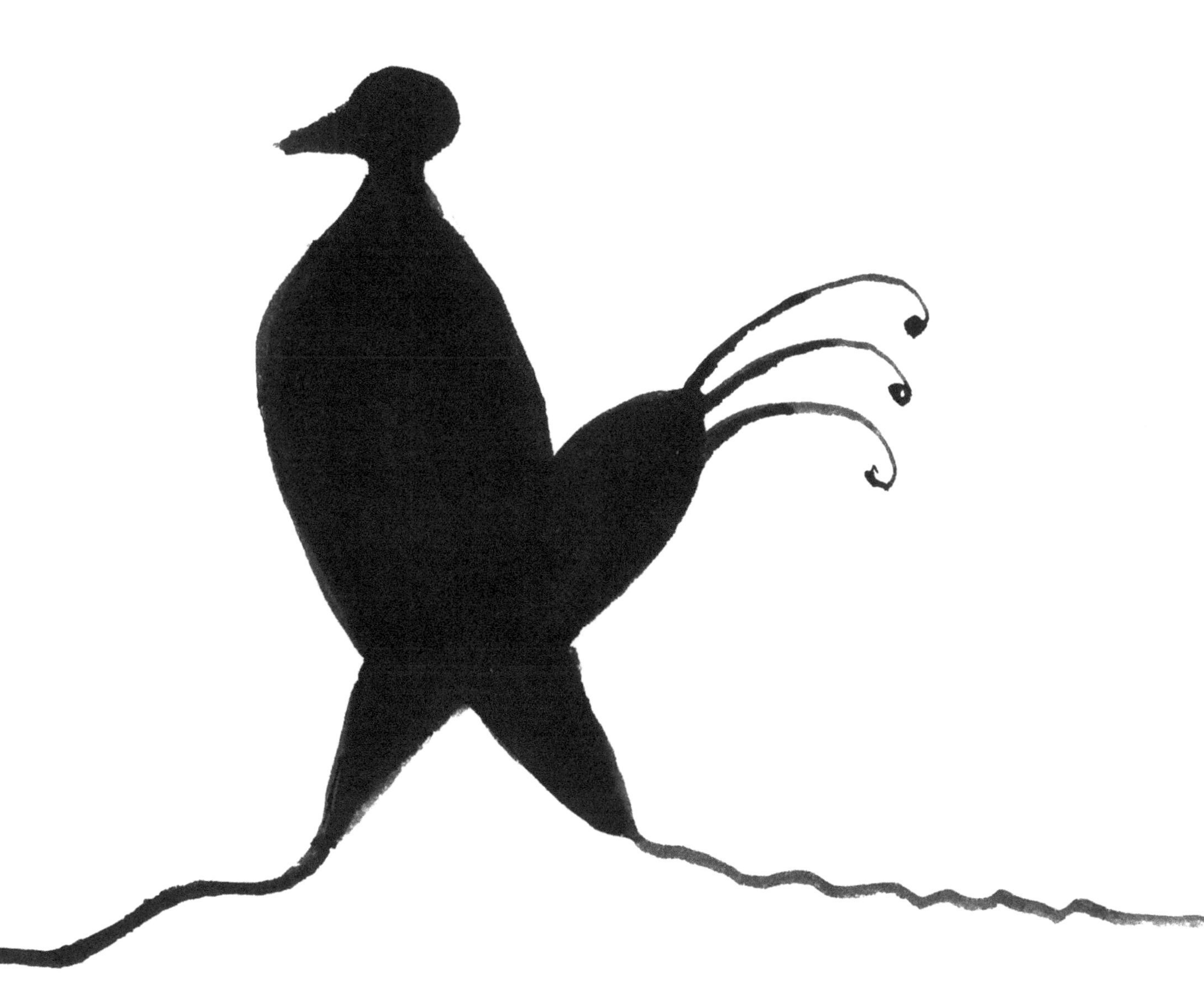

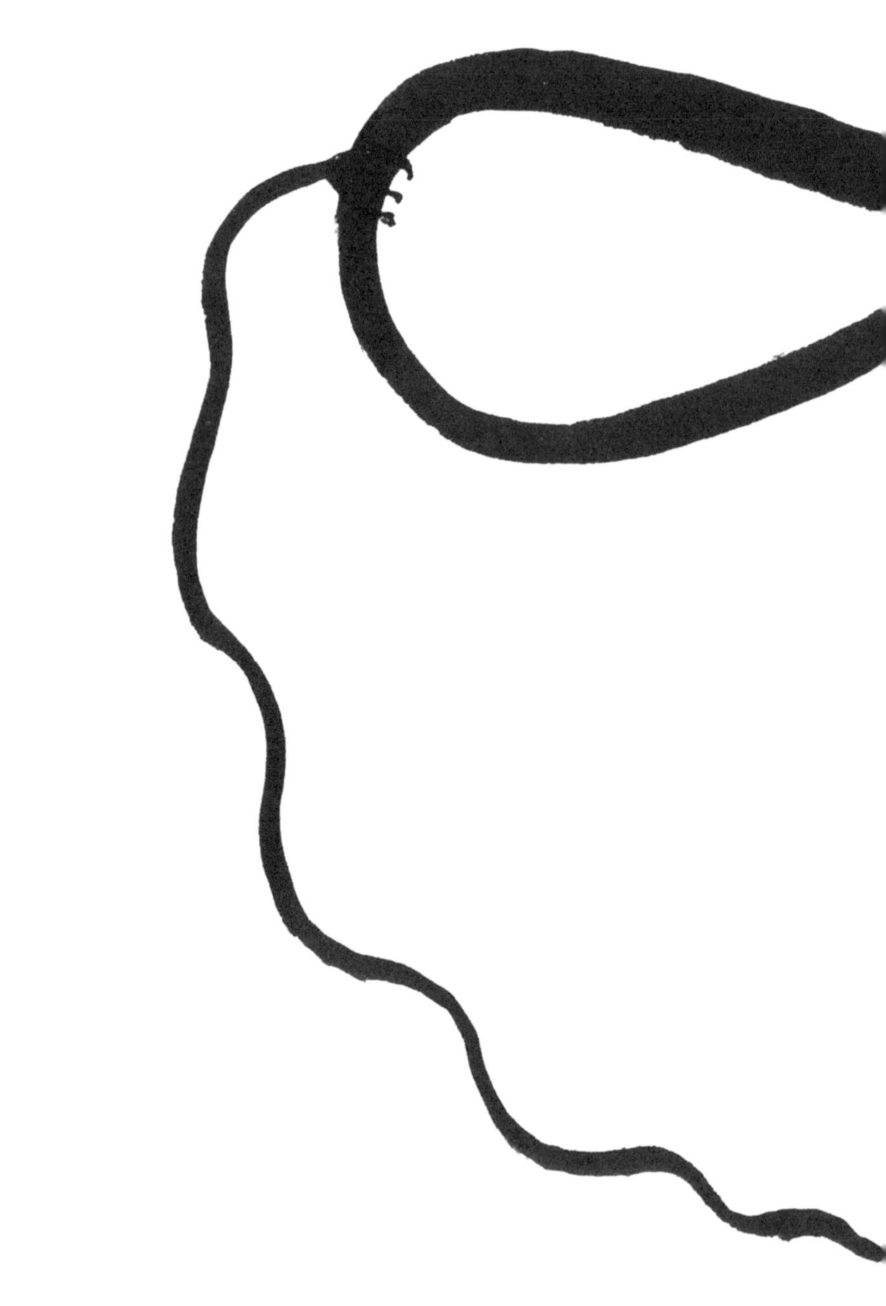

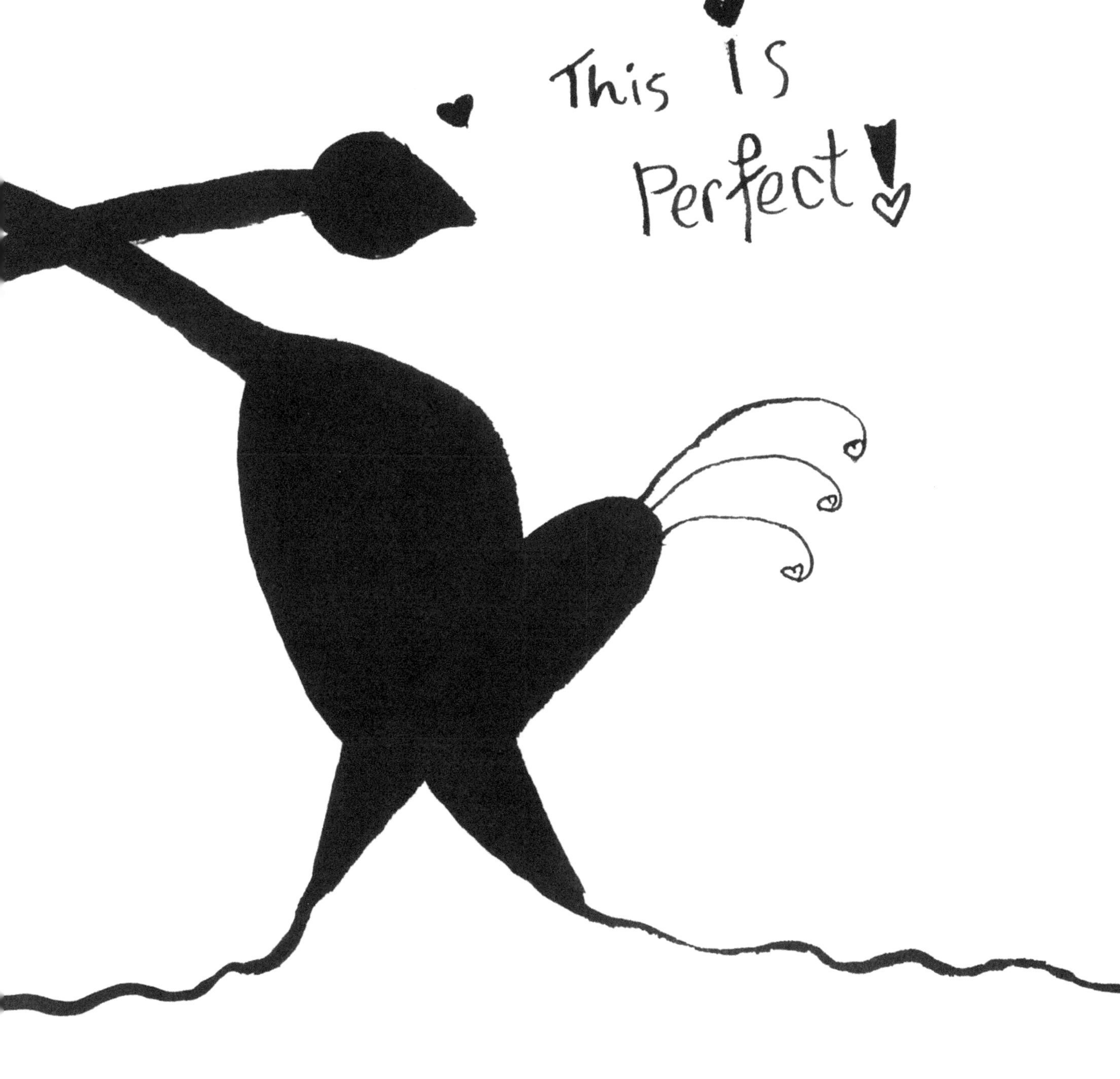

This is
Perfect!

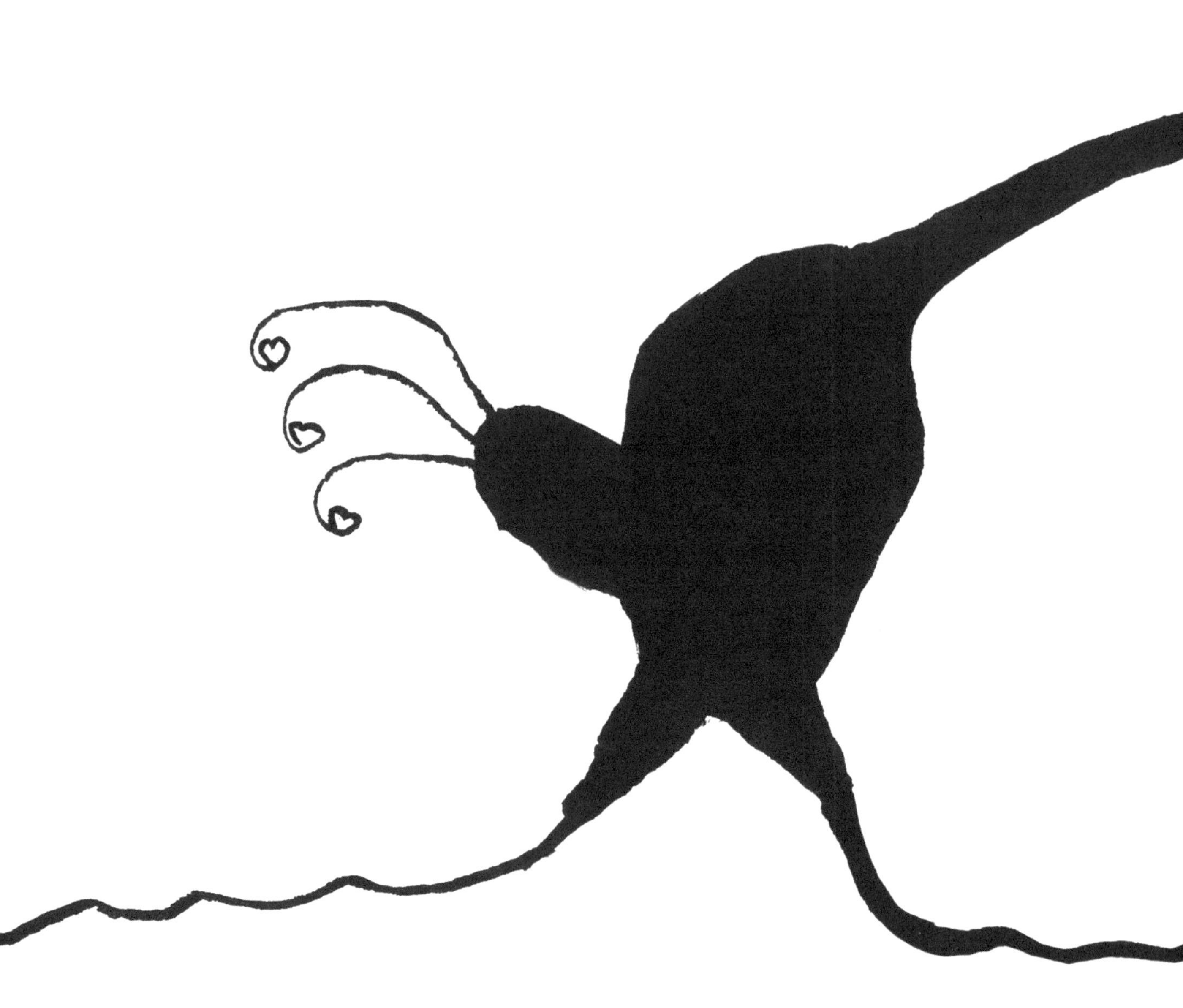

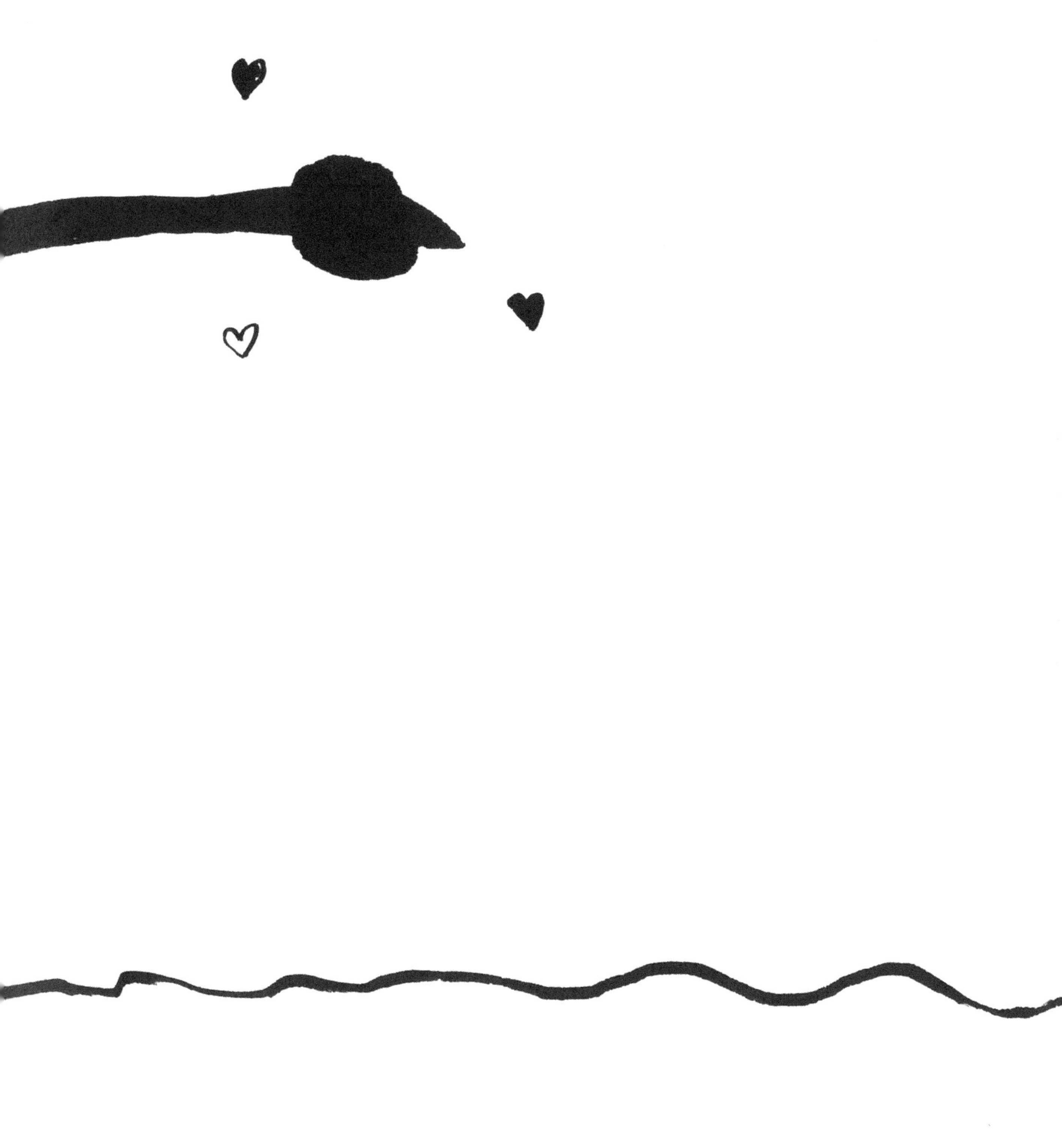

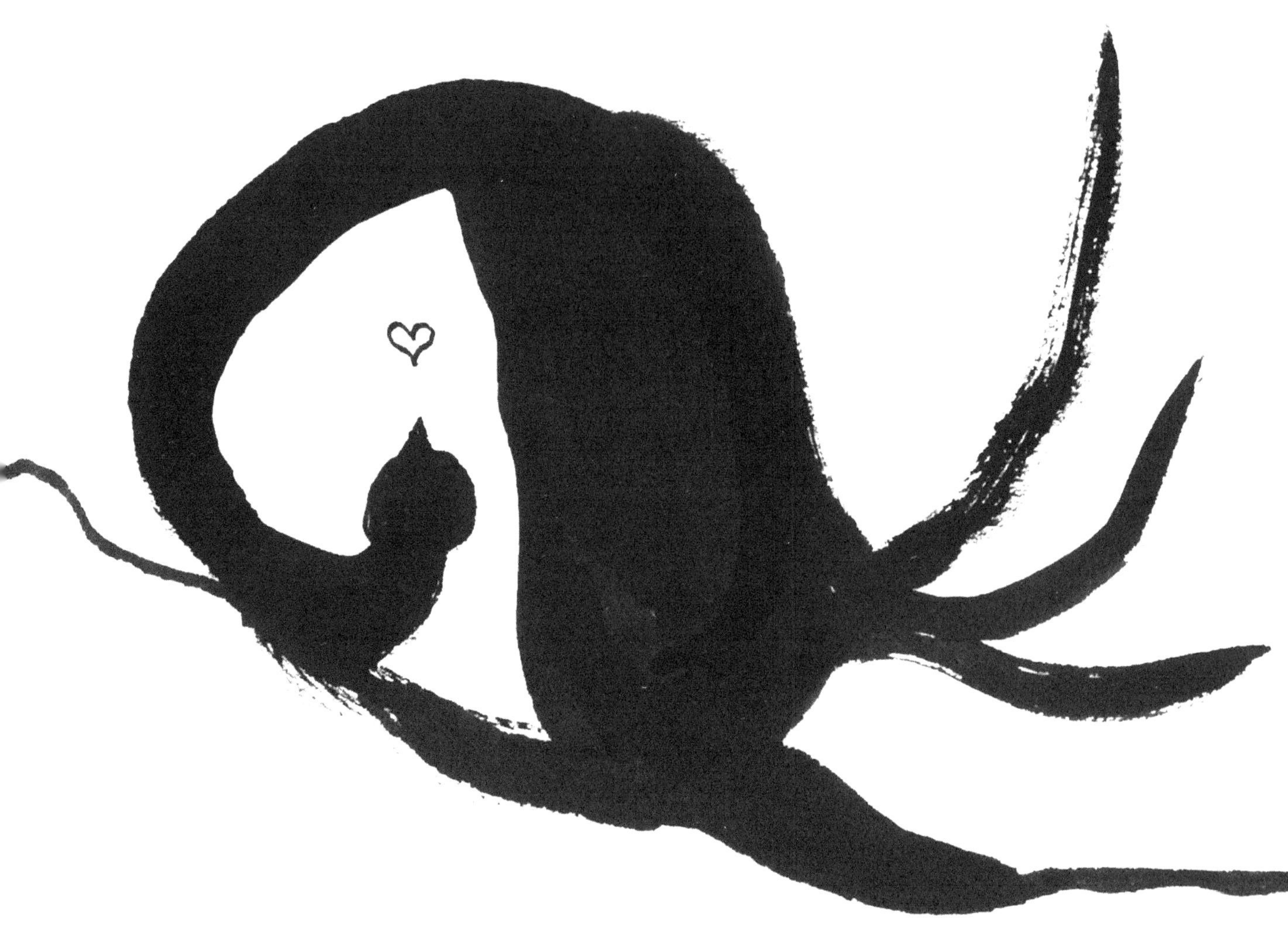

WOW
look at my
lovely long neck!

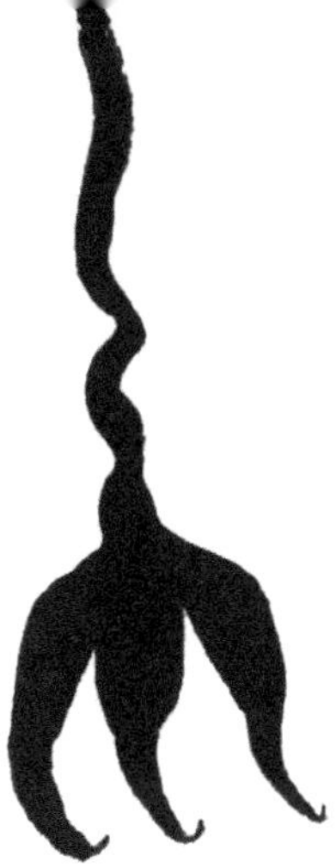

"Just call me
the
long neck bird"

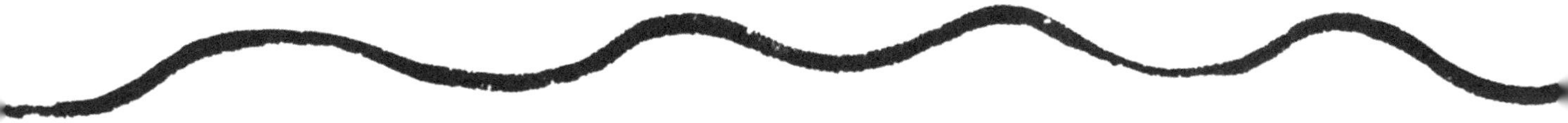

"But, your name is Faada!"

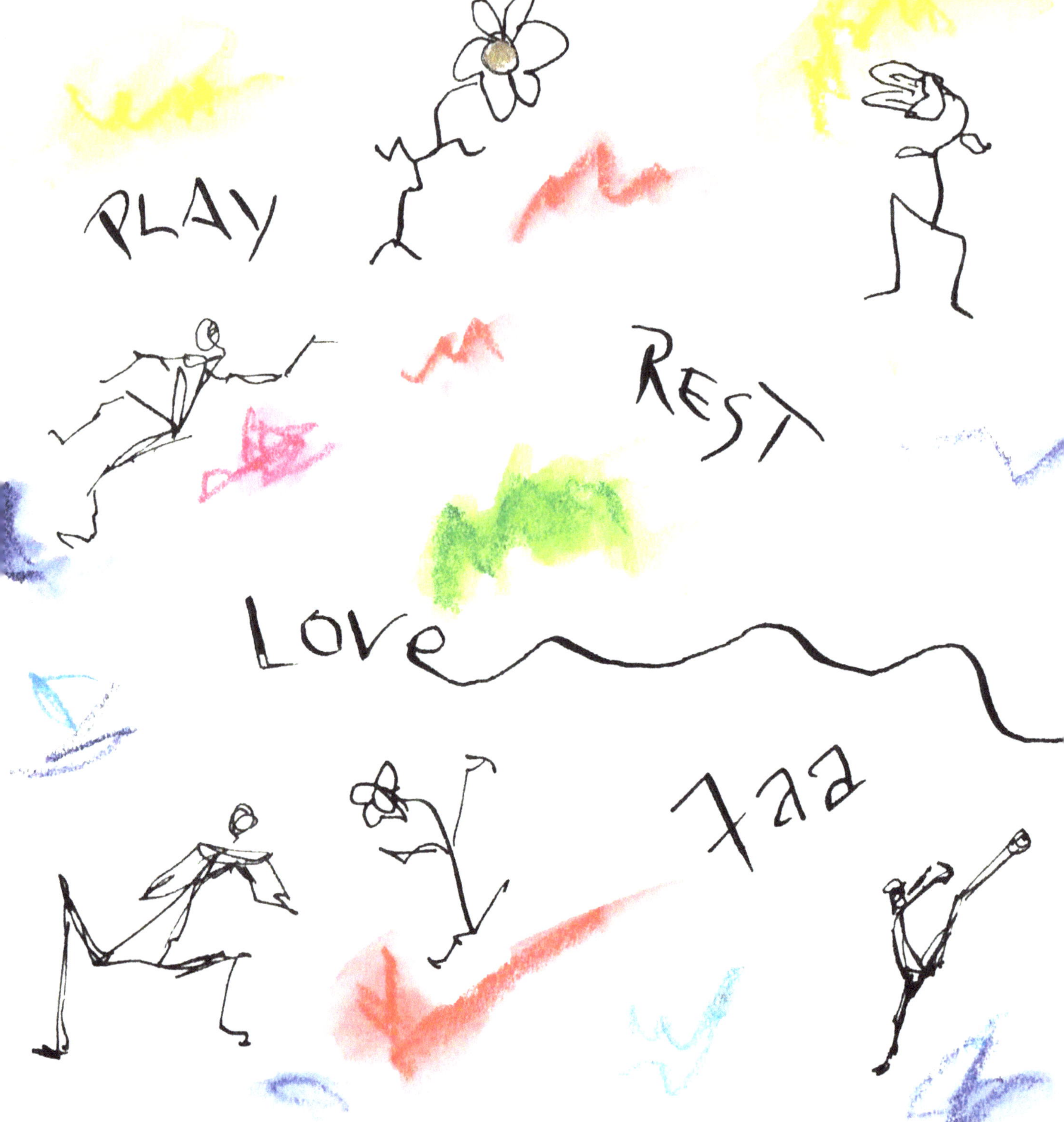

PLAY
REST
LOVE
Jaa

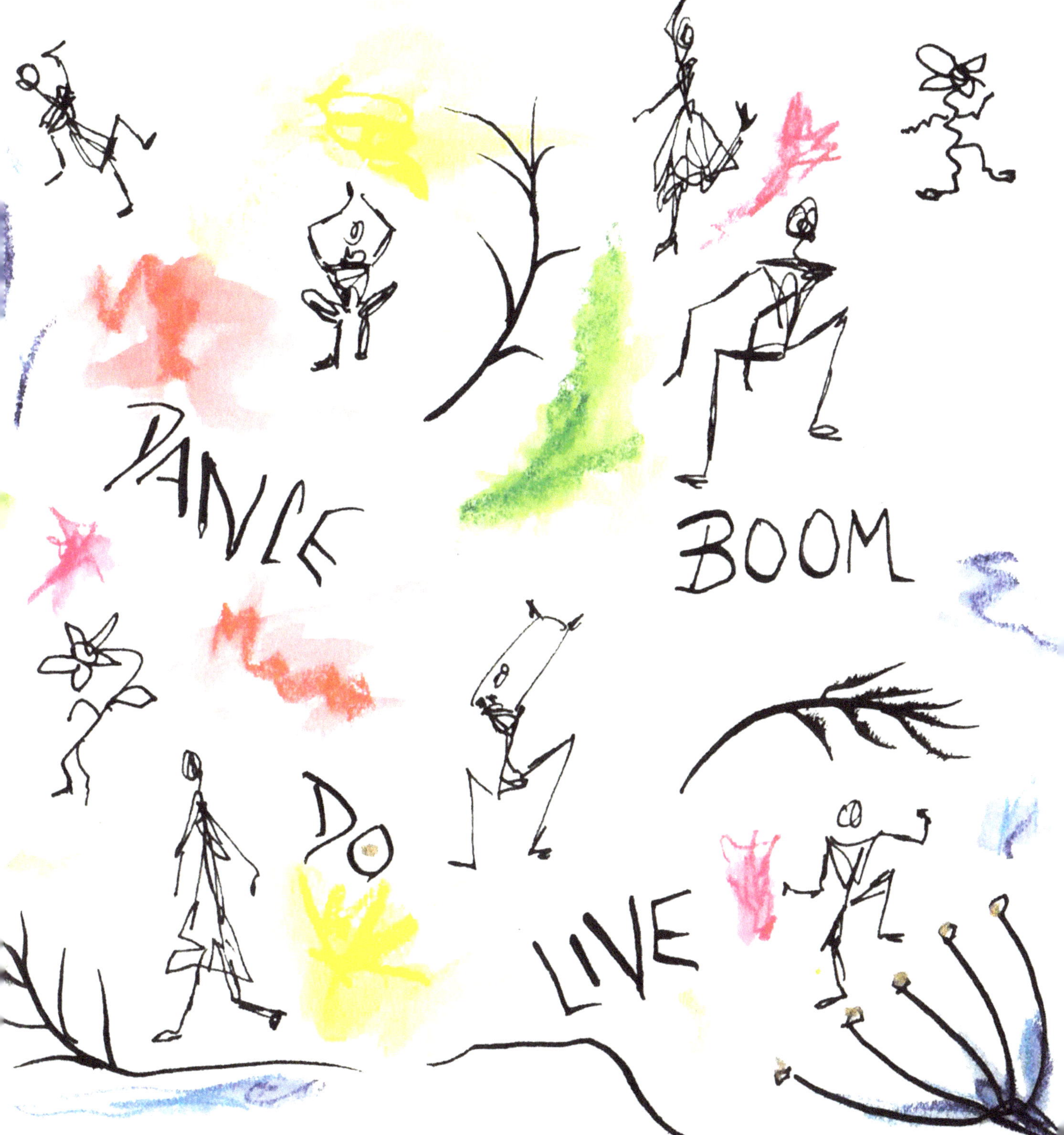

DANCE
BOOM
DO
LIVE